CHAPTER 1: ADELEINE IN LOVE WITH LOVE

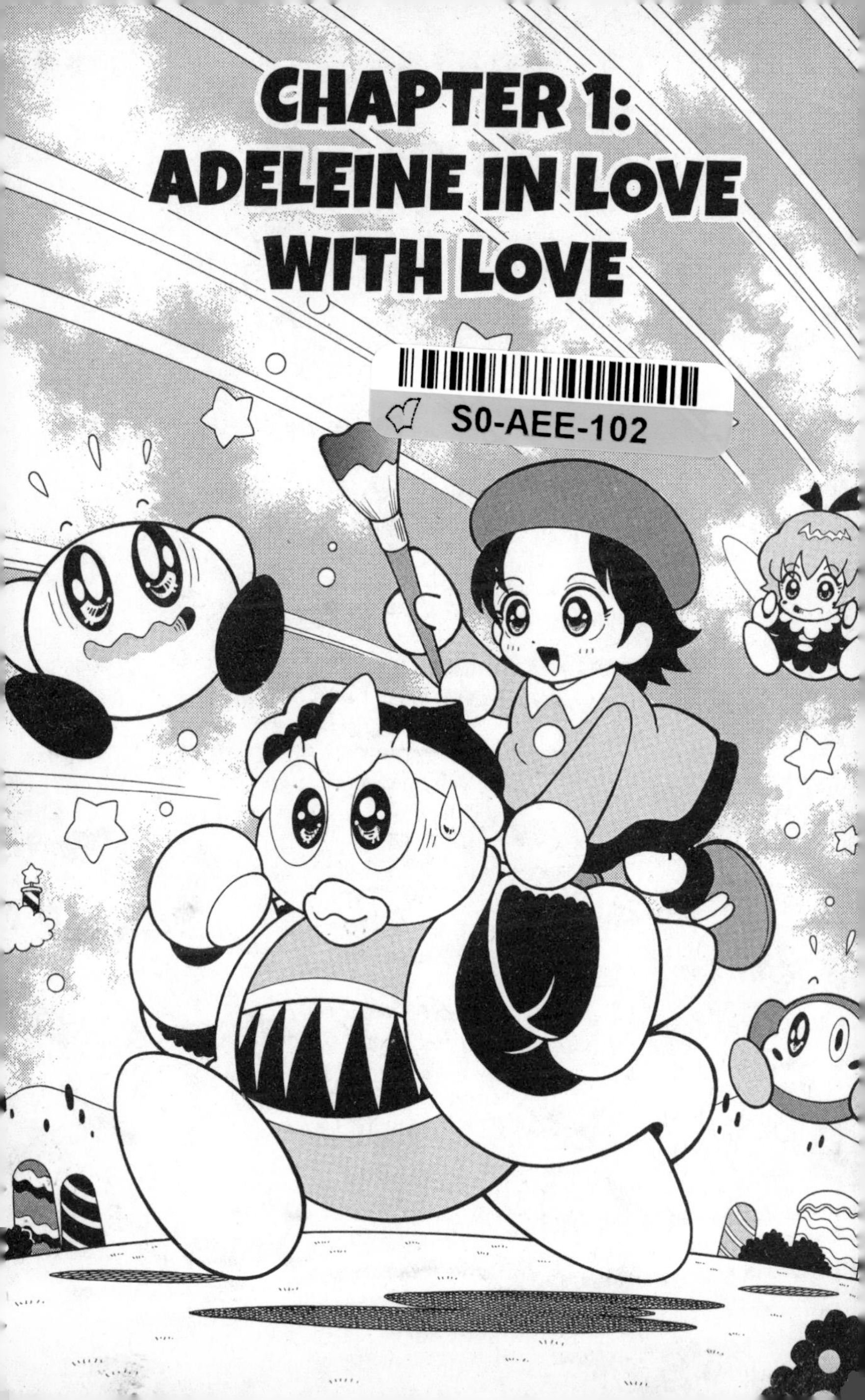

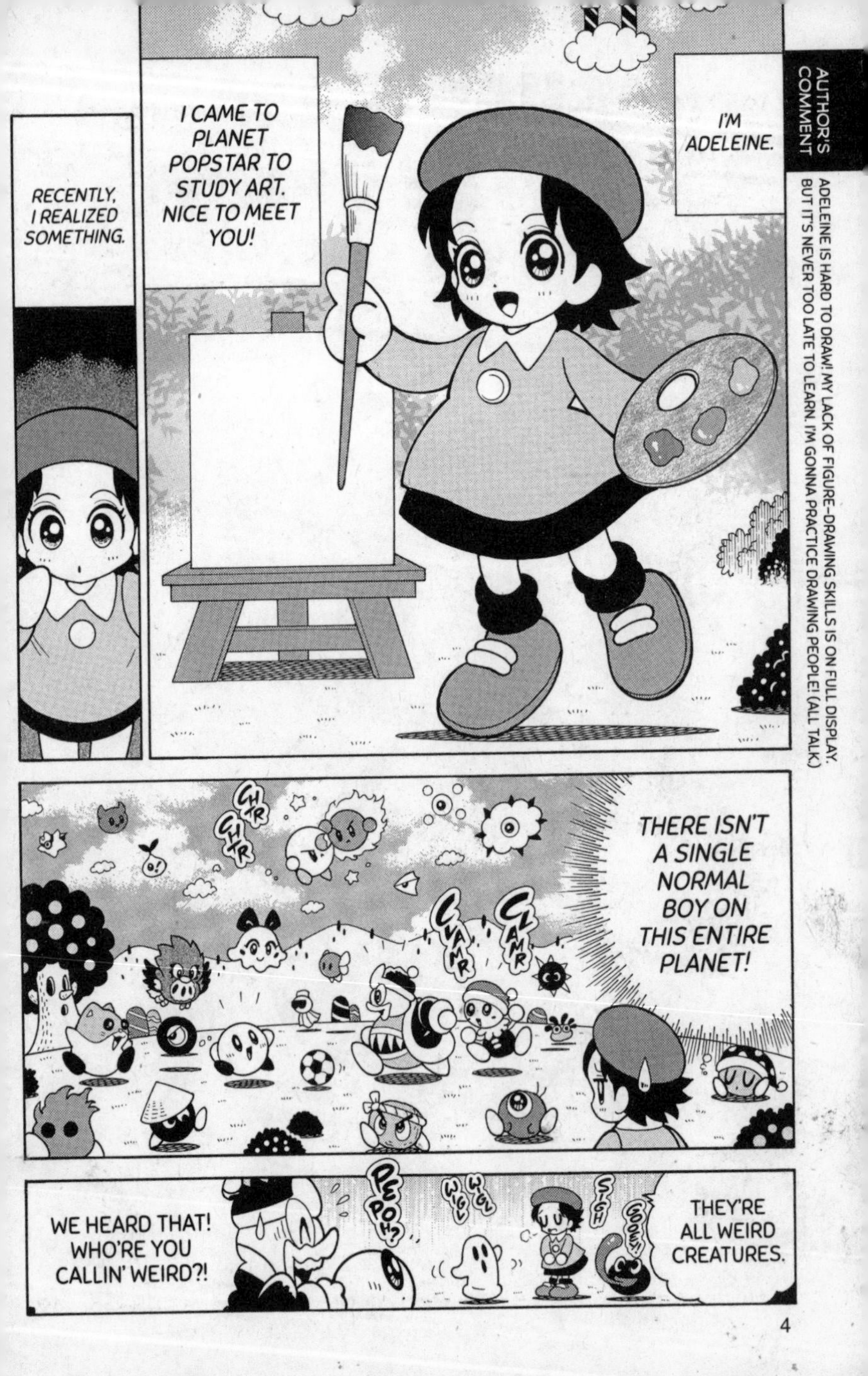
I'M ADELEINE.
I CAME TO PLANET POPSTAR TO STUDY ART. NICE TO MEET YOU!
RECENTLY, I REALIZED SOMETHING.
CHR CHR
THERE ISN'T A SINGLE NORMAL BOY ON THIS ENTIRE PLANET!
THEY'RE ALL WEIRD CREATURES.
SIGH
WE HEARD THAT! WHO'RE YOU CALLIN' WEIRD?!

AUTHOR'S COMMENT

ADELEINE IS HARD TO DRAW! MY LACK OF FIGURE-DRAWING SKILLS IS ON FULL DISPLAY. BUT IT'S NEVER TOO LATE TO LEARN. I'M GONNA PRACTICE DRAWING PEOPLE! (ALL TALK.)

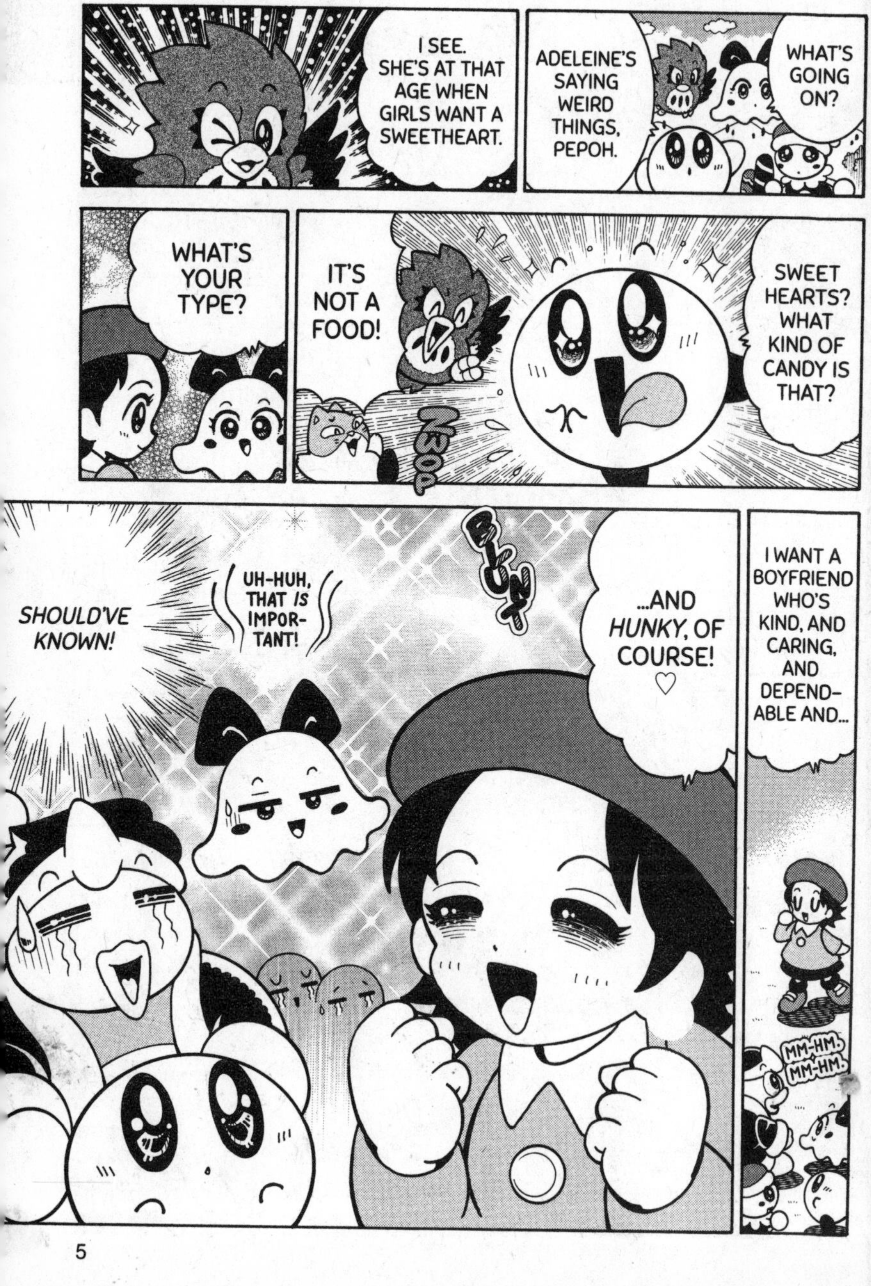
WHAT'S GOING ON?
ADELEINE'S SAYING WEIRD THINGS, PEPOH.
I SEE. SHE'S AT THAT AGE WHEN GIRLS WANT A SWEETHEART.
SWEET HEARTS? WHAT KIND OF CANDY IS THAT?
IT'S NOT A FOOD!
WOOP
WHAT'S YOUR TYPE?
I WANT A BOYFRIEND WHO'S KIND, AND CARING, AND DEPENDABLE AND...
MM-HM. MM-HM.
...AND *HUNKY*, OF COURSE! ♡
BLUNT
UH-HUH, THAT *IS* IMPORTANT!
SHOULD'VE KNOWN!

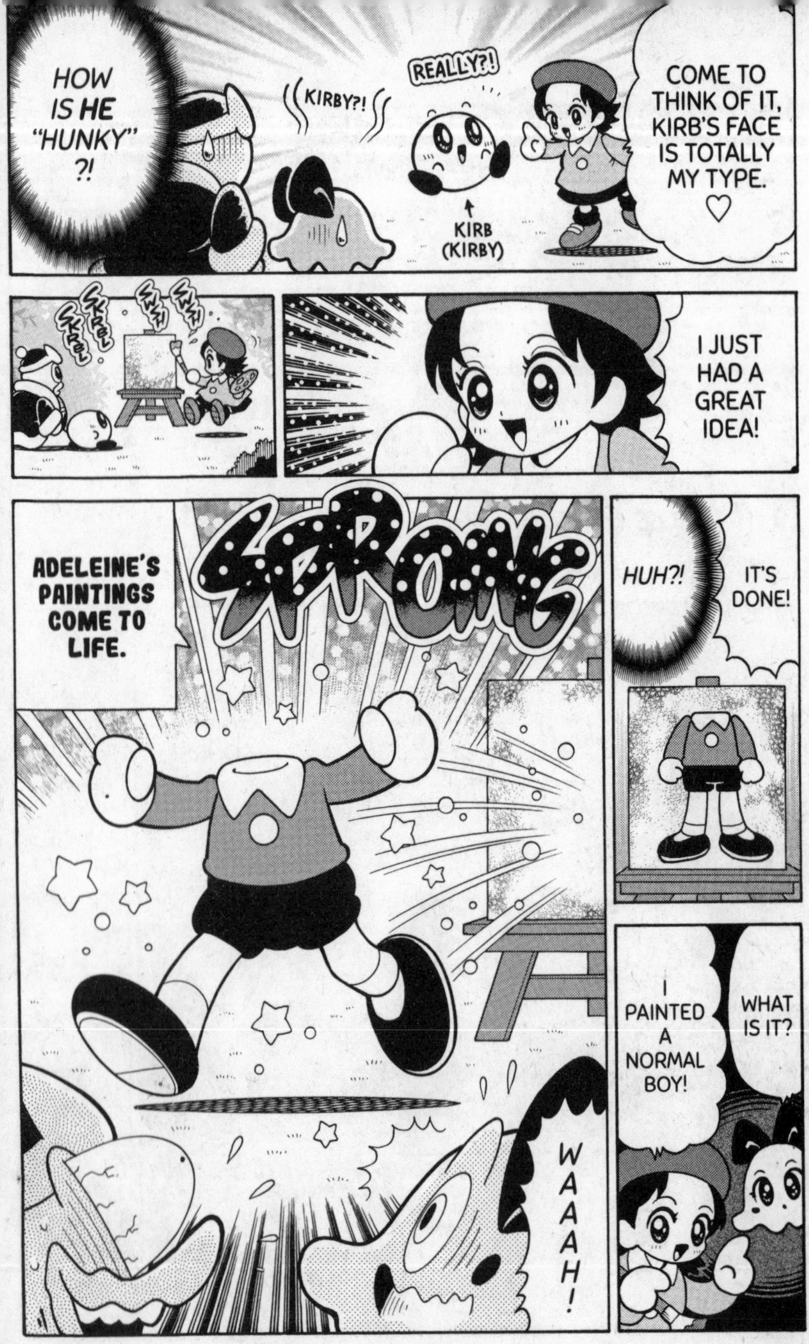
COME TO THINK OF IT, KIRB'S FACE IS TOTALLY MY TYPE. ♡
REALLY?!
KIRB (KIRBY)
KIRBY?!
HOW IS HE "HUNKY" ?!
I JUST HAD A GREAT IDEA!
SWSH SWSH
SKREL SKREL SKREL
IT'S DONE!
HUH?!
WHAT IS IT?
I PAINTED A NORMAL BOY!
ADELEINE'S PAINTINGS COME TO LIFE.
WAAAAH!

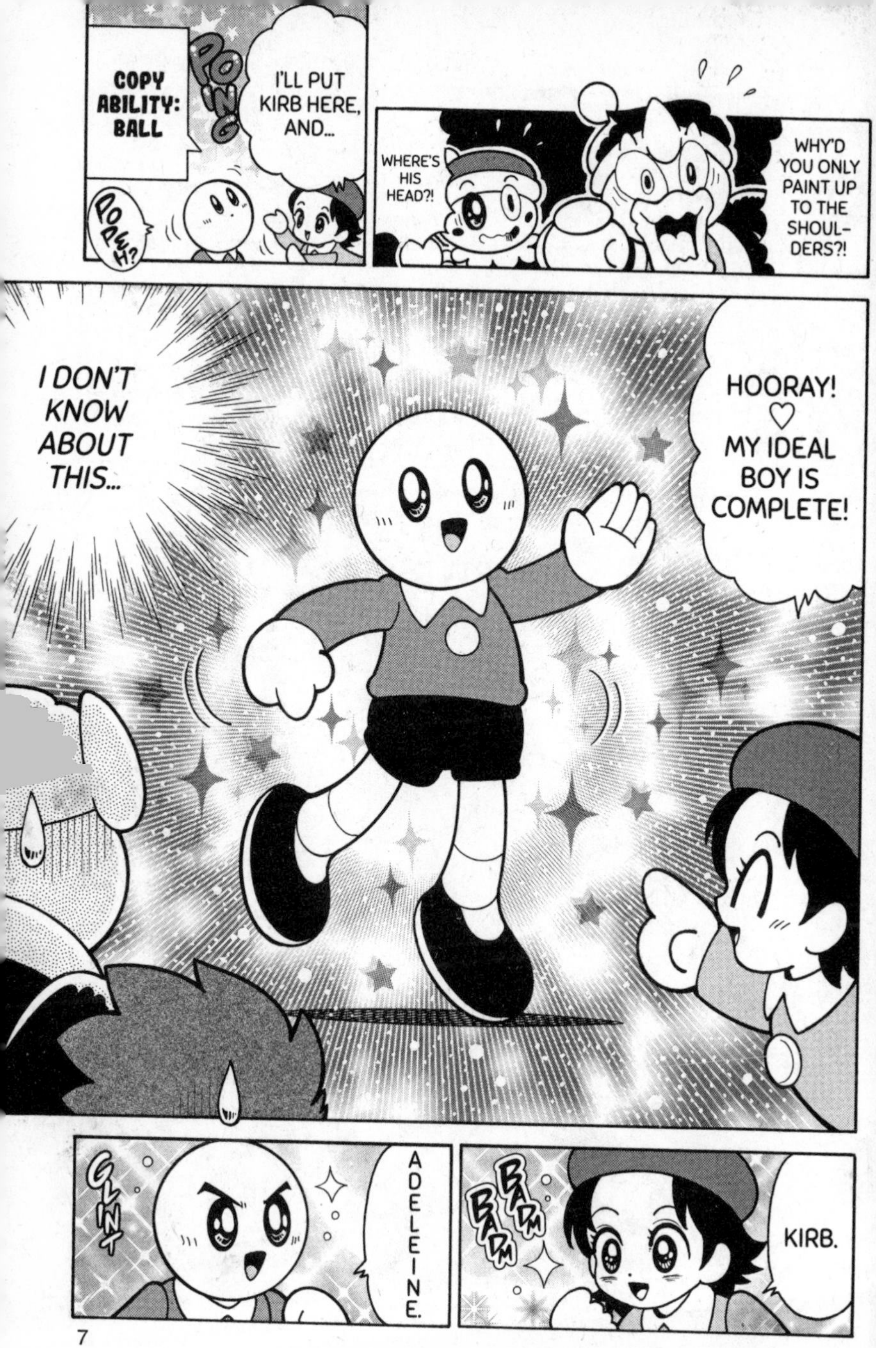
WHY'D YOU ONLY PAINT UP TO THE SHOULDERS?!
WHERE'S HIS HEAD?!
I'LL PUT KIRB HERE, AND...
POING
COPY ABILITY: BALL
POPEH?
HOORAY! ♡ MY IDEAL BOY IS COMPLETE!
I DON'T KNOW ABOUT THIS...
KIRB.
BADM
BADM
ADELEINE.
GLINT

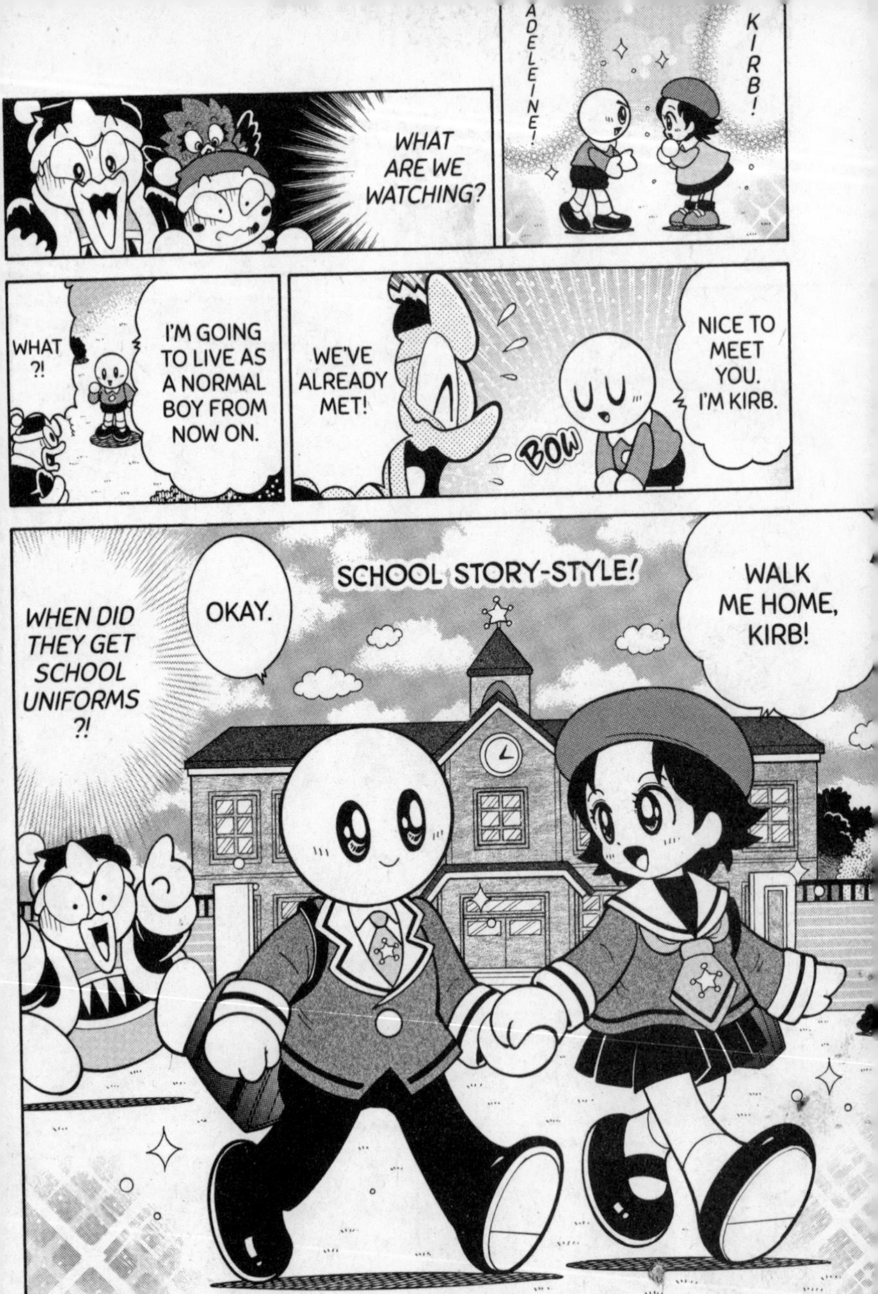
KIRB!
ADELEINE!
WHAT ARE WE WATCHING?
NICE TO MEET YOU. I'M KIRB.
BOW
WE'VE ALREADY MET!
I'M GOING TO LIVE AS A NORMAL BOY FROM NOW ON.
WHAT ?!
WALK ME HOME, KIRB!
SCHOOL STORY-STYLE!
OKAY.
WHEN DID THEY GET SCHOOL UNIFORMS ?!

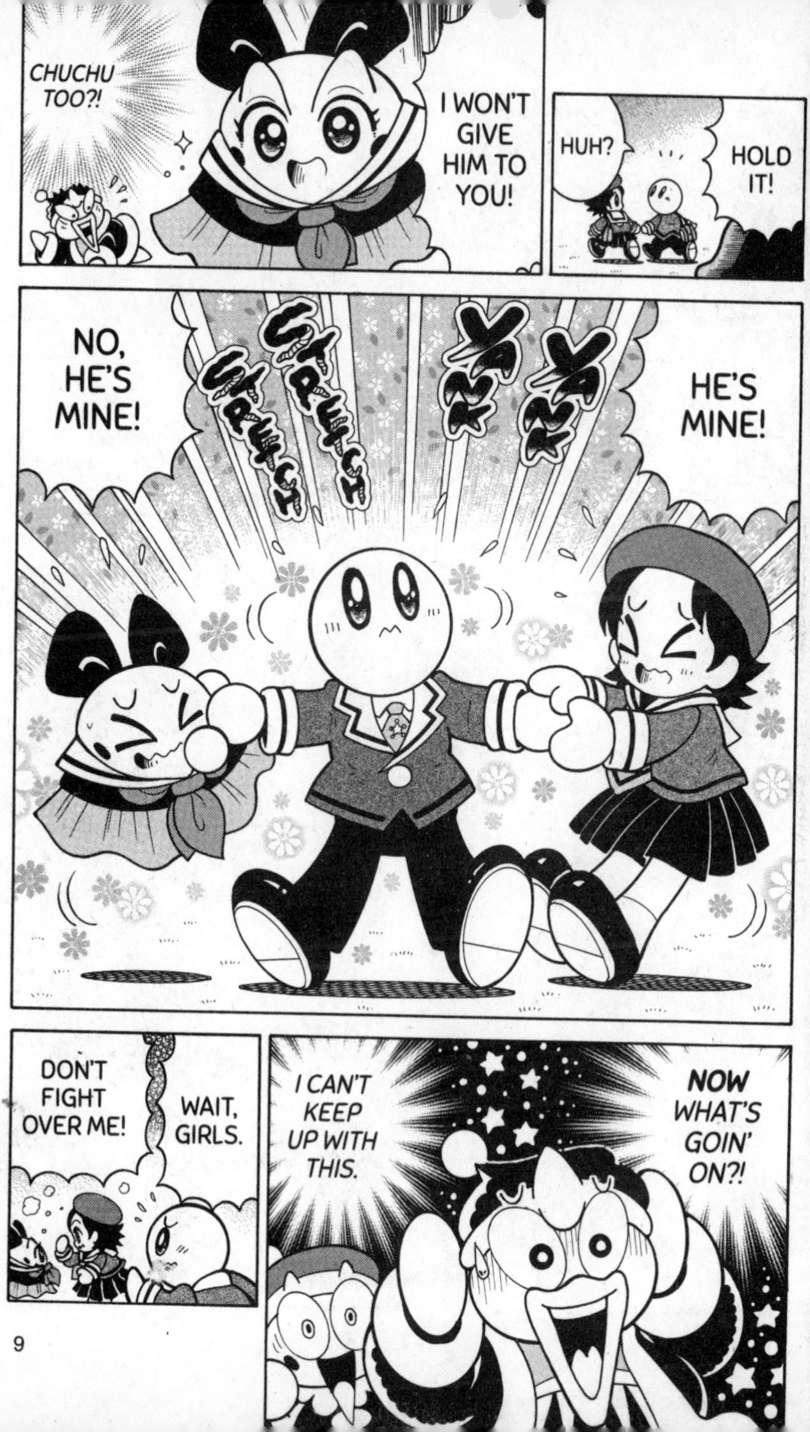
HOLD IT!
HUH?
I WON'T GIVE HIM TO YOU!
CHUCHU TOO?!
HE'S MINE!
YANK
YANK
STRETCH
STRETCH
NO, HE'S MINE!
NOW WHAT'S GOIN' ON?!
I CAN'T KEEP UP WITH THIS.
WAIT, GIRLS.
DON'T FIGHT OVER ME!

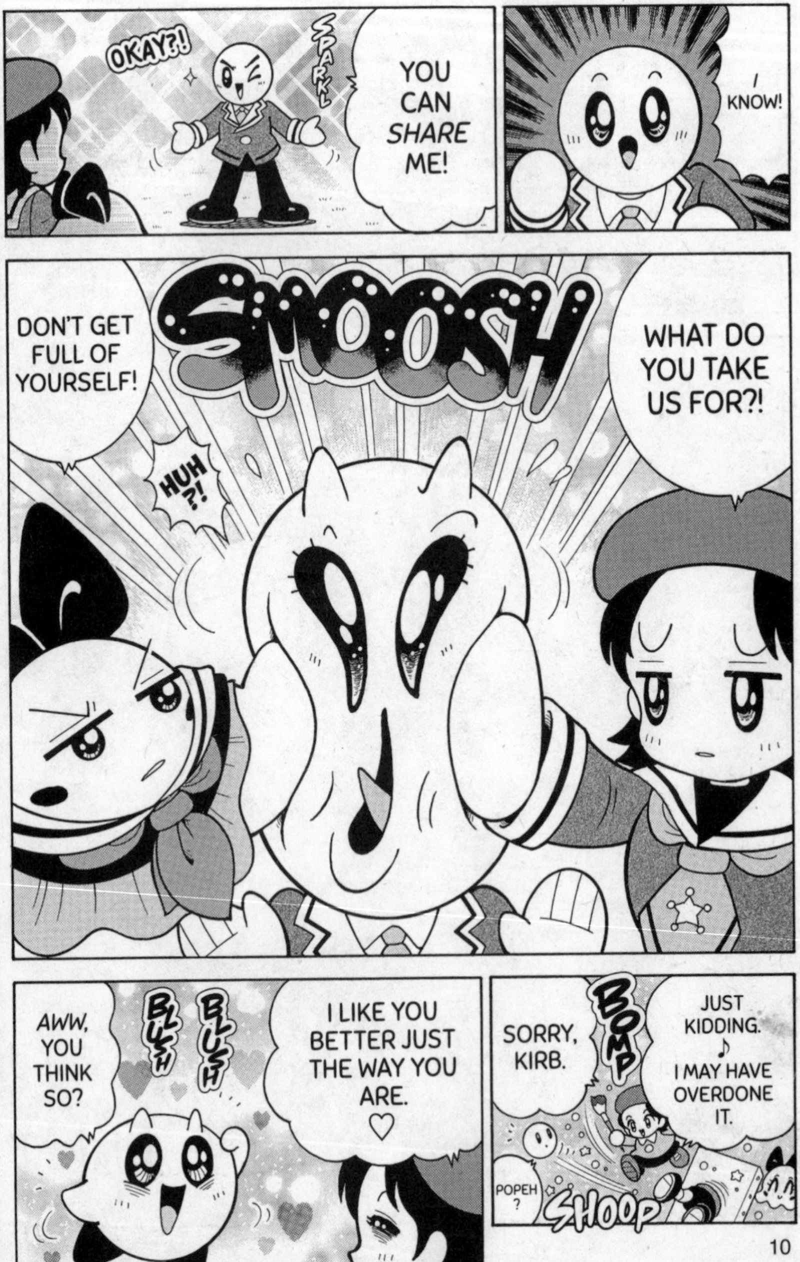
I KNOW!
YOU CAN SHARE ME!
SPARKL
OKAY?!
WHAT DO YOU TAKE US FOR?!
SMOOSH
DON'T GET FULL OF YOURSELF!
HUH?!
JUST KIDDING. ♪ I MAY HAVE OVERDONE IT.
BOMP
SORRY, KIRB.
POPEH ?
SHOOP
I LIKE YOU BETTER JUST THE WAY YOU ARE. ♡
BLUSH
BLUSH
AWW, YOU THINK SO?

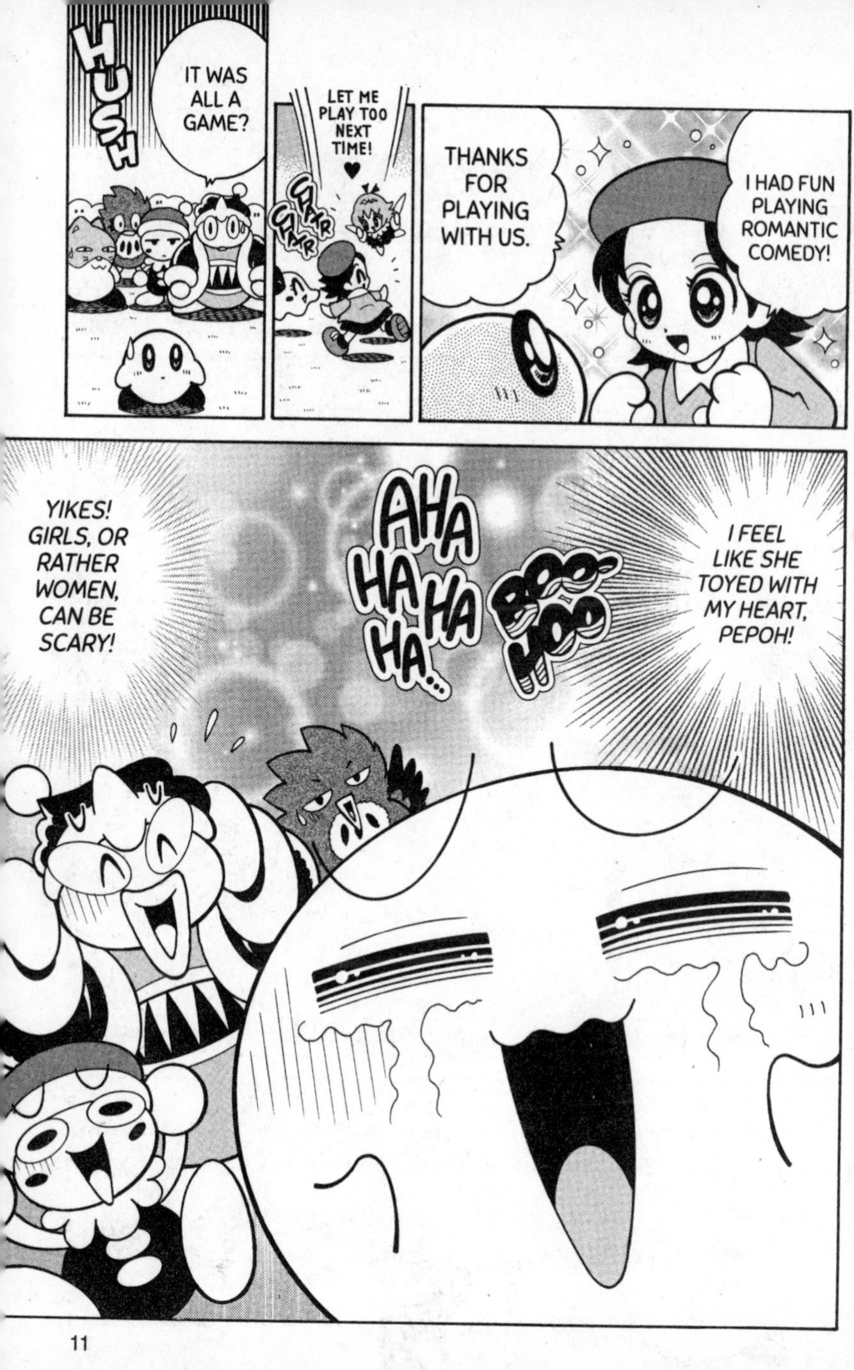
I HAD FUN PLAYING ROMANTIC COMEDY!
THANKS FOR PLAYING WITH US.
LET ME PLAY TOO NEXT TIME! ♥
CHAAR
CHAAR
HUSH
IT WAS ALL A GAME?
I FEEL LIKE SHE TOYED WITH MY HEART, PEPOH!
BOO HOO
AHAHAHAHA HA...
YIKES! GIRLS, OR RATHER WOMEN, CAN BE SCARY!

KIRBY'S PEEK BEHIND THE SCENES 1

IT'S TIME FOR A BRIEF LOOK INTO THE MAKING OF THE *KIRBY* MANGA!

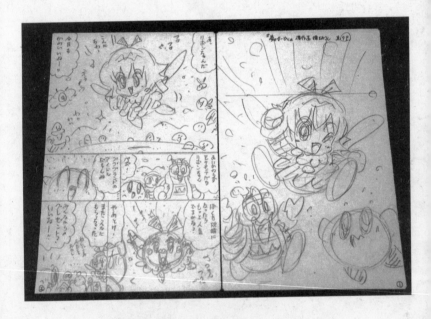

I START BY DRAFTING A STORY. THIS IS THE TOUGHEST PART OF MAKING MANGA. WHEN I CAN'T COME UP WITH A STORY, EVEN WITH A DEADLINE LOOMING, IT REALLY MAKES ME WANT TO RUN AWAY!

CHAPTER 2: THE BIGGEST CAT CRAZE OF ALL TIME?!

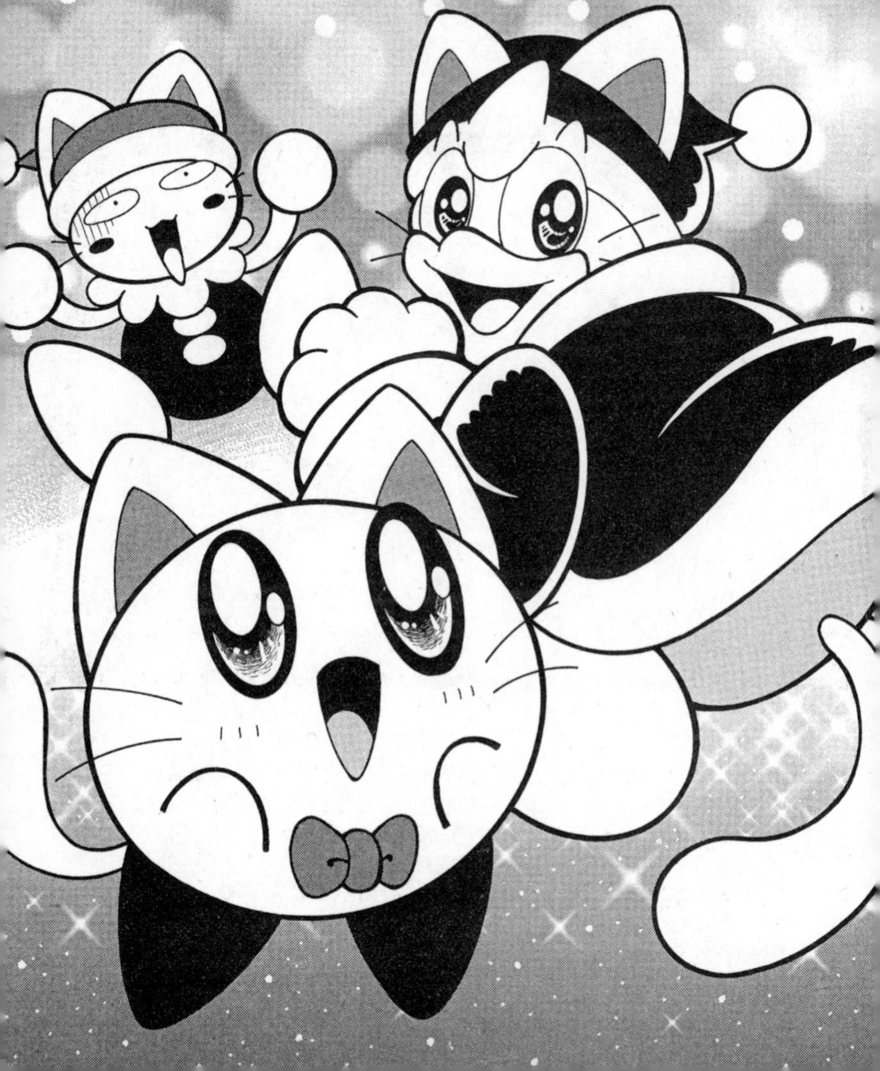

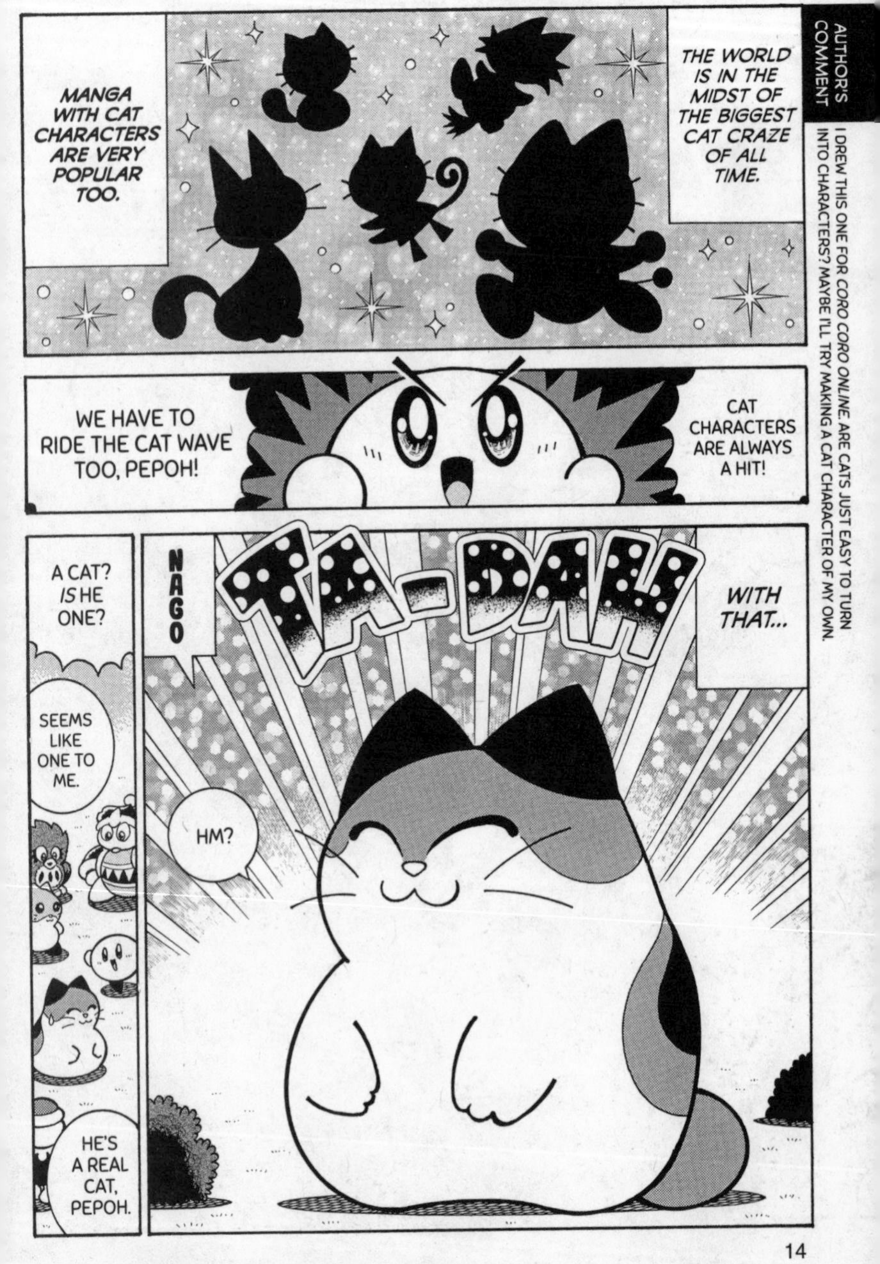
THE WORLD IS IN THE MIDST OF THE BIGGEST CAT CRAZE OF ALL TIME.
MANGA WITH CAT CHARACTERS ARE VERY POPULAR TOO.
CAT CHARACTERS ARE ALWAYS A HIT!
WE HAVE TO RIDE THE CAT WAVE TOO, PEPOH!
WITH THAT...
TA-DAH
NAGO
HM?
A CAT? *IS* HE ONE?
SEEMS LIKE ONE TO ME.
HE'S A REAL CAT, PEPOH.

AUTHOR'S COMMENT

I DREW THIS ONE FOR *CORO CORO ONLINE*. ARE CATS JUST EASY TO TURN INTO CHARACTERS? MAYBE I'LL TRY MAKING A CAT CHARACTER OF MY OWN.

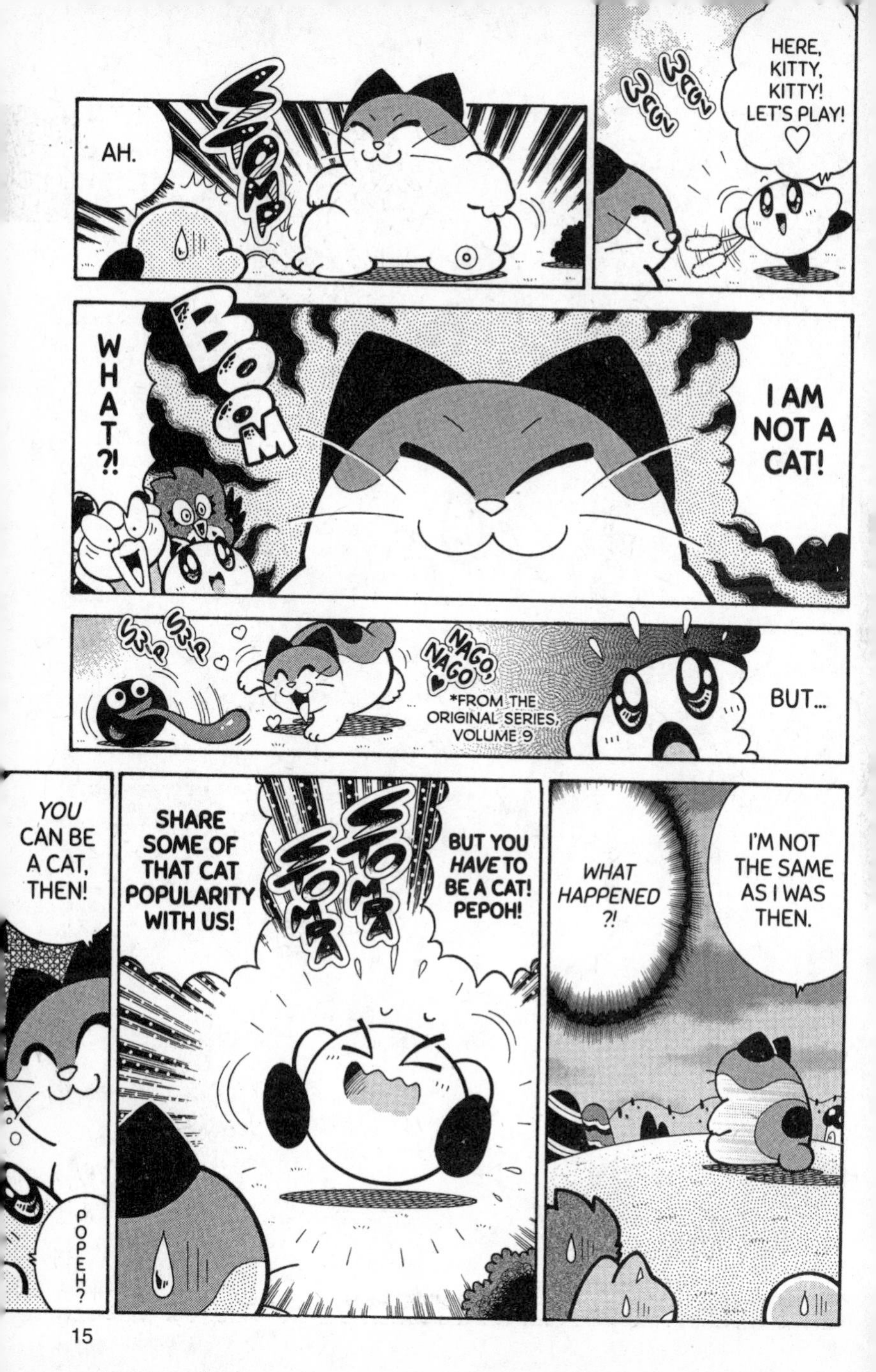
HERE, KITTY, KITTY! LET'S PLAY! ♡
STOMP
AH.
I AM NOT A CAT!
BOOM
WHAT?!
BUT...
NAGO, NAGO ♥
*FROM THE ORIGINAL SERIES, VOLUME 9
I'M NOT THE SAME AS I WAS THEN.
WHAT HAPPENED ?!
BUT YOU *HAVE* TO BE A CAT! PEPOH!
STOMP
STOMP
SHARE SOME OF THAT CAT POPULARITY WITH US!
YOU CAN BE A CAT, THEN!
POPEH?

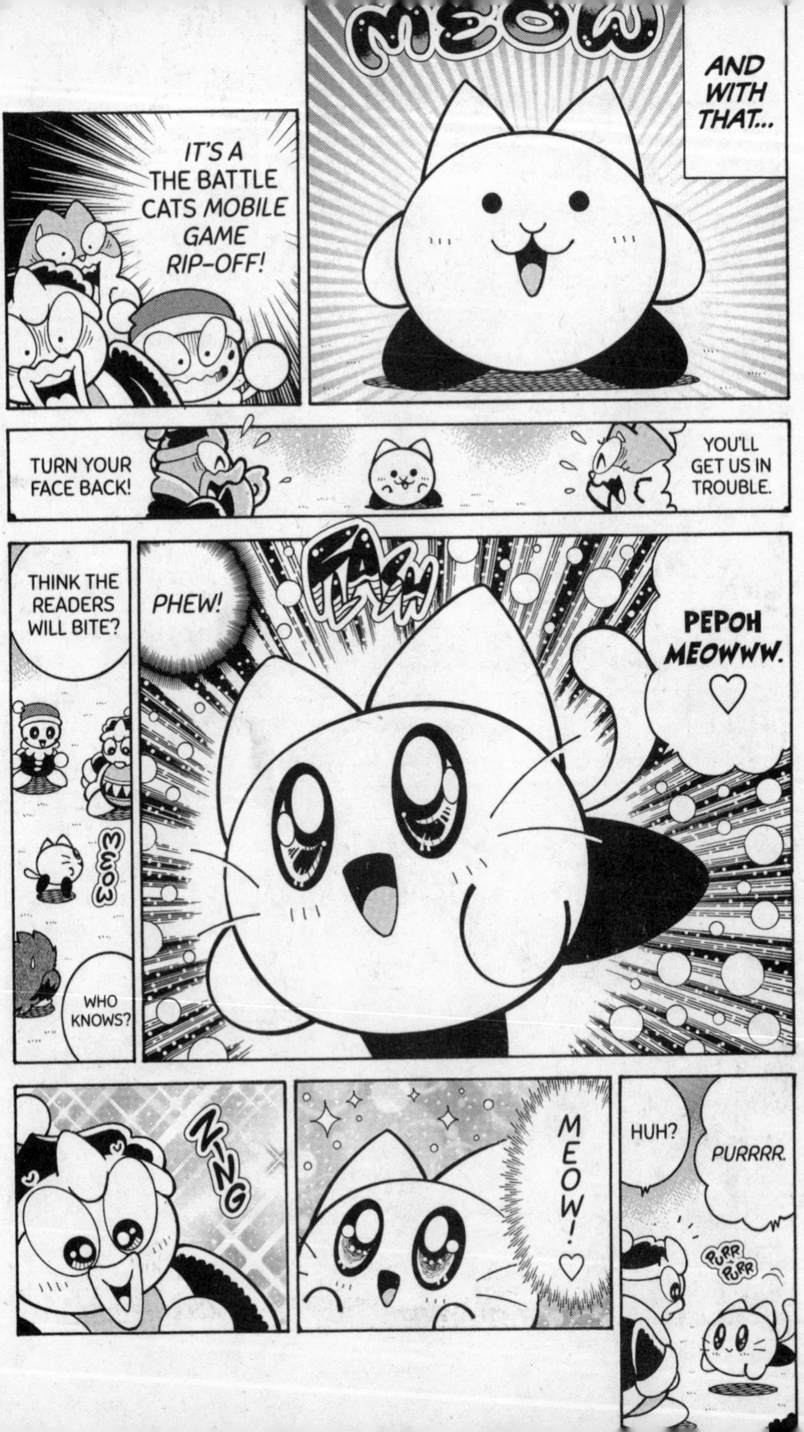
MEOW
AND WITH THAT...
IT'S A THE BATTLE CATS MOBILE GAME RIP-OFF!
YOU'LL GET US IN TROUBLE.
TURN YOUR FACE BACK!
PEPOH MEOWWW. ♥
PHEW!
THINK THE READERS WILL BITE?
MEOW
WHO KNOWS?
PURRRR.
HUH?
PURR PURR
MEOW! ♥

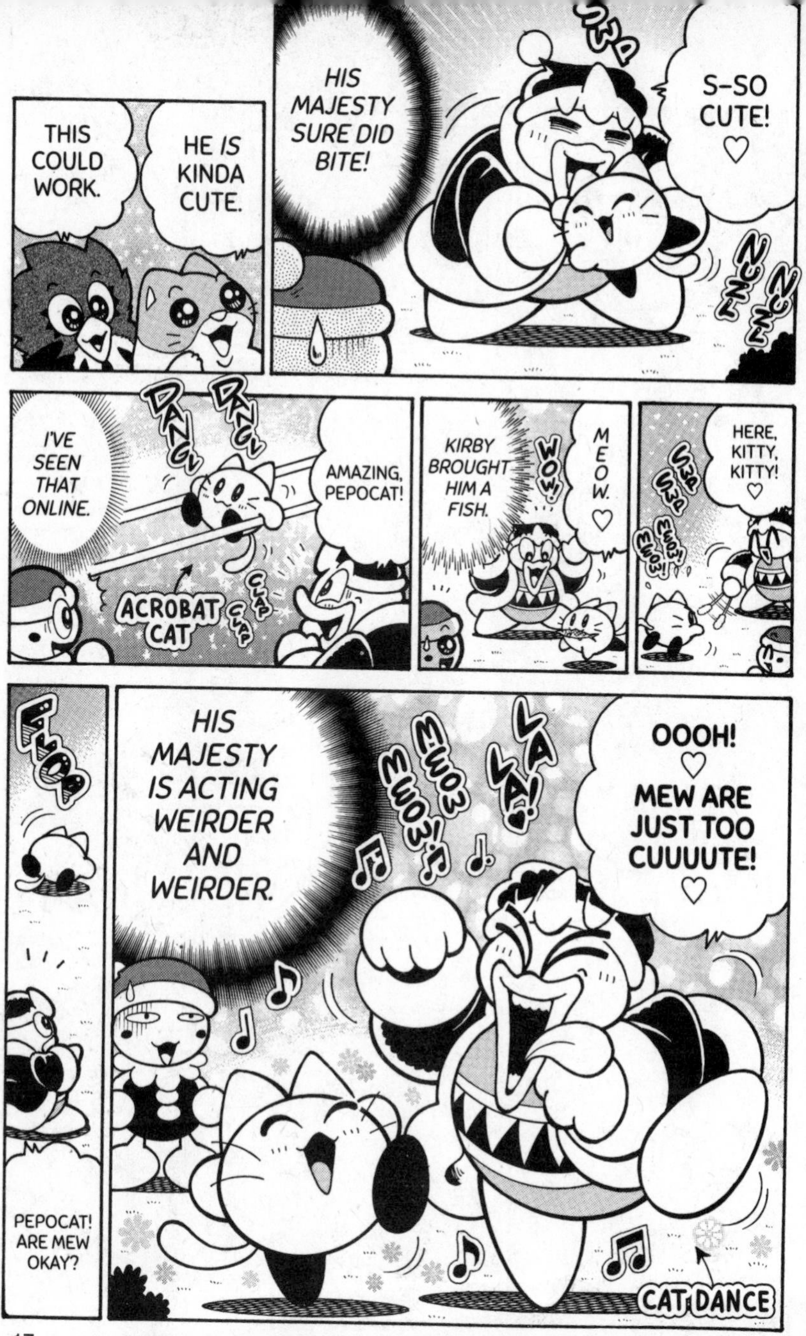
S-SO CUTE! ♡
HIS MAJESTY SURE DID BITE!
NUZZLE NUZZLE
HE IS KINDA CUTE.
THIS COULD WORK.
HERE, KITTY, KITTY! ♡
MEOW. ♡
WOW!
KIRBY BROUGHT HIM A FISH.
AMAZING, PEPOCAT!
I'VE SEEN THAT ONLINE.
ACROBAT CAT
CLAP CLAP
OOOH! ♡ MEW ARE JUST TOO CUUUUTE! ♡
LA LA!
HIS MAJESTY IS ACTING WEIRDER AND WEIRDER.
CAT DANCE
PEPOCAT! ARE MEW OKAY?

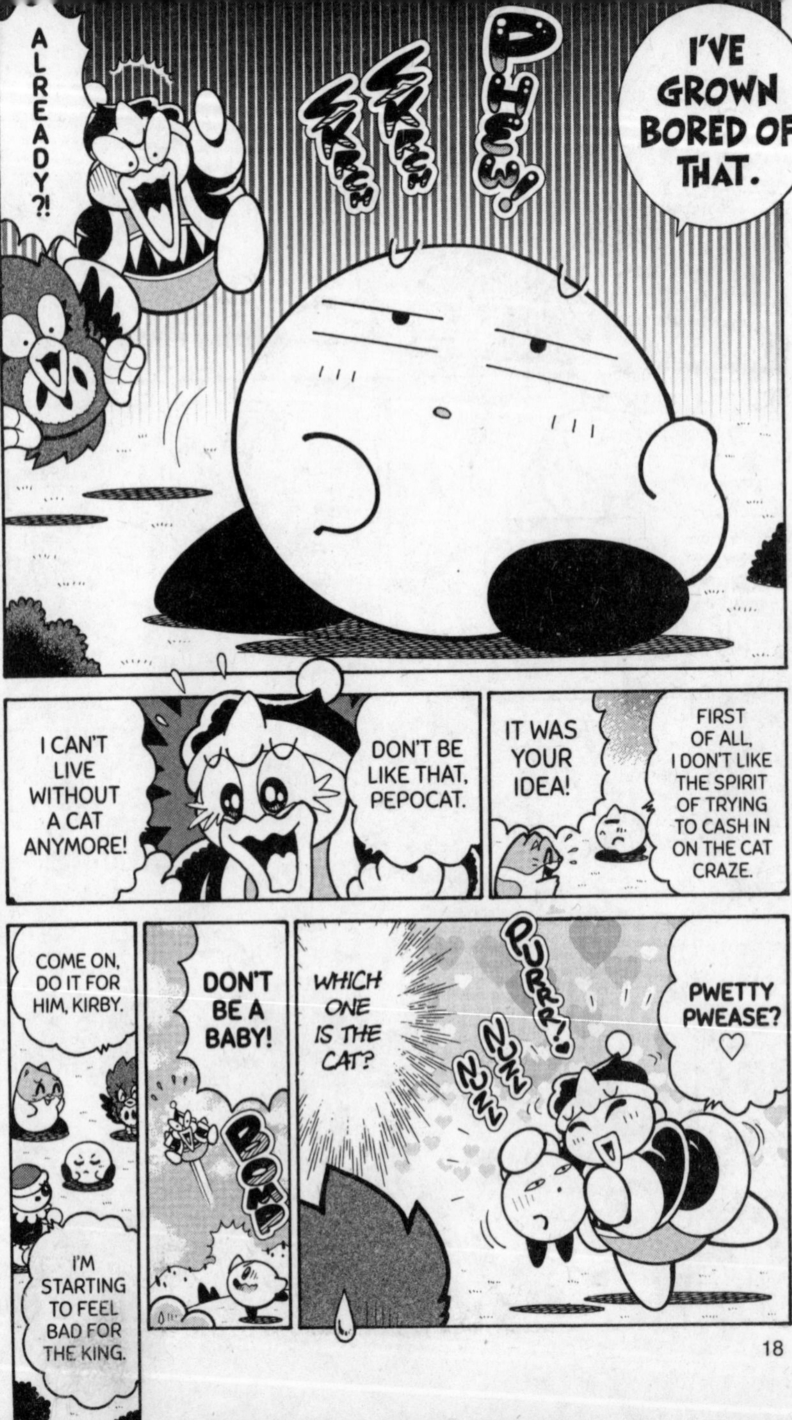
I'VE GROWN BORED OF THAT.
PHEW!
SKRCH
SKRCH
ALREADY?!
FIRST OF ALL, I DON'T LIKE THE SPIRIT OF TRYING TO CASH IN ON THE CAT CRAZE.
IT WAS YOUR IDEA!
DON'T BE LIKE THAT, PEPOCAT.
I CAN'T LIVE WITHOUT A CAT ANYMORE!
PWETTY PWEASE? ♡
PURRR!♥
NUZZ
NUZZ
WHICH ONE IS THE CAT?
DON'T BE A BABY!
BOMP
COME ON, DO IT FOR HIM, KIRBY.
I'M STARTING TO FEEL BAD FOR THE KING.

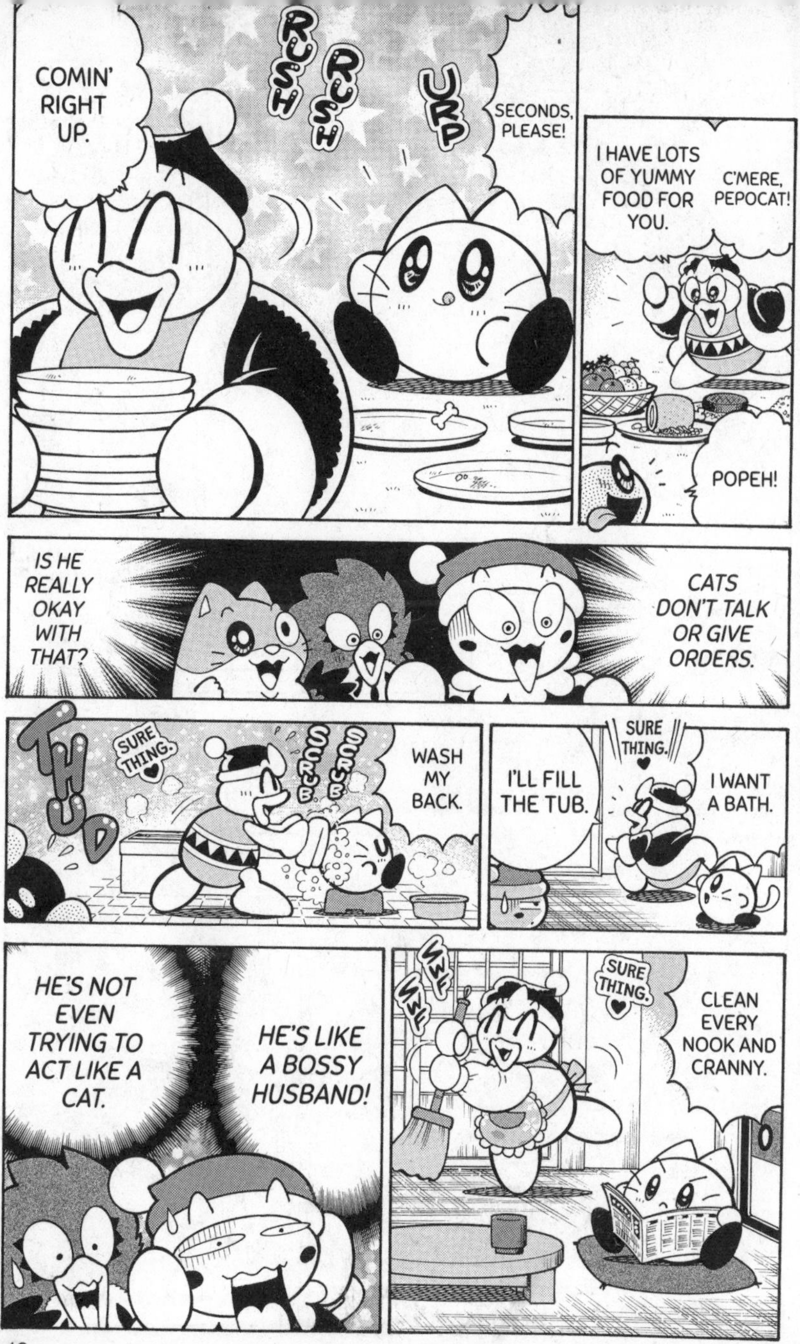
C'MERE, PEPOCAT!
I HAVE LOTS OF YUMMY FOOD FOR YOU.
POPEH!
SECONDS, PLEASE!
URP
RUSH RUSH
COMIN' RIGHT UP.
CATS DON'T TALK OR GIVE ORDERS.
IS HE REALLY OKAY WITH THAT?
I WANT A BATH.
SURE THING.
I'LL FILL THE TUB.
WASH MY BACK.
SCRUB SCRUB
SURE THING.
THUD
CLEAN EVERY NOOK AND CRANNY.
SURE THING.
SWF SWF
HE'S LIKE A BOSSY HUSBAND!
HE'S NOT EVEN TRYING TO ACT LIKE A CAT.

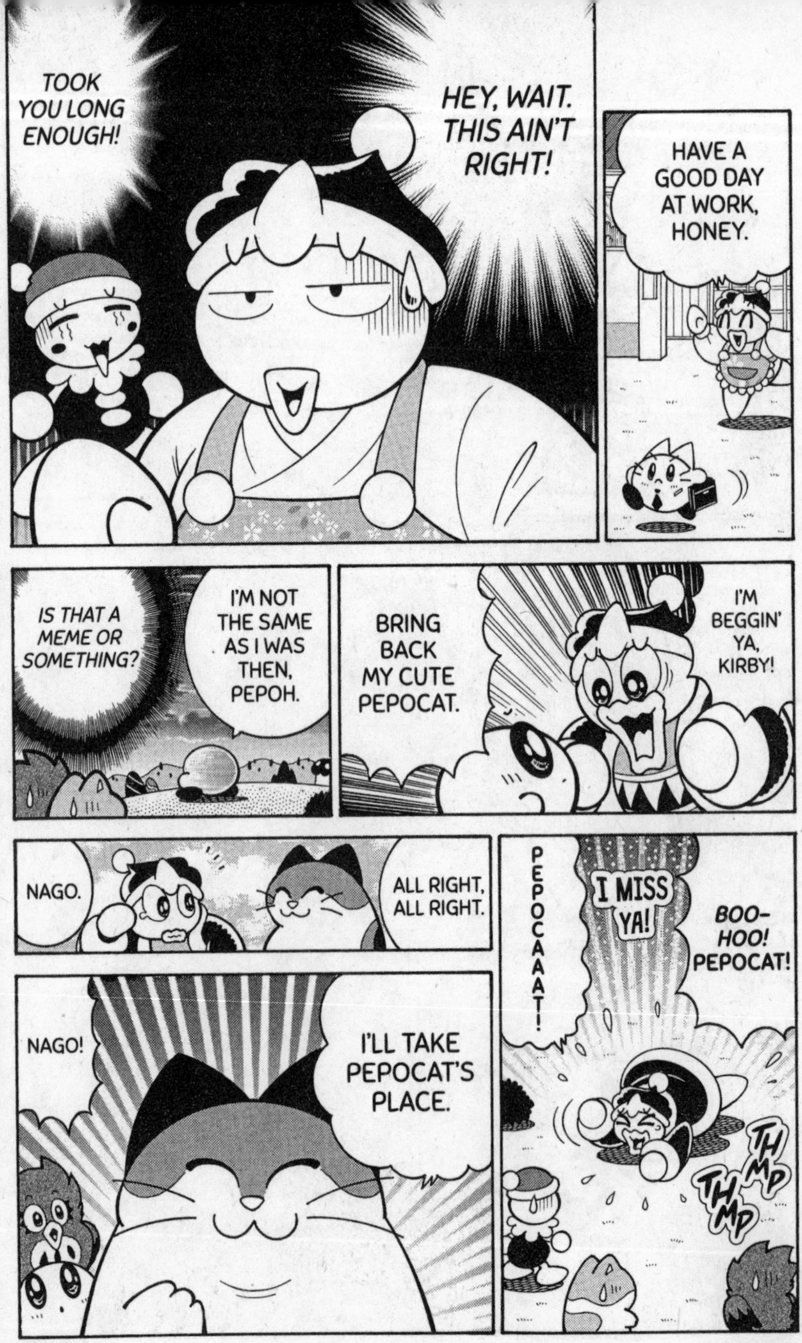
HAVE A GOOD DAY AT WORK, HONEY.
HEY, WAIT. THIS AIN'T RIGHT!
TOOK YOU LONG ENOUGH!
I'M BEGGIN' YA, KIRBY!
BRING BACK MY CUTE PEPOCAT.
I'M NOT THE SAME AS I WAS THEN, PEPOH.
IS THAT A MEME OR SOMETHING?
BOO-HOO! PEPOCAT!
I MISS YA!
PEPOCAAAT!
THMP
THMP
ALL RIGHT, ALL RIGHT.
NAGO.
I'LL TAKE PEPOCAT'S PLACE.
NAGO!

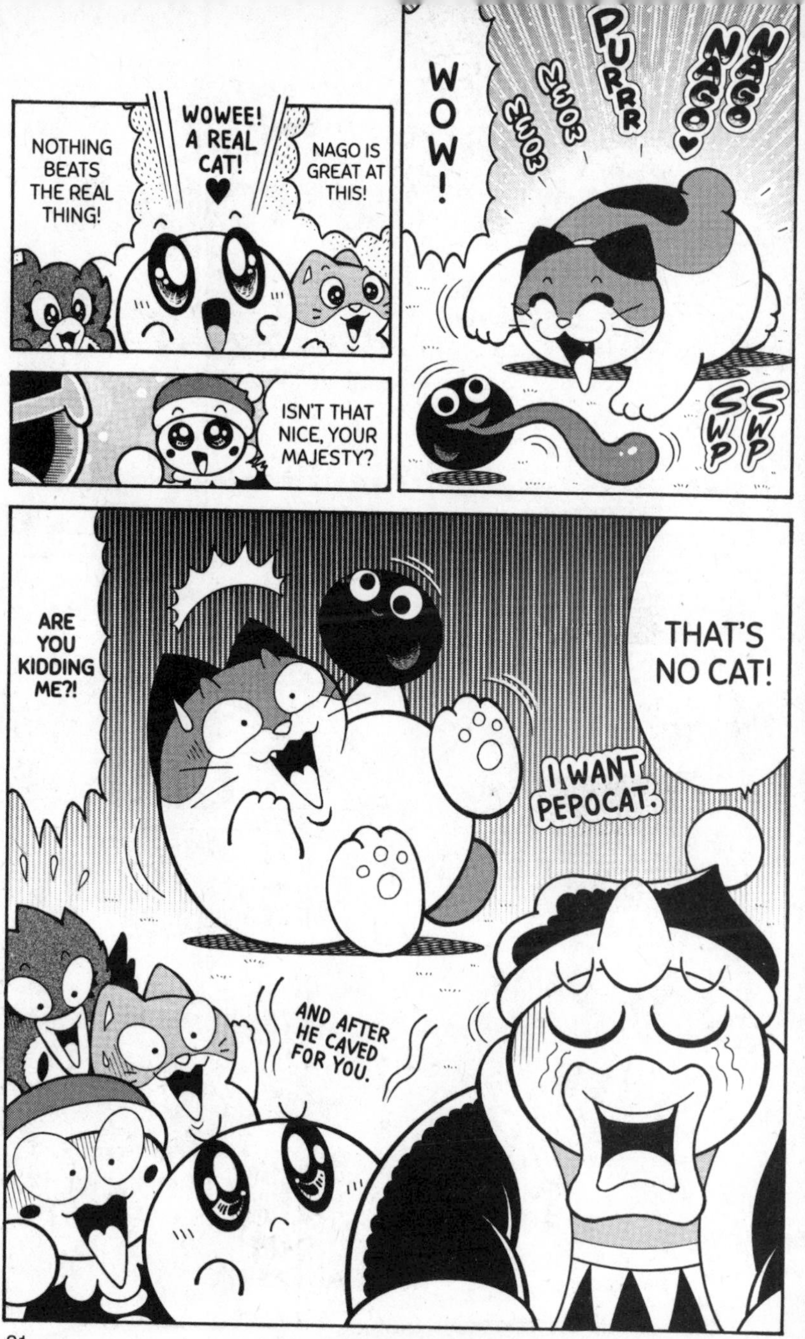
NAGO NAGO ♥
PURRR
MEOW MEOW
WOW!
SWP SWP
NAGO IS GREAT AT THIS!
WOWEE! A REAL CAT! ♥
NOTHING BEATS THE REAL THING!
ISN'T THAT NICE, YOUR MAJESTY?
THAT'S NO CAT!
I WANT PEPOCAT.
ARE YOU KIDDING ME?!
AND AFTER HE CAVED FOR YOU.

KIRBY'S PEEK
BEHIND THE SCENES 2

AFTER I GET THE OKAY FROM MY
EDITOR AND NINTENDO, I DO THE
PENCILS ON A4-SIZE COPY PAPER.

SINCE I'M A WEAK ARTIST, IT TAKES ME A
LONG TIME! ONCE IT'S DONE, I PHOTOCOPY
IT ENLARGED TO B4-SIZE AND THEN TRACE IT
ONTO MANGA DRAFT PAPER WITH A 2B
MECHANICAL PENCIL.

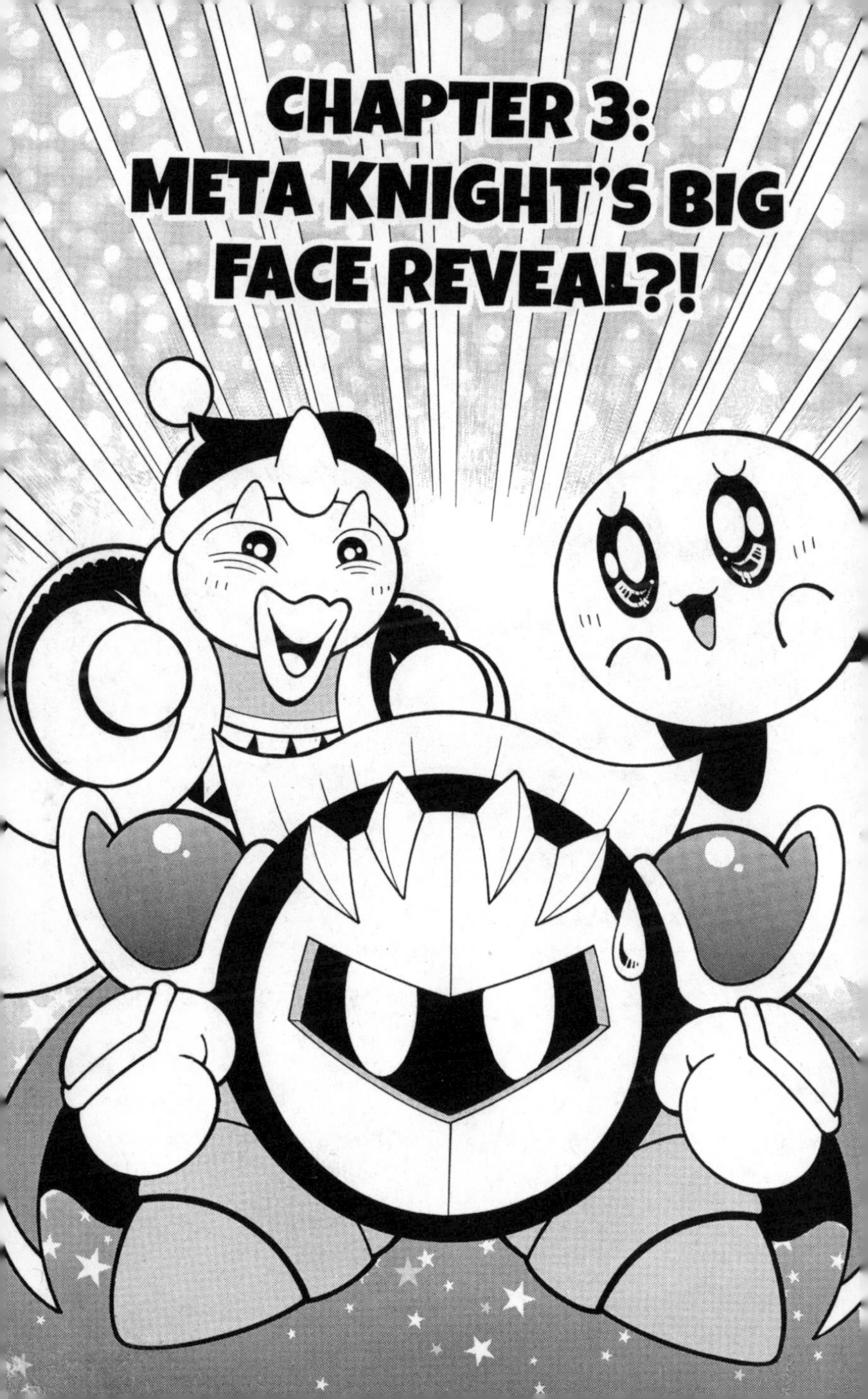
CHAPTER 3:
META KNIGHT'S BIG
FACE REVEAL?!

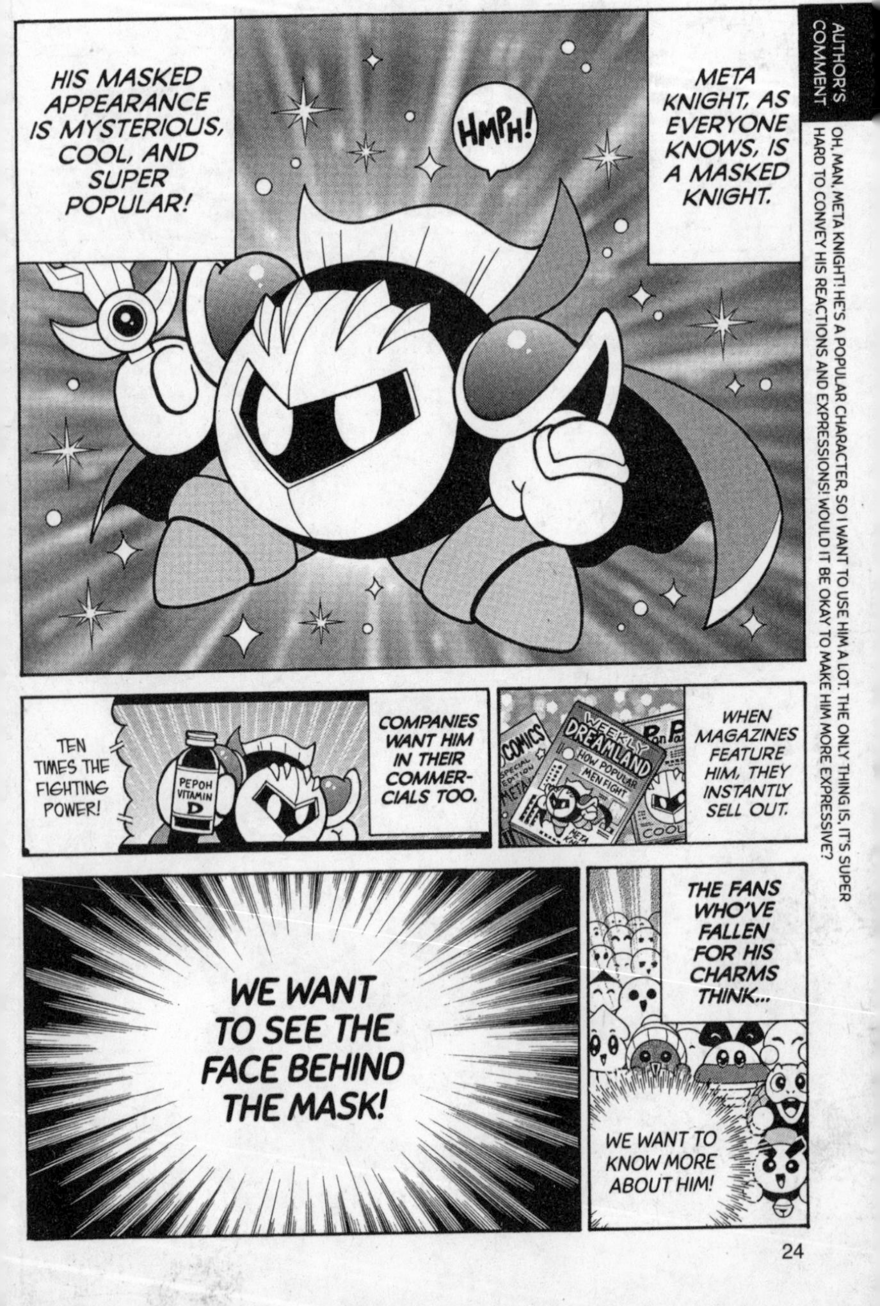
META KNIGHT, AS EVERYONE KNOWS, IS A MASKED KNIGHT.
HMPH!
HIS MASKED APPEARANCE IS MYSTERIOUS, COOL, AND SUPER POPULAR!
WHEN MAGAZINES FEATURE HIM, THEY INSTANTLY SELL OUT.
WEEKLY DREAMLAND
HOW POPULAR MEN FIGHT
META KNIGHT
COMICS
SPECIAL EDITION
META
COOL
COMPANIES WANT HIM IN THEIR COMMERCIALS TOO.
TEN TIMES THE FIGHTING POWER!
PEPOH VITAMIN D
THE FANS WHO'VE FALLEN FOR HIS CHARMS THINK...
WE WANT TO KNOW MORE ABOUT HIM!
WE WANT TO SEE THE FACE BEHIND THE MASK!

AUTHOR'S COMMENT

OH, MAN, META KNIGHT! HE'S A POPULAR CHARACTER, SO I WANT TO USE HIM A LOT. THE ONLY THING IS, IT'S SUPER HARD TO CONVEY HIS REACTIONS AND EXPRESSIONS! WOULD IT BE OKAY TO MAKE HIM MORE EXPRESSIVE?

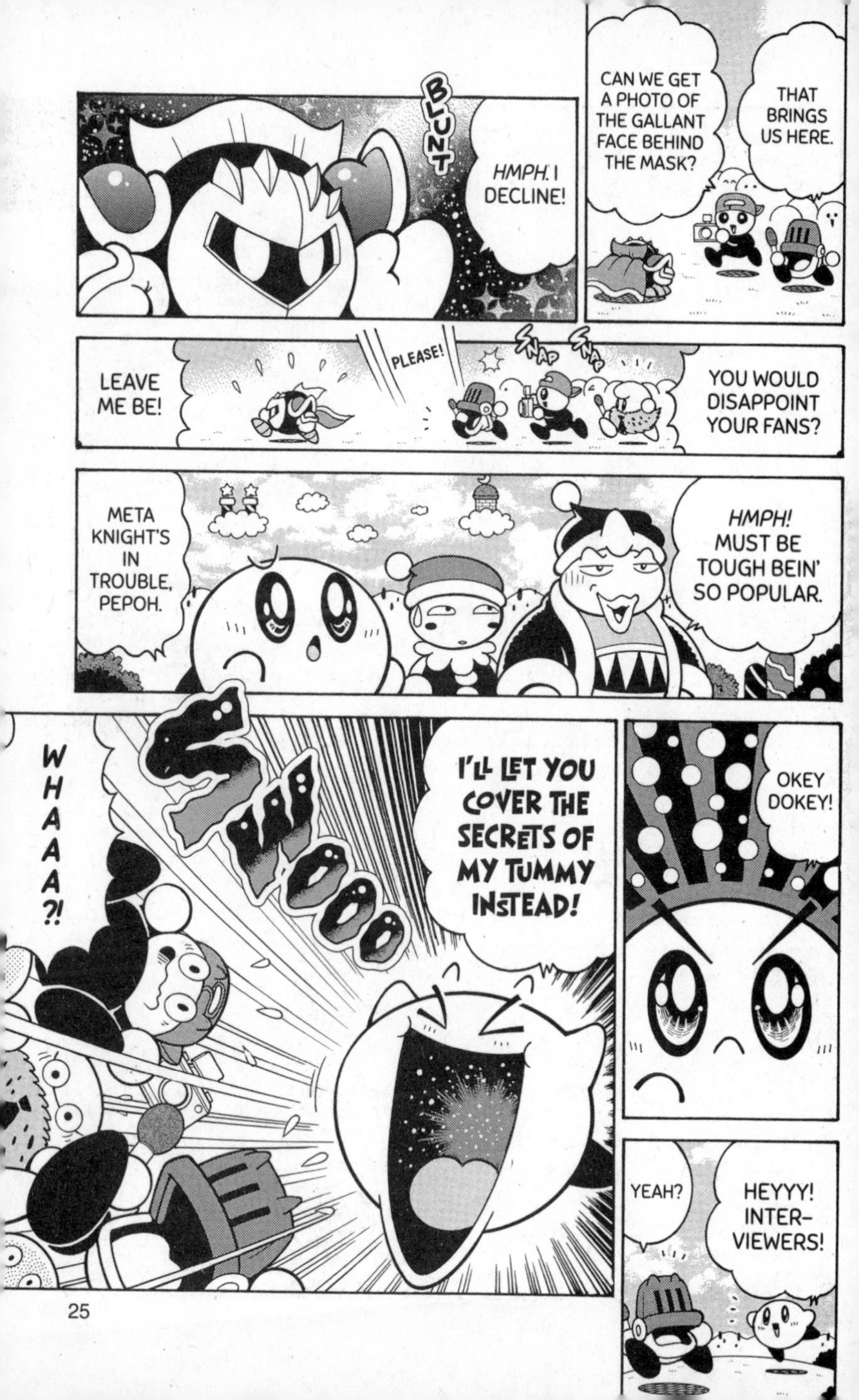
THAT BRINGS US HERE.
CAN WE GET A PHOTO OF THE GALLANT FACE BEHIND THE MASK?
BLUNT
HMPH. I DECLINE!
YOU WOULD DISAPPOINT YOUR FANS?
SNAP
SNAP
PLEASE!
LEAVE ME BE!
HMPH! MUST BE TOUGH BEIN' SO POPULAR.
META KNIGHT'S IN TROUBLE, PEPOH.
OKEY DOKEY!
HEYYY! INTER-VIEWERS!
YEAH?
I'LL LET YOU COVER THE SECRETS OF MY TUMMY INSTEAD!
SWOOO
WHAAAA?!

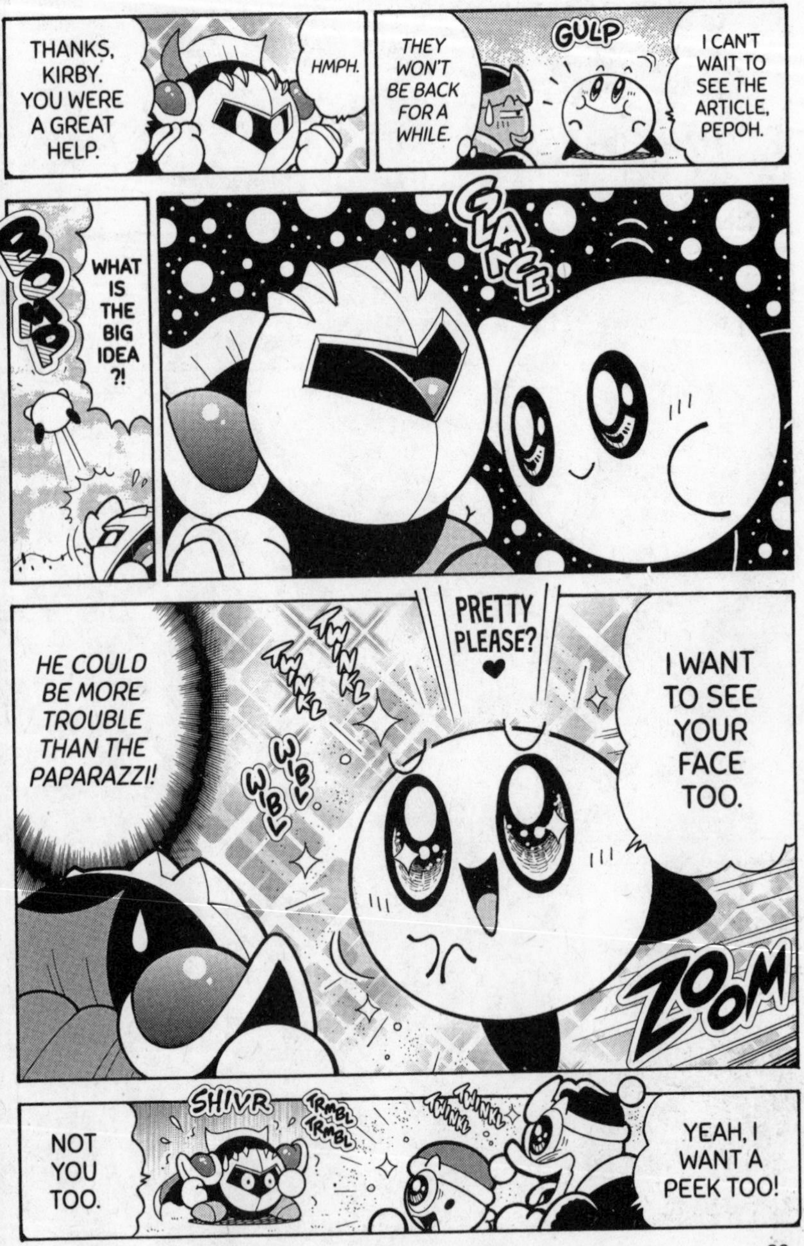
GULP
I CAN'T WAIT TO SEE THE ARTICLE, PEPOH.
THEY WON'T BE BACK FOR A WHILE.
HMPH.
THANKS, KIRBY. YOU WERE A GREAT HELP.
GLANCE
WHAT IS THE BIG IDEA ?!
I WANT TO SEE YOUR FACE TOO.
PRETTY PLEASE? ♥
TWINKL TWINKL
WIBL WIBL
HE COULD BE MORE TROUBLE THAN THE PAPARAZZI!
ZOOM
YEAH, I WANT A PEEK TOO!
TWINKL TWINKL
TRMBL TRMBL
SHIVR
NOT YOU TOO.

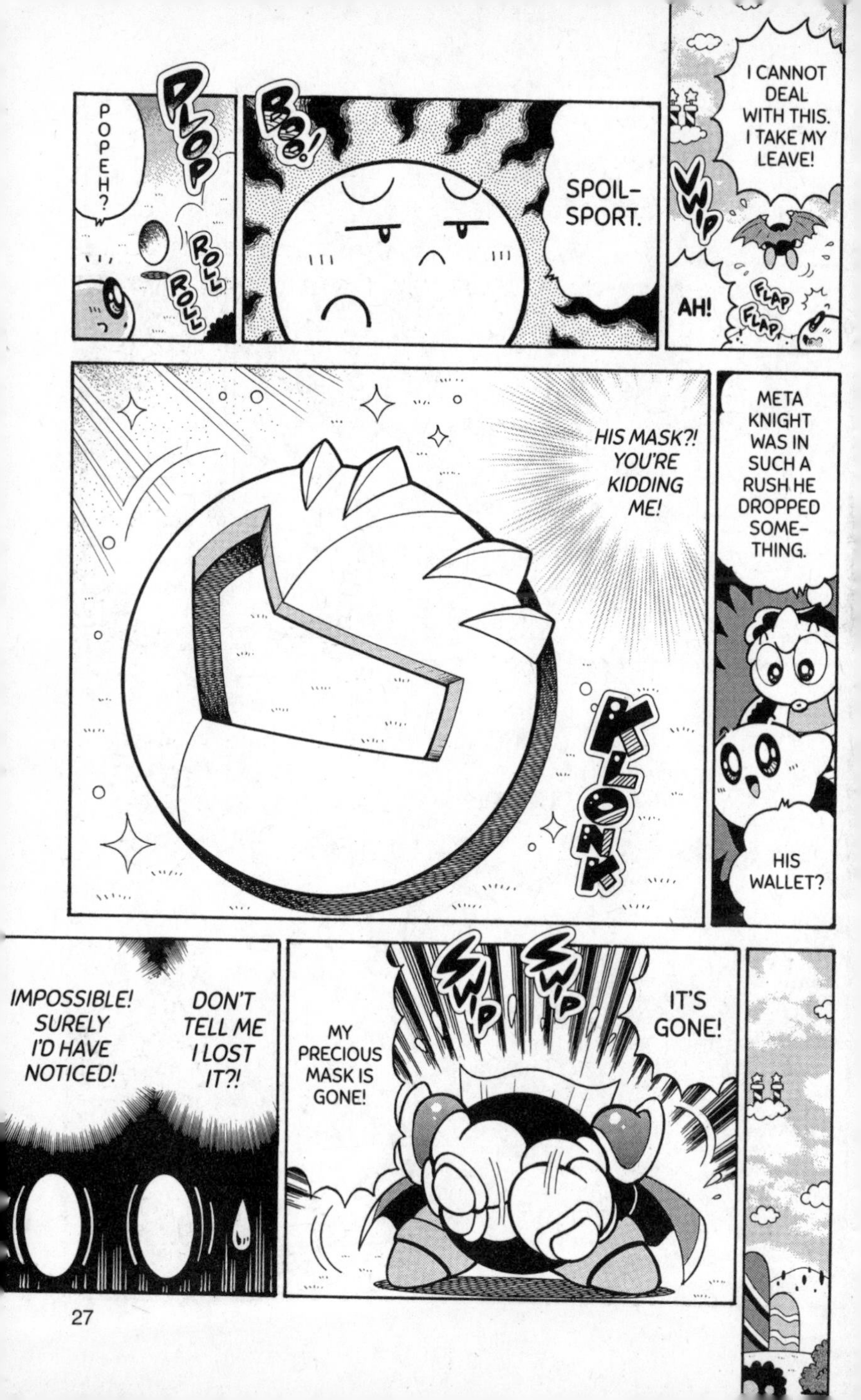
I CANNOT DEAL WITH THIS. I TAKE MY LEAVE!
VWIP
AH!
FLAP FLAP
BOO!
SPOIL-SPORT.
PLOP
POPEH?
ROLL ROLL
META KNIGHT WAS IN SUCH A RUSH HE DROPPED SOME-THING.
HIS WALLET?
HIS MASK?! YOU'RE KIDDING ME!
KLONK
SWIP SWIP
IT'S GONE!
MY PRECIOUS MASK IS GONE!
DON'T TELL ME I LOST IT?!
IMPOSSIBLE! SURELY I'D HAVE NOTICED!

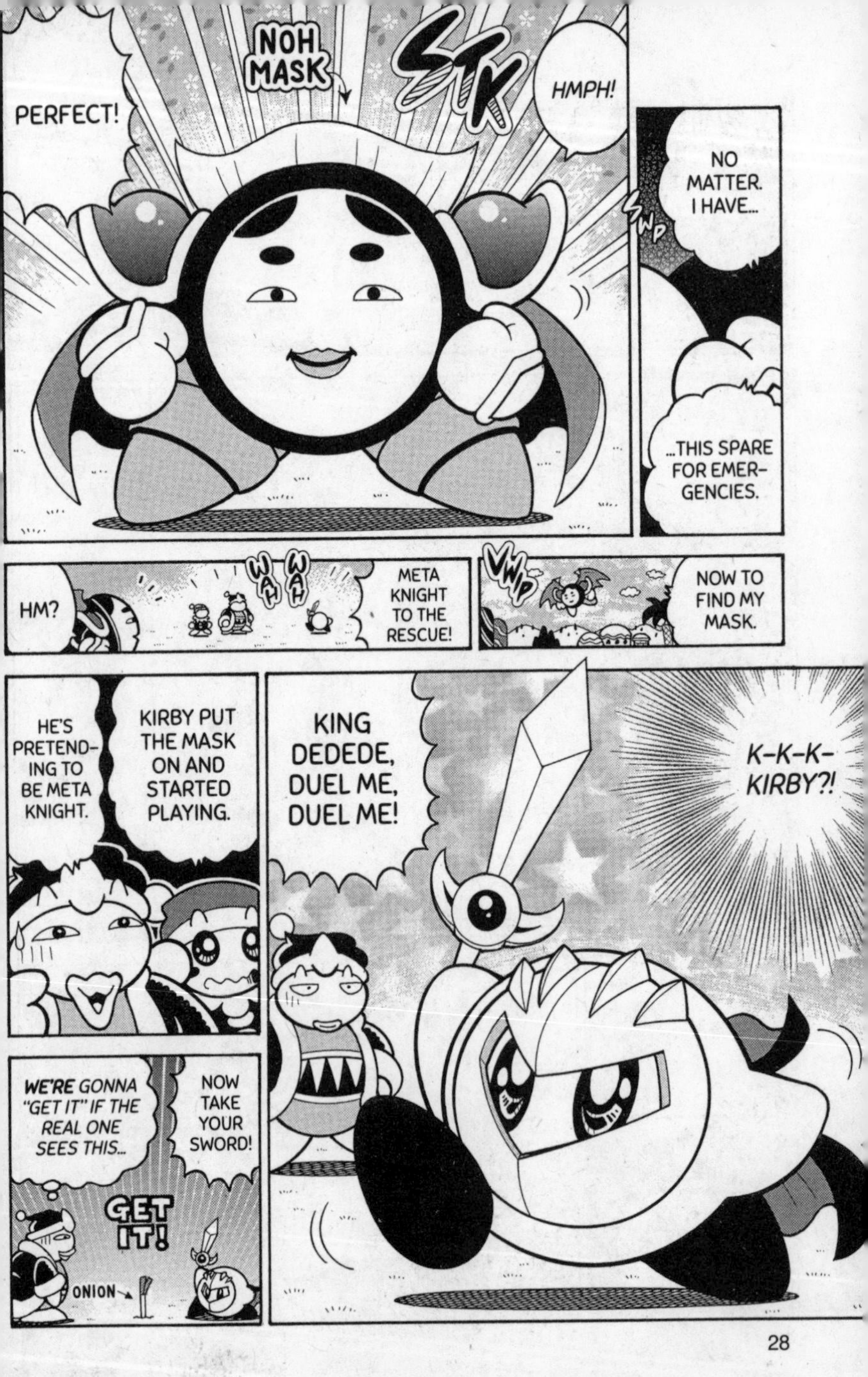
NO MATTER. I HAVE...
SNP
...THIS SPARE FOR EMER-GENCIES.
HMPH!
STK
NOH MASK
PERFECT!
NOW TO FIND MY MASK.
VWIP
META KNIGHT TO THE RESCUE!
WAH
WAH
HM?
K-K-K-KIRBY?!
KING DEDEDE, DUEL ME, DUEL ME!
KIRBY PUT THE MASK ON AND STARTED PLAYING.
HE'S PRETEND-ING TO BE META KNIGHT.
NOW TAKE YOUR SWORD!
WE'RE GONNA "GET IT" IF THE REAL ONE SEES THIS...
GET IT!
ONION

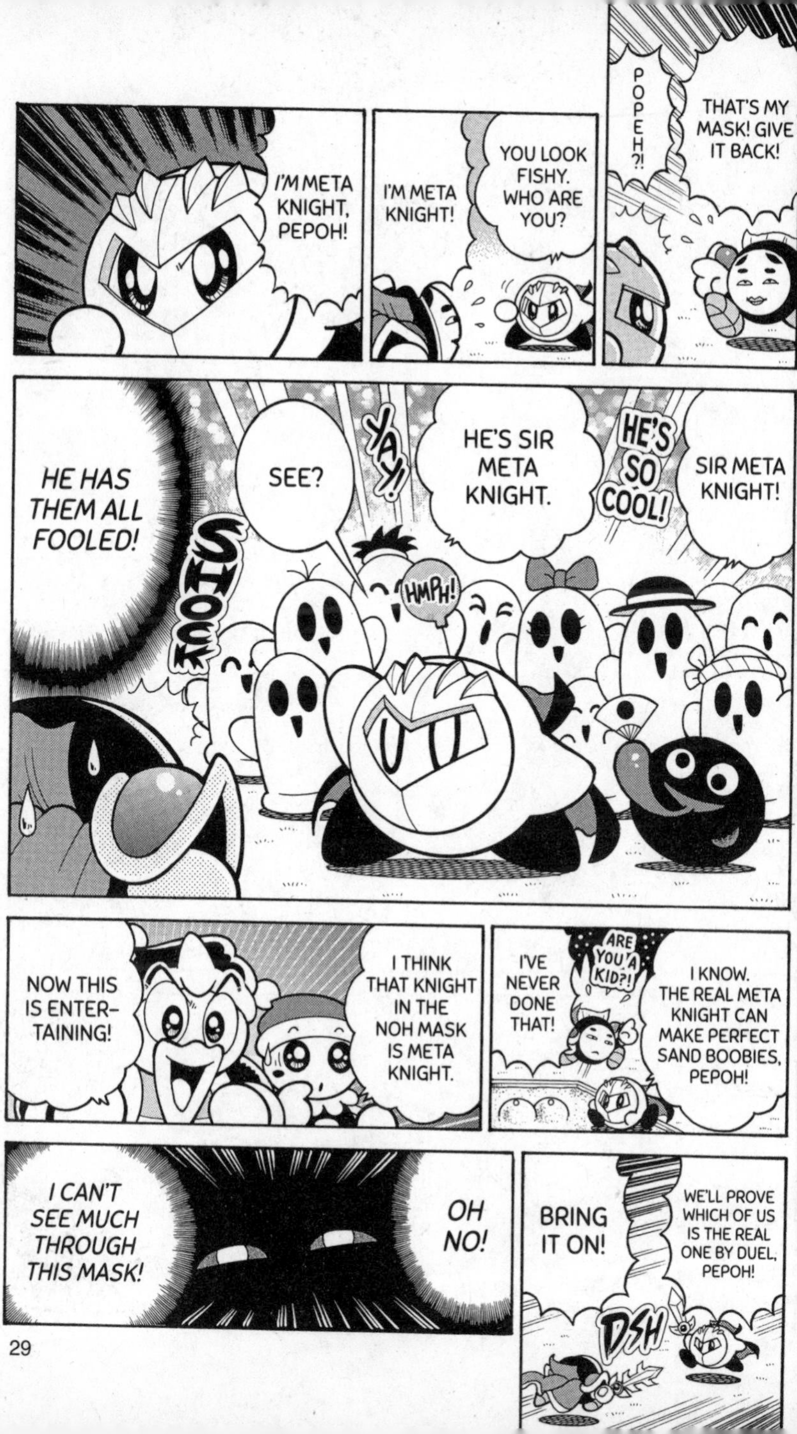
THAT'S MY MASK! GIVE IT BACK!
POPEH?!
YOU LOOK FISHY. WHO ARE YOU?
I'M META KNIGHT!
I'M META KNIGHT, PEPOH!
SIR META KNIGHT!
HE'S SO COOL!
HE'S SIR META KNIGHT.
YAY!
SEE?
HMPH!
SHOCK
HE HAS THEM ALL FOOLED!
I KNOW. THE REAL META KNIGHT CAN MAKE PERFECT SAND BOOBIES, PEPOH!
ARE YOU A KID?!
I'VE NEVER DONE THAT!
I THINK THAT KNIGHT IN THE NOH MASK IS META KNIGHT.
NOW THIS IS ENTER-TAINING!
WE'LL PROVE WHICH OF US IS THE REAL ONE BY DUEL, PEPOH!
BRING IT ON!
DSH
OH NO!
I CAN'T SEE MUCH THROUGH THIS MASK!

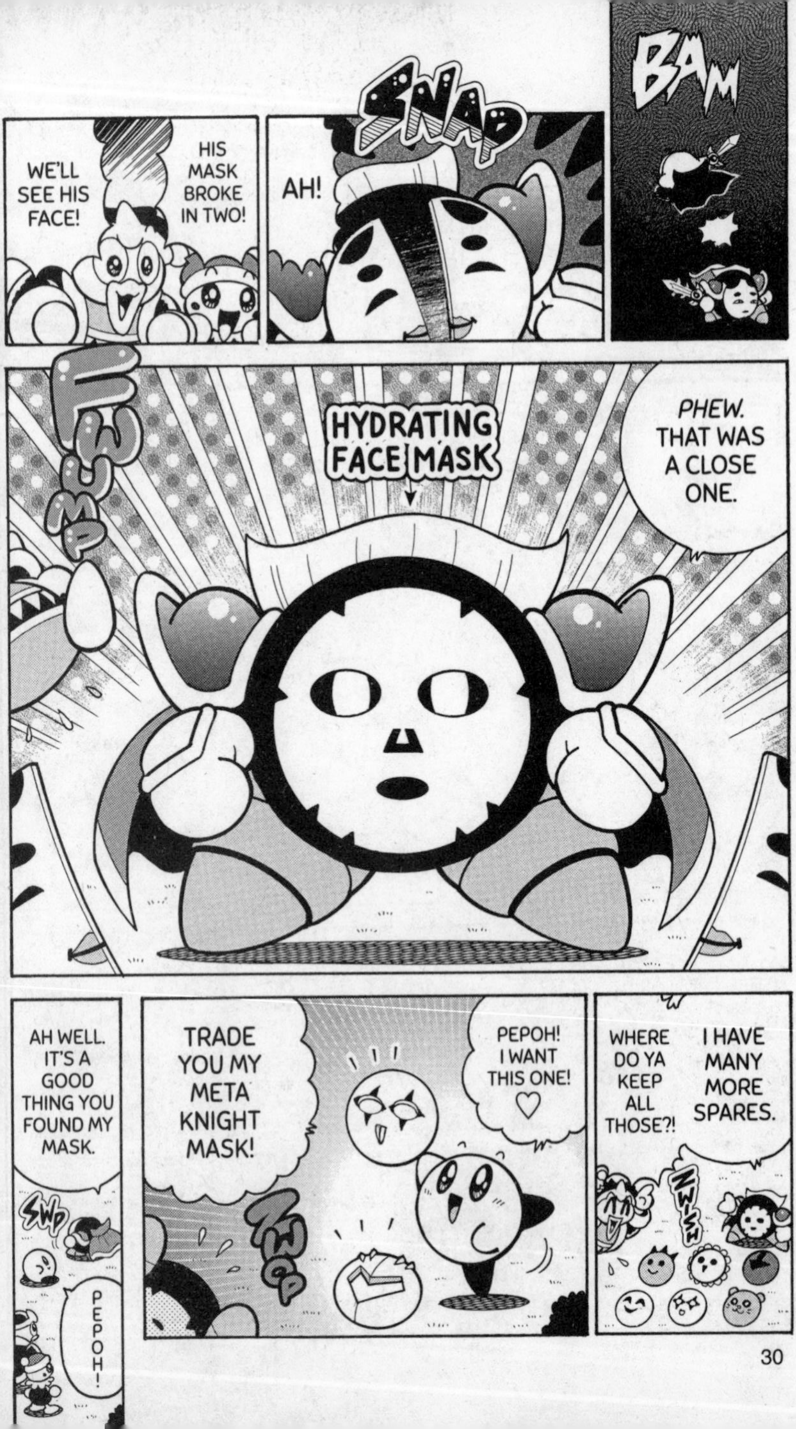
BAM
SNAP
AH!
HIS MASK BROKE IN TWO!
WE'LL SEE HIS FACE!
PHEW. THAT WAS A CLOSE ONE.
HYDRATING FACE MASK
FWUMP
I HAVE MANY MORE SPARES.
WHERE DO YA KEEP ALL THOSE?!
ZWISH
PEPOH! I WANT THIS ONE! ♡
TRADE YOU MY META KNIGHT MASK!
TWOP
AH WELL. IT'S A GOOD THING YOU FOUND MY MASK.
SWP
PEPOH!

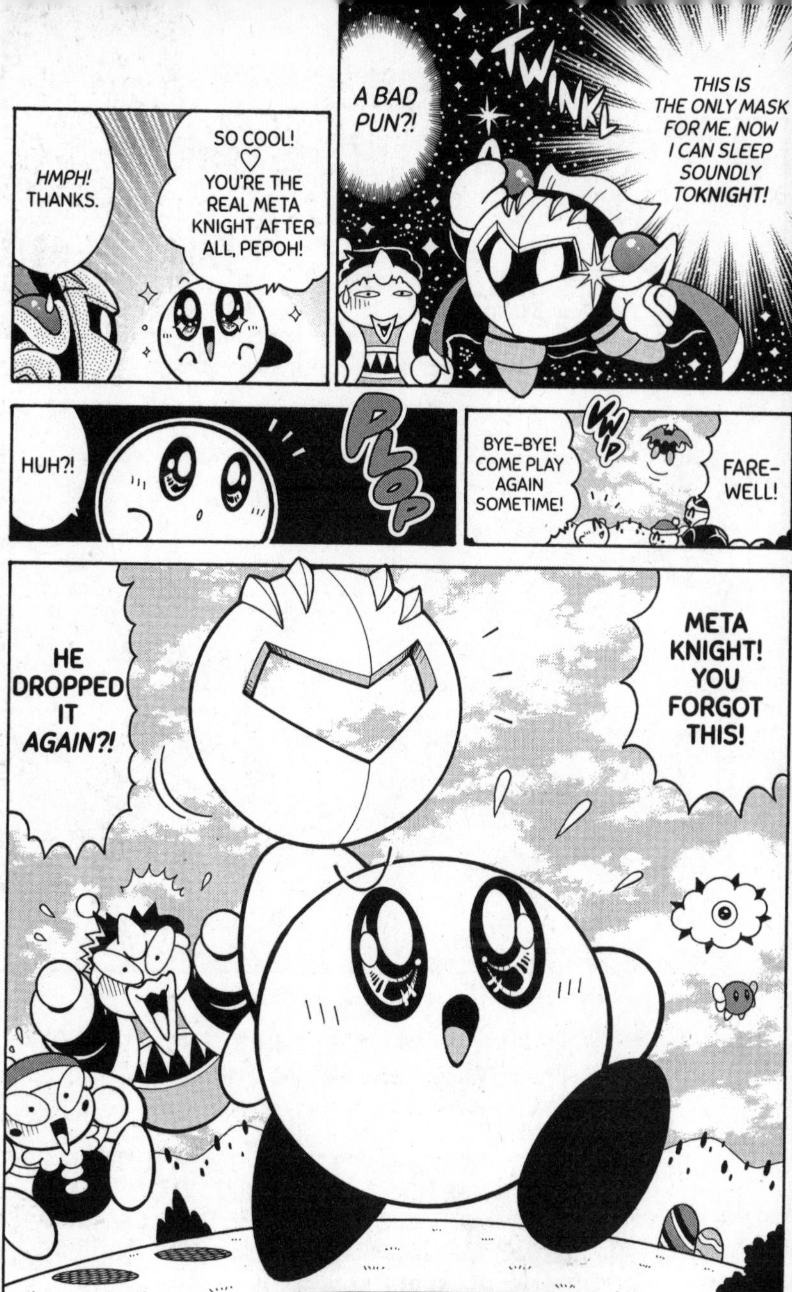
THIS IS THE ONLY MASK FOR ME. NOW I CAN SLEEP SOUNDLY TOKNIGHT!
TWINKL
A BAD PUN?!
SO COOL! ♡ YOU'RE THE REAL META KNIGHT AFTER ALL, PEPOH!
HMPH! THANKS.
FARE-WELL!
VWIP
BYE-BYE! COME PLAY AGAIN SOMETIME!
PLOP
HUH?!
META KNIGHT! YOU FORGOT THIS!
HE DROPPED IT AGAIN?!

KIRBY'S PEEK BEHIND THE SCENES 3

IT'S FINALLY TIME FOR INKING.
USING ELLIPSE AND CLOUD STENCILS,
I CAREFULLY GO OVER THE PENCIL
LINES WITH 0.03 TO 0.8 MILLIMETER
DRAWING PENS.

WHEN THAT'S DONE, I MOVE ON TO
FINISHING TOUCHES. FROM THIS POINT ON,
MY WORK IS HAPPY AND FUN.☺

THE LAST TOUCH IS TO PUT THE WHITE IN
THE EYES! AFTER I CAREFULLY DOUBLE-
CHECK THAT I DIDN'T FORGET TO DRAW
ANYTHING OR REMOVE UNNEEDED PARTS
OF THE SCREENTONE STICKERS, ETC.,
IT'S DONE. GREAT JOB!

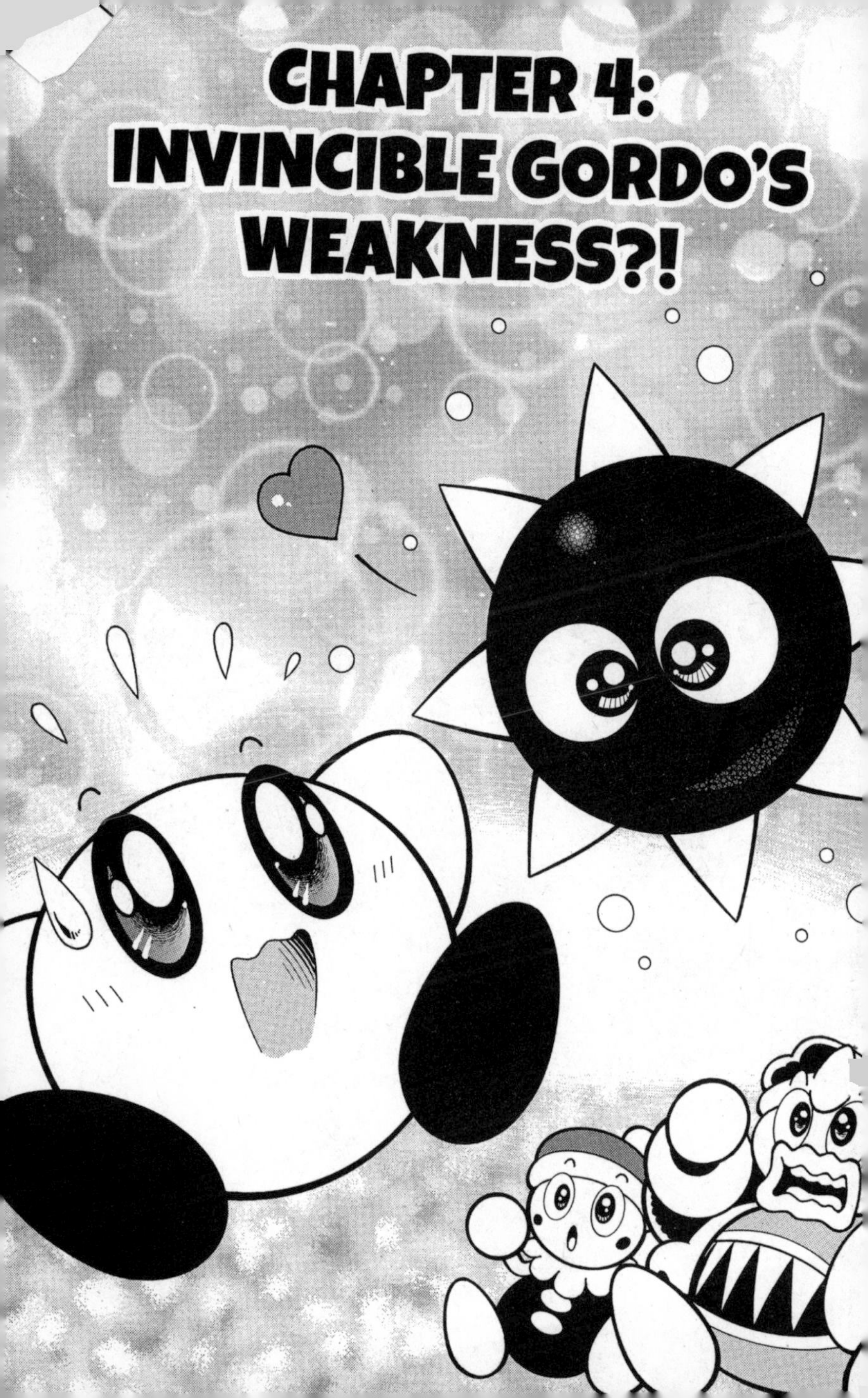
CHAPTER 4:
INVINCIBLE GORDO'S
WEAKNESS?!

AUTHOR'S COMMENT

THE INVINCIBLE GORDO. I TRIED MAKING HIM A BIT CUTE FOR THIS CHAPTER. AS SOMEONE WITH LOW SELF-ESTEEM, I'D LIKE TO BE STRONGER MENTALLY.

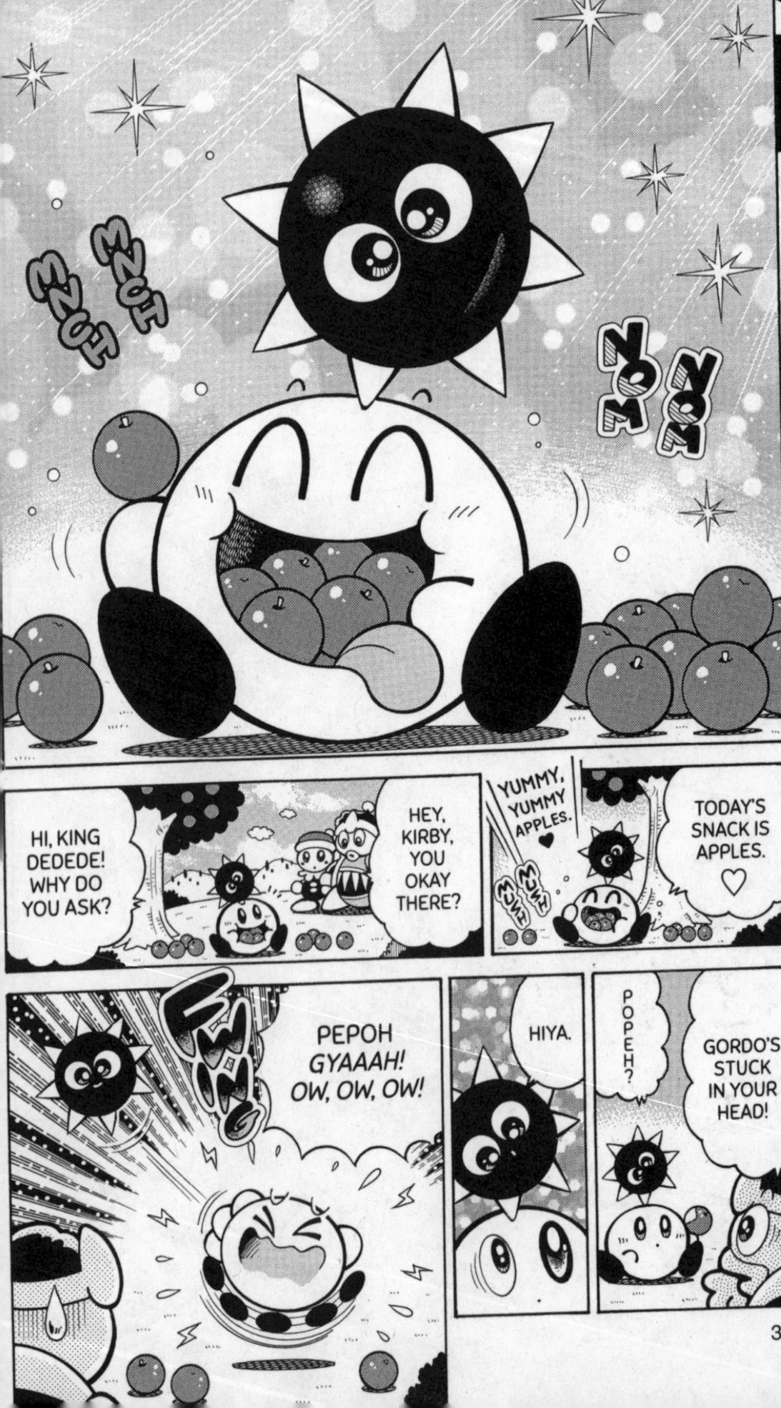

NOM NOM
MUNCH MUNCH
TODAY'S SNACK IS APPLES. ♡
YUMMY, YUMMY APPLES. ♥
MUNCH MUNCH
HEY, KIRBY, YOU OKAY THERE?
HI, KING DEDEDE! WHY DO YOU ASK?
GORDO'S STUCK IN YOUR HEAD!
POPEH?
HIYA.
PEPOH GYAAAH! OW, OW, OW!

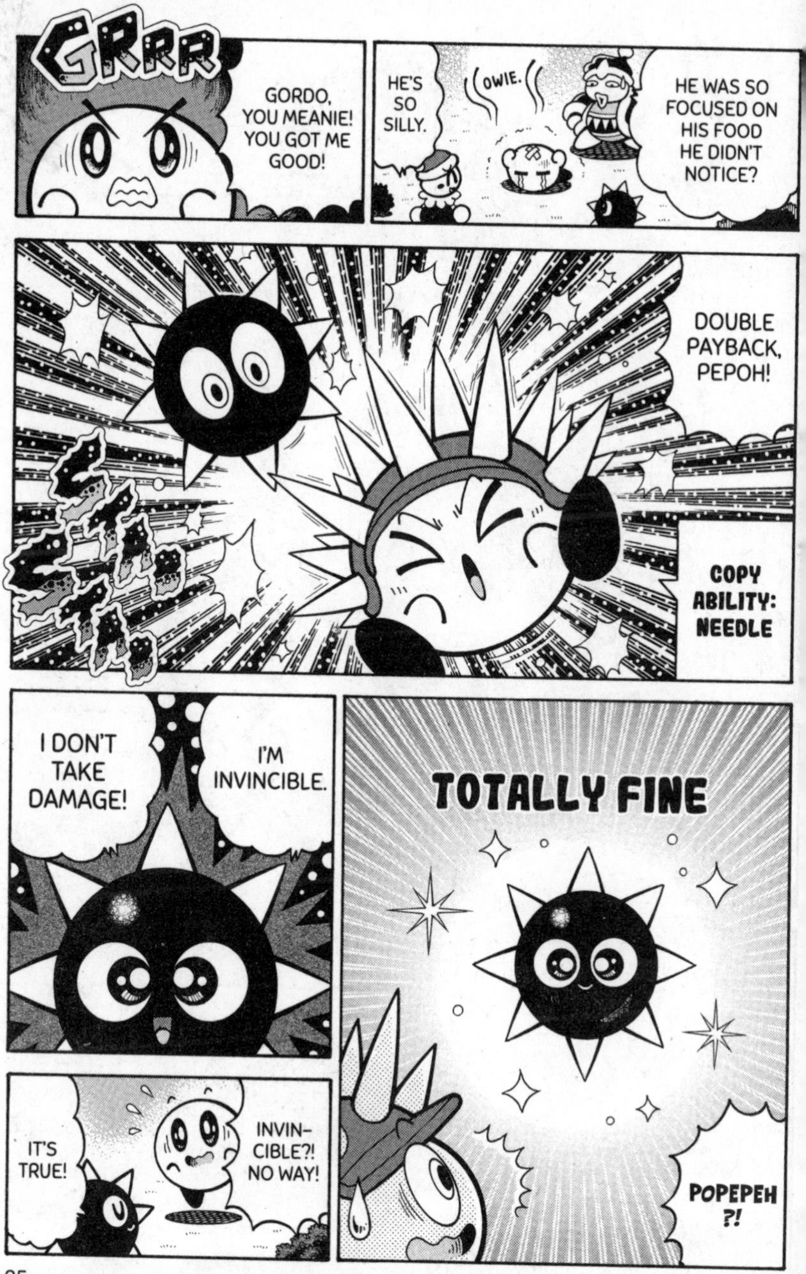
HE WAS SO FOCUSED ON HIS FOOD HE DIDN'T NOTICE?
OWIE.
HE'S SO SILLY.
GRRR
GORDO, YOU MEANIE! YOU GOT ME GOOD!
DOUBLE PAYBACK, PEPOH!
COPY ABILITY: NEEDLE
TOTALLY FINE
POPEPEH ?!
I'M INVINCIBLE.
I DON'T TAKE DAMAGE!
INVIN-CIBLE?! NO WAY!
IT'S TRUE!

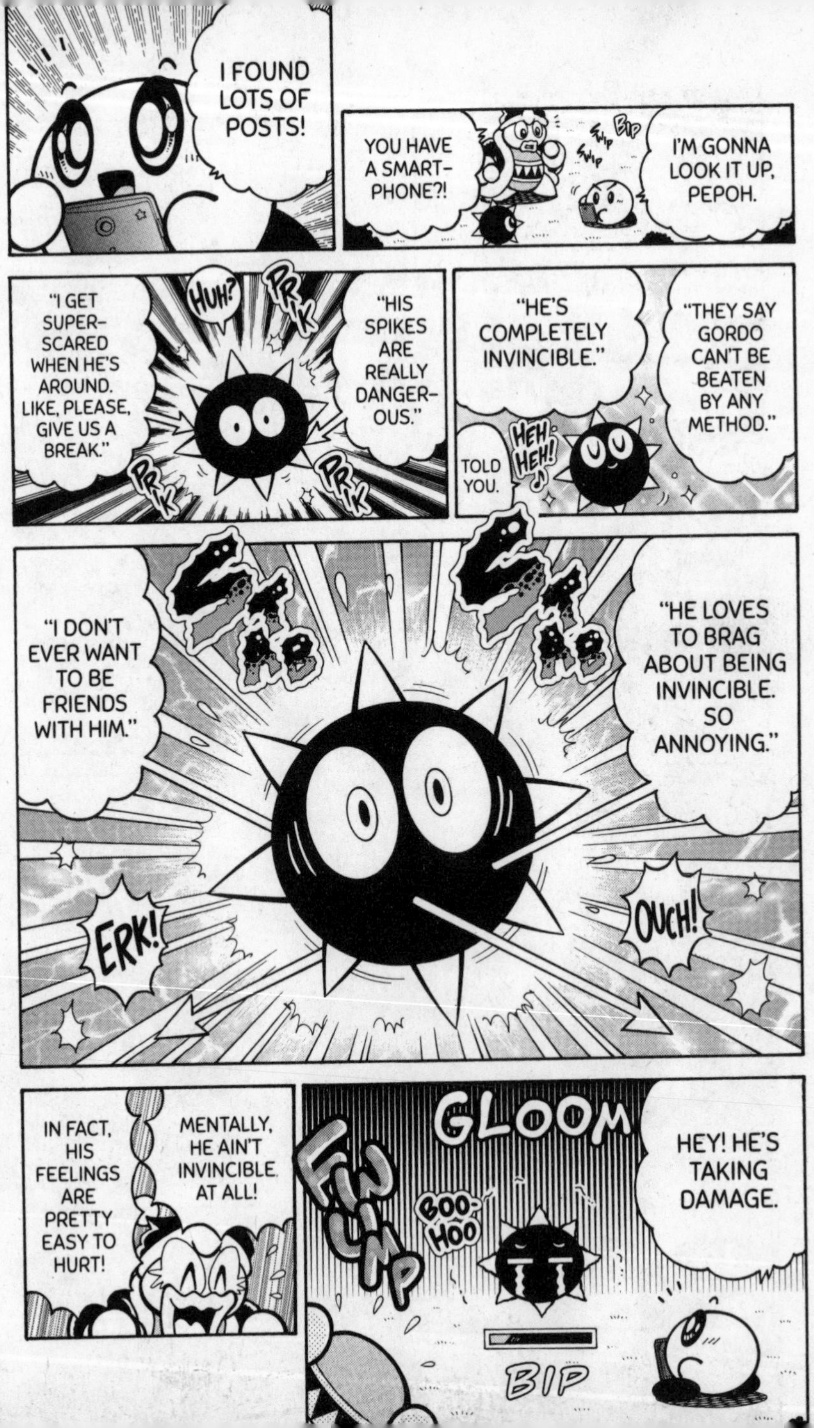
I'M GONNA LOOK IT UP, PEPOH.
BIP
SWIP
SWIP
YOU HAVE A SMART-PHONE?!
I FOUND LOTS OF POSTS!
"THEY SAY GORDO CAN'T BE BEATEN BY ANY METHOD."
"HE'S COMPLETELY INVINCIBLE."
HEH HEH!
TOLD YOU.
"HIS SPIKES ARE REALLY DANGER-OUS."
PRIK
HUH?
"I GET SUPER-SCARED WHEN HE'S AROUND. LIKE, PLEASE, GIVE US A BREAK."
PRIK
PRIK
"HE LOVES TO BRAG ABOUT BEING INVINCIBLE. SO ANNOYING."
"I DON'T EVER WANT TO BE FRIENDS WITH HIM."
OUCH!
ERK!
HEY! HE'S TAKING DAMAGE.
GLOOM
BOO-HOO
FWUMP
BIP
MENTALLY, HE AIN'T INVINCIBLE AT ALL!
IN FACT, HIS FEELINGS ARE PRETTY EASY TO HURT!

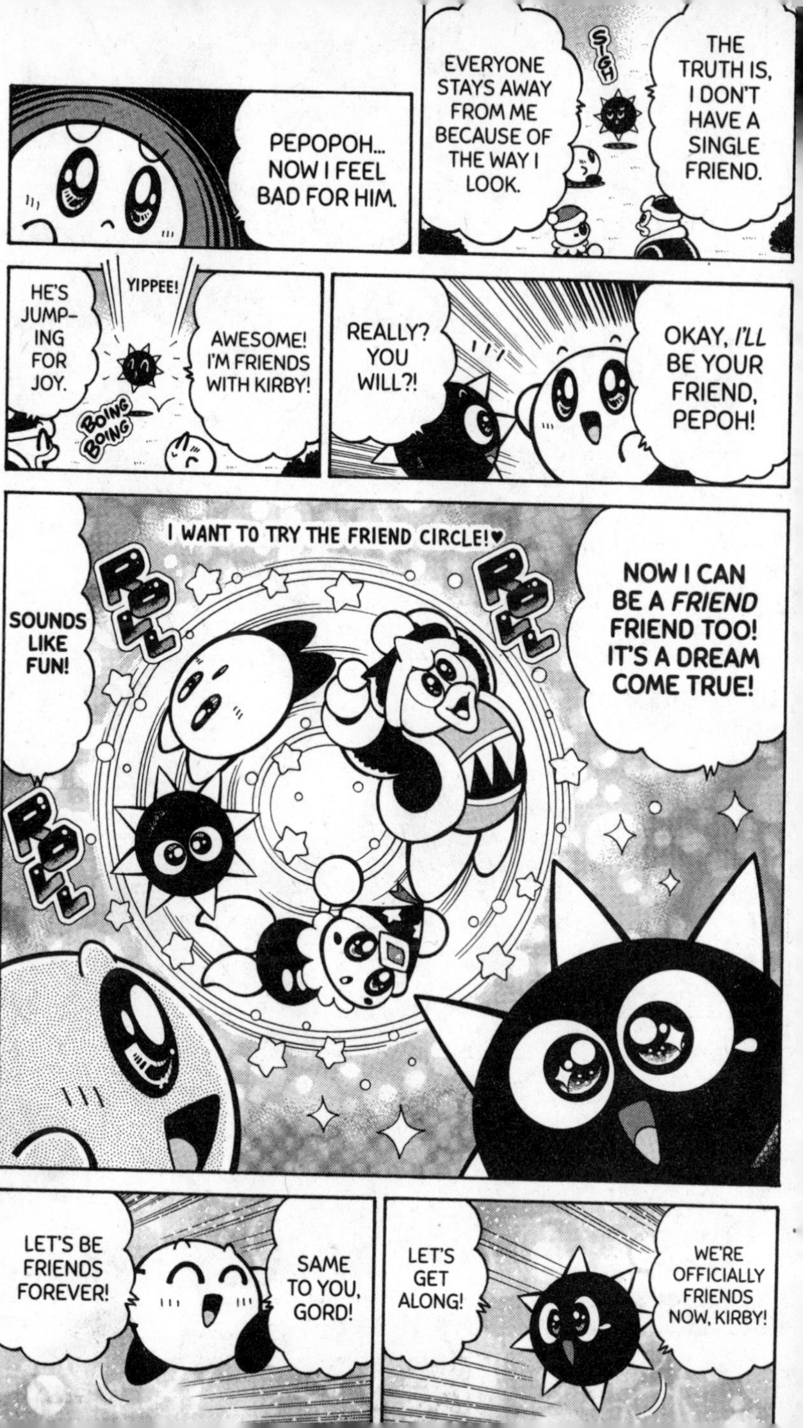
THE TRUTH IS, I DON'T HAVE A SINGLE FRIEND.
SIGH
EVERYONE STAYS AWAY FROM ME BECAUSE OF THE WAY I LOOK.
PEPOPOH... NOW I FEEL BAD FOR HIM.
OKAY, *I'LL* BE YOUR FRIEND, PEPOH!
REALLY? YOU WILL?!
AWESOME! I'M FRIENDS WITH KIRBY!
YIPPEE!
BOING BOING
HE'S JUMP-ING FOR JOY.
NOW I CAN BE A *FRIEND* FRIEND TOO! IT'S A DREAM COME TRUE!
I WANT TO TRY THE FRIEND CIRCLE!♥
ROLL
ROLL
SOUNDS LIKE FUN!
ROLL
WE'RE OFFICIALLY FRIENDS NOW, KIRBY!
LET'S GET ALONG!
SAME TO YOU, GORD!
LET'S BE FRIENDS FOREVER!

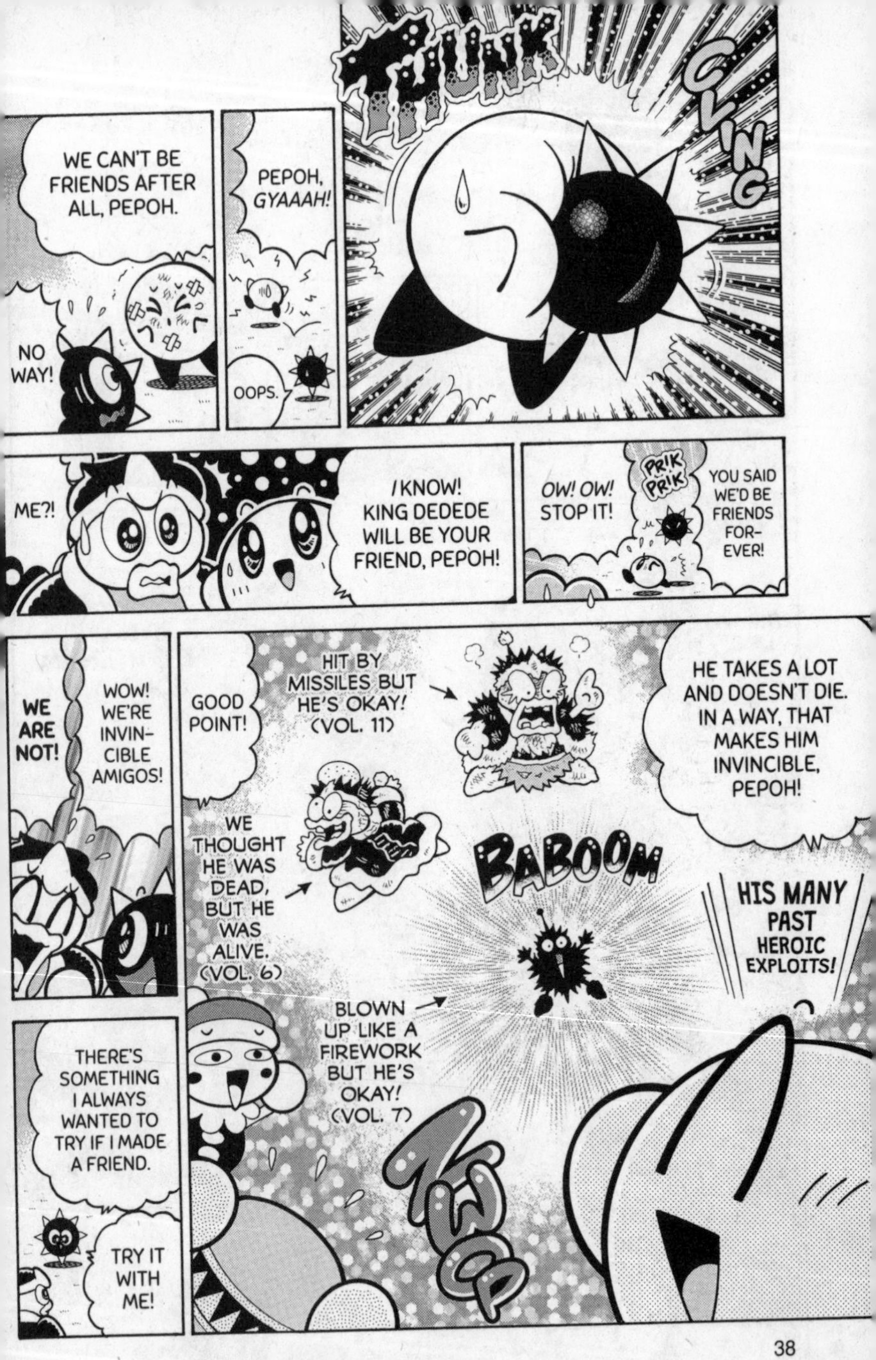
THUNK
CLING
PEPOH, *GYAAAH!*
OOPS.
WE CAN'T BE FRIENDS AFTER ALL, PEPOH.
NO WAY!
YOU SAID WE'D BE FRIENDS FOR-EVER!
PRIK PRIK
OW! OW! STOP IT!
I KNOW! KING DEDEDE WILL BE YOUR FRIEND, PEPOH!
ME?!
HE TAKES A LOT AND DOESN'T DIE. IN A WAY, THAT MAKES HIM INVINCIBLE, PEPOH!
HIS MANY PAST HEROIC EXPLOITS!
HIT BY MISSILES BUT HE'S OKAY! (VOL. 11)
BABOOM
GOOD POINT!
WE THOUGHT HE WAS DEAD, BUT HE WAS ALIVE. (VOL. 6)
BLOWN UP LIKE A FIREWORK BUT HE'S OKAY! (VOL. 7)
KWOP
WOW! WE'RE INVIN-CIBLE AMIGOS!
WE ARE NOT!
THERE'S SOMETHING I ALWAYS WANTED TO TRY IF I MADE A FRIEND.
TRY IT WITH ME!

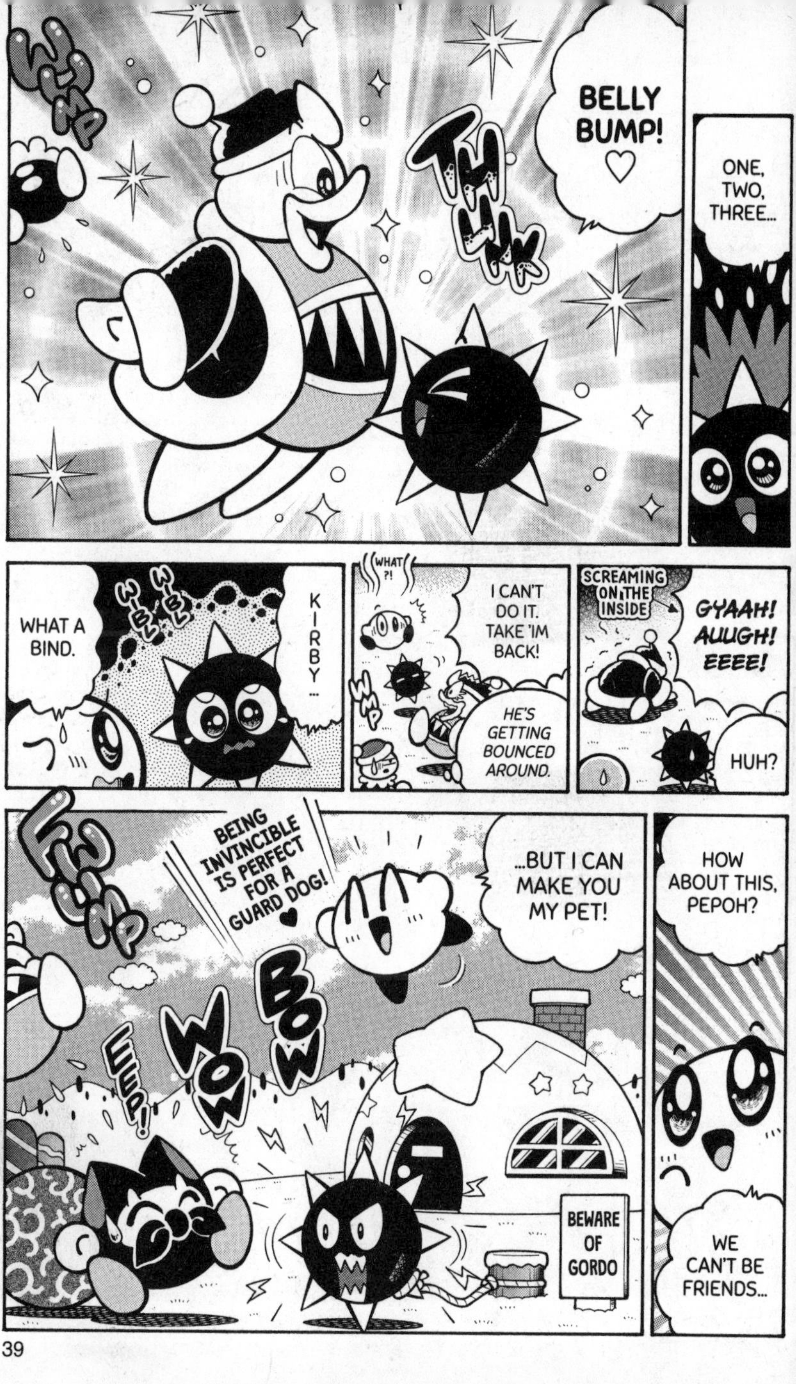
ONE, TWO, THREE...
BELLY BUMP! ♥
WUMP
SCREAMING ON THE INSIDE
GYAAH! AUUGH! EEEE!
HUH?
WHAT?!
I CAN'T DO IT. TAKE 'IM BACK!
WMP
HE'S GETTING BOUNCED AROUND.
KIRBY...
WIBL WIBL
WHAT A BIND.
HOW ABOUT THIS, PEPOH?
WE CAN'T BE FRIENDS...
...BUT I CAN MAKE YOU MY PET!
BEING INVINCIBLE IS PERFECT FOR A GUARD DOG! ♥
FWUMP
BOW WOW
EEEP!
BEWARE OF GORDO

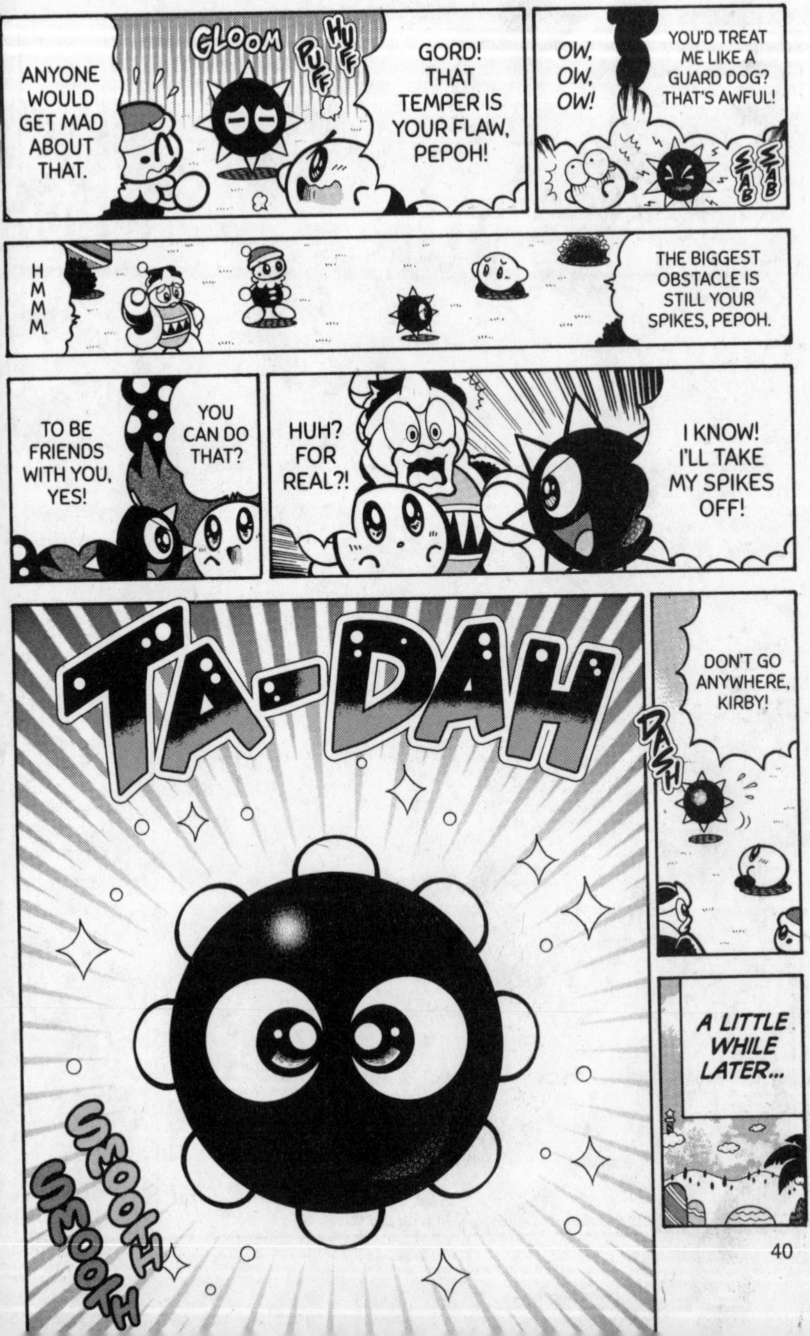
YOU'D TREAT ME LIKE A GUARD DOG? THAT'S AWFUL!
OW, OW, OW!
STAB
STAB
GORD! THAT TEMPER IS YOUR FLAW, PEPOH!
HUFF
PUFF
GLOOM
ANYONE WOULD GET MAD ABOUT THAT.
THE BIGGEST OBSTACLE IS STILL YOUR SPIKES, PEPOH.
HMMM.
I KNOW! I'LL TAKE MY SPIKES OFF!
HUH? FOR REAL?!
YOU CAN DO THAT?
TO BE FRIENDS WITH YOU, YES!
DON'T GO ANYWHERE, KIRBY!
DASH
A LITTLE WHILE LATER...
TA-DAH
SMOOOH
SMOOOH

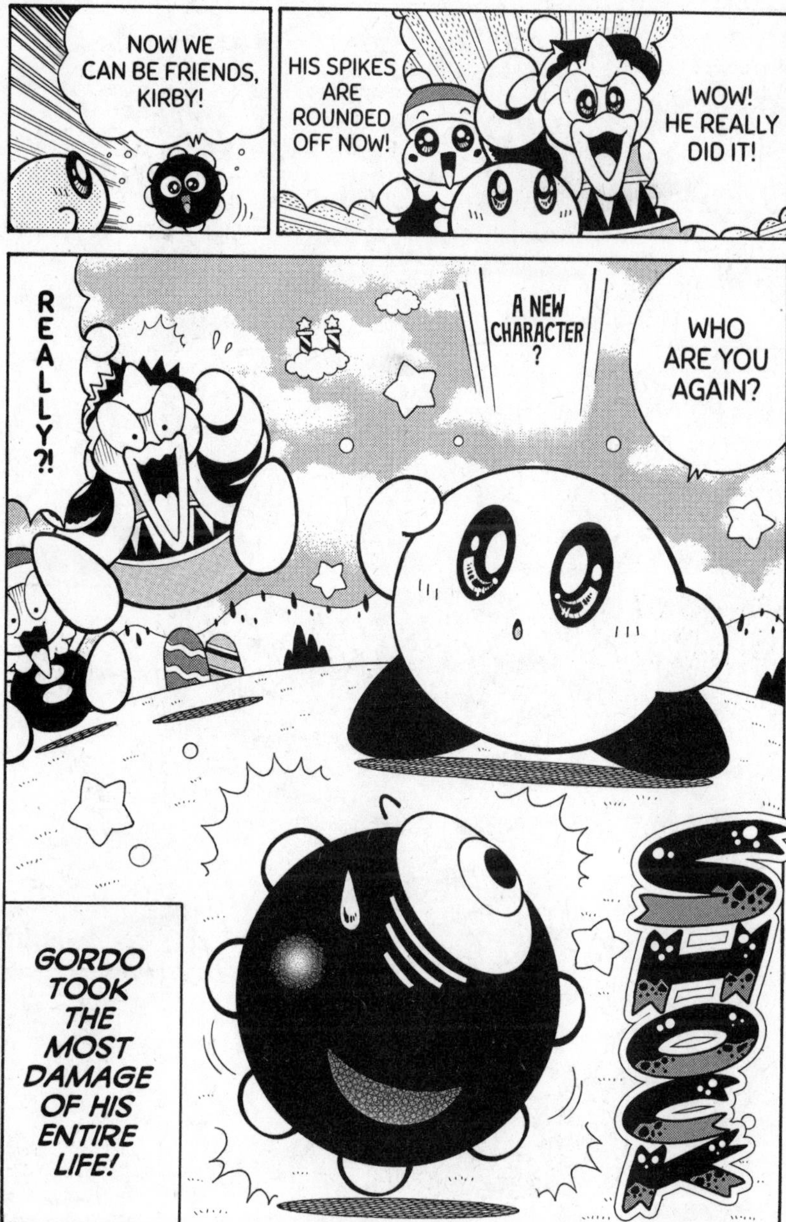
WOW! HE REALLY DID IT!
HIS SPIKES ARE ROUNDED OFF NOW!
NOW WE CAN BE FRIENDS, KIRBY!
WHO ARE YOU AGAIN?
A NEW CHARACTER?
REALLY?!
SHOCK
GORDO TOOK THE MOST DAMAGE OF HIS ENTIRE LIFE!

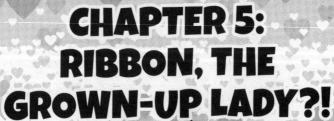

CHAPTER 5: RIBBON, THE GROWN-UP LADY?!

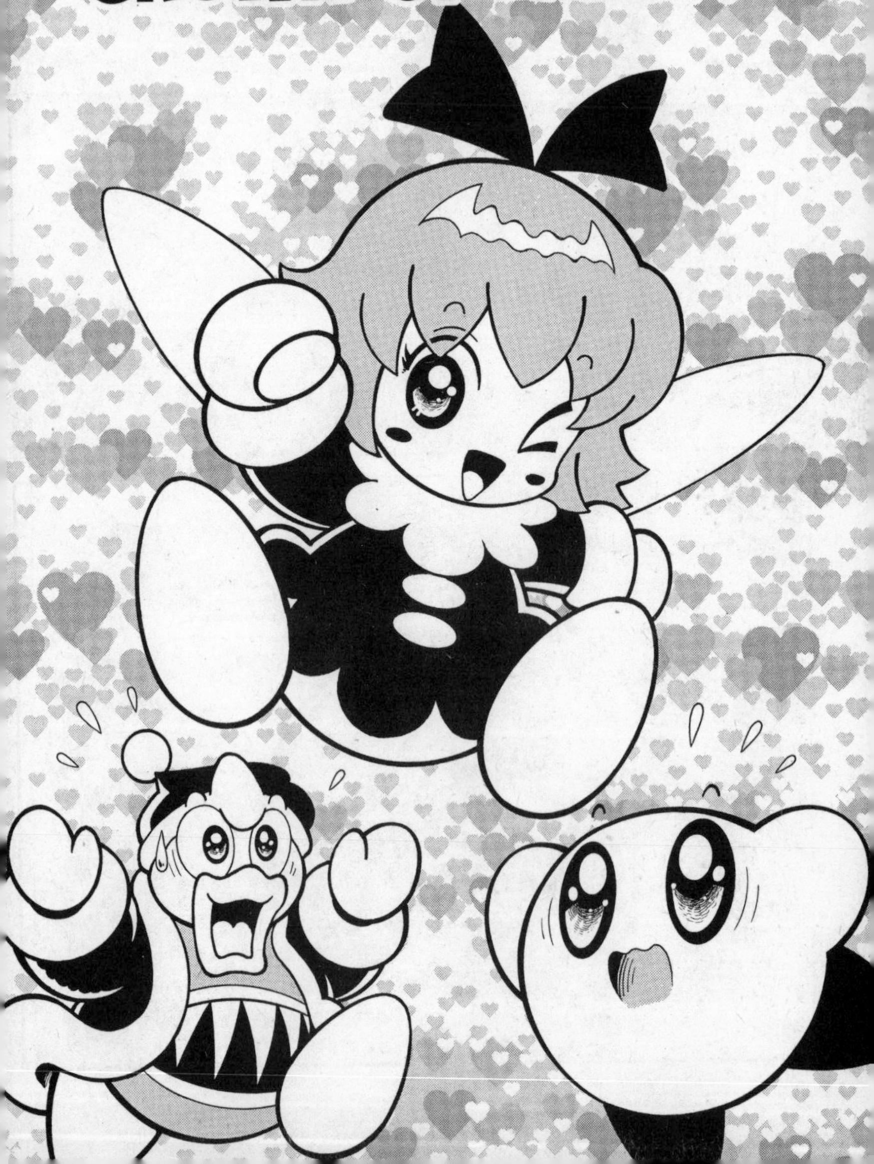

AUTHOR'S COMMENT

THIS ONE'S A RIBBON STORY. I HAD A LOT OF FUN DRAFTING IT. SHE'S EASIER TO DRAW THAN ADELEINE. I WONDER WHY THAT IS?

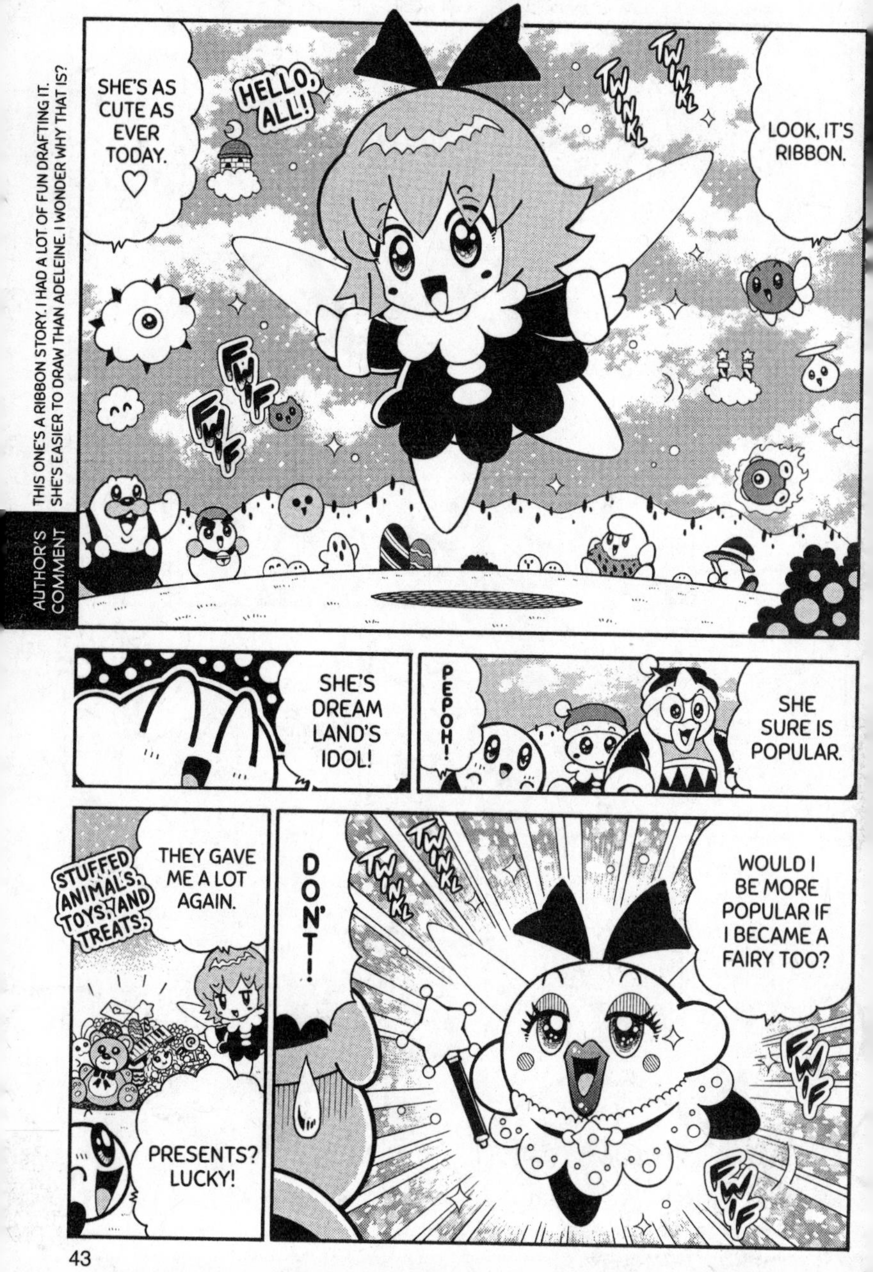
LOOK, IT'S RIBBON.
TWINKL TWINKL
HELLO, ALL!
SHE'S AS CUTE AS EVER TODAY. ♡
FWIF FWIF
SHE SURE IS POPULAR.
PEPOH!
SHE'S DREAM LAND'S IDOL!
WOULD I BE MORE POPULAR IF I BECAME A FAIRY TOO?
TWINKL TWINKL
FWIF FWIF
DON'T!
THEY GAVE ME A LOT AGAIN.
STUFFED ANIMALS, TOYS, AND TREATS.
PRESENTS? LUCKY!

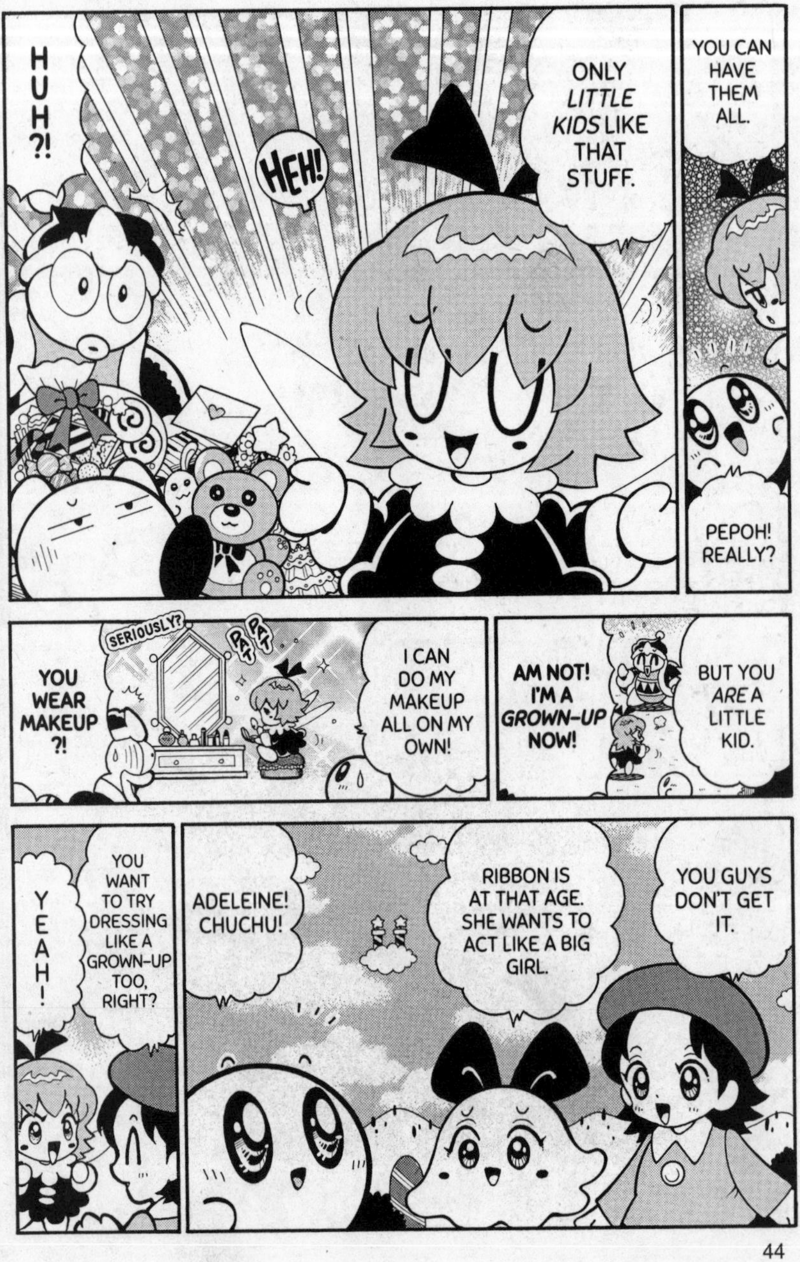
YOU CAN HAVE THEM ALL.
PEPOH! REALLY?
ONLY *LITTLE KIDS* LIKE THAT STUFF.
HEH!
HUH?!
BUT YOU *ARE* A LITTLE KID.
AM NOT! I'M A *GROWN-UP* NOW!
I CAN DO MY MAKEUP ALL ON MY OWN!
PAT PAT
SERIOUSLY?
YOU WEAR MAKEUP?!
YOU GUYS DON'T GET IT.
RIBBON IS AT THAT AGE. SHE WANTS TO ACT LIKE A BIG GIRL.
ADELEINE! CHUCHU!
YOU WANT TO TRY DRESSING LIKE A GROWN-UP TOO, RIGHT?
YEAH!

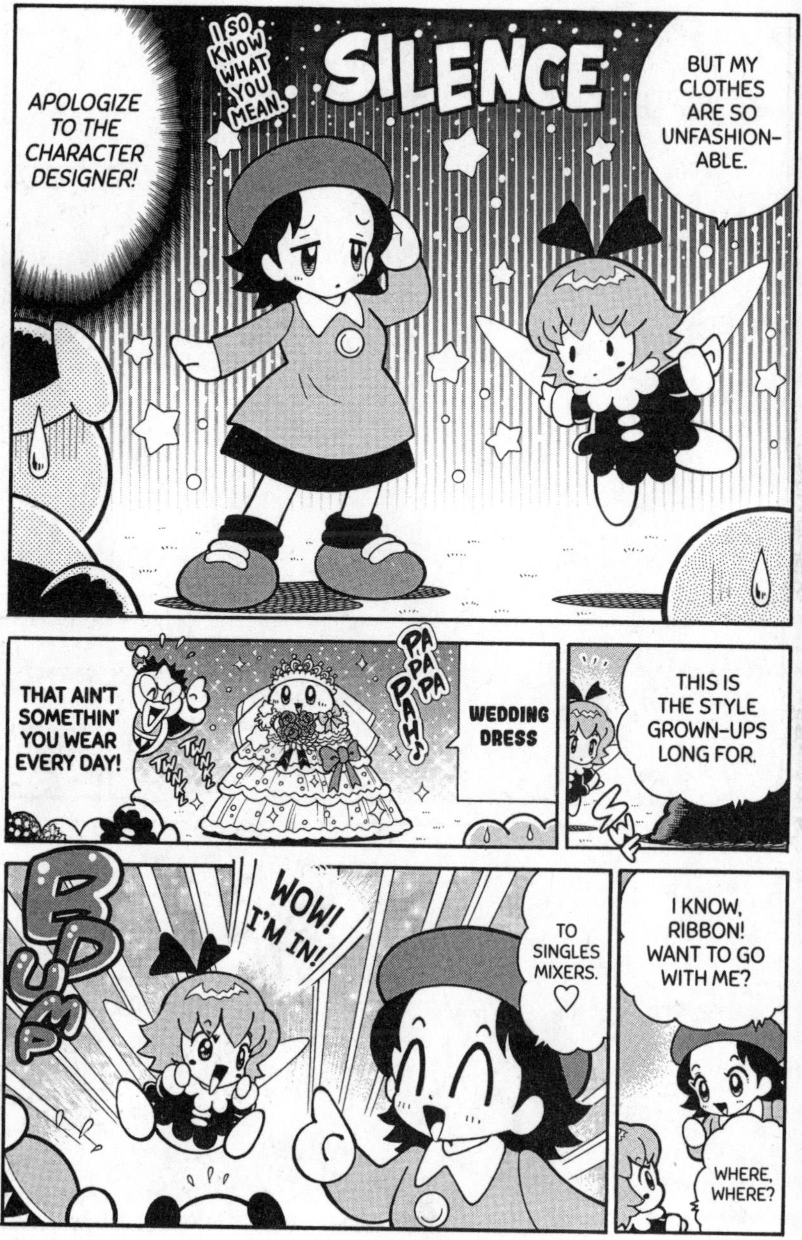
BUT MY CLOTHES ARE SO UNFASHIONABLE.
SILENCE
I SO KNOW WHAT YOU MEAN.
APOLOGIZE TO THE CHARACTER DESIGNER!
THIS IS THE STYLE GROWN-UPS LONG FOR.
PAPAPAPAH♪
WEDDING DRESS
THAT AIN'T SOMETHIN' YOU WEAR EVERY DAY!
TWINK
TWINK
I KNOW, RIBBON! WANT TO GO WITH ME?
WHERE, WHERE?
TO SINGLES MIXERS. ♡
WOW! I'M IN!
BADUMP

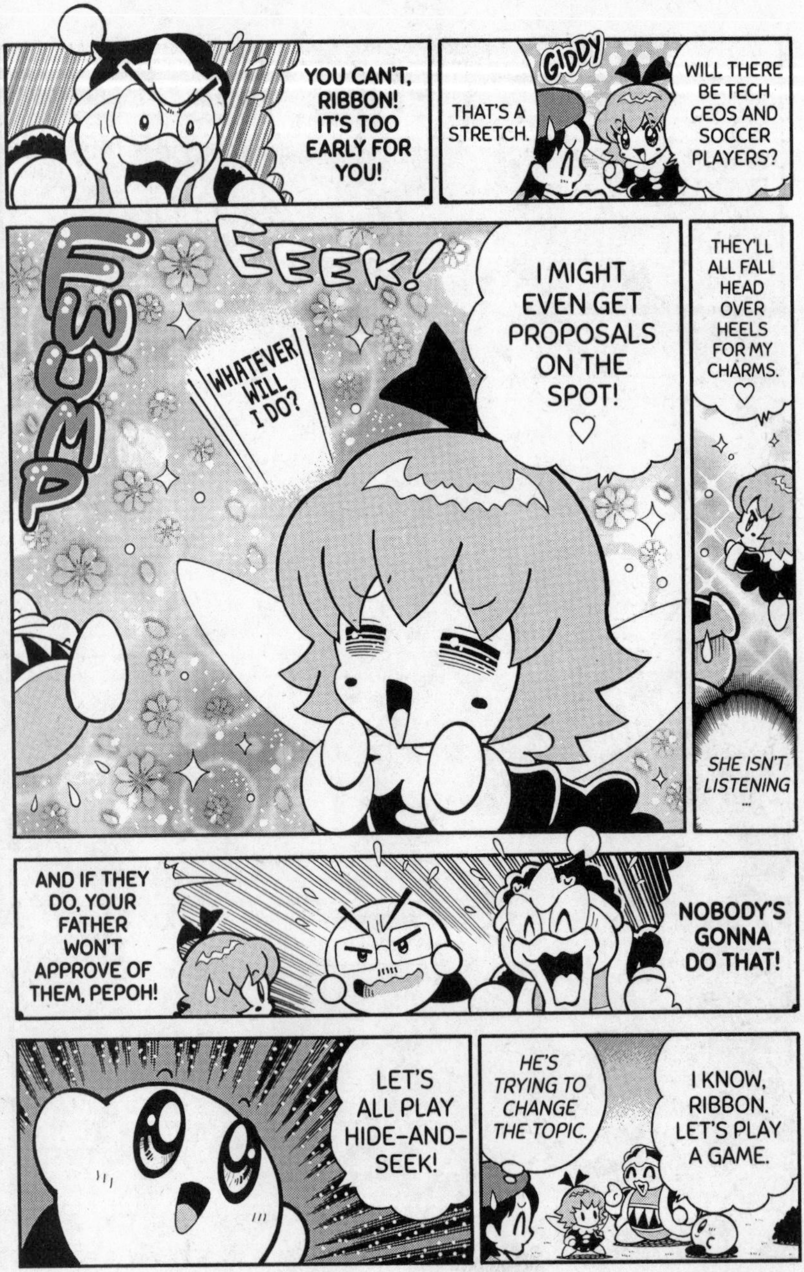
WILL THERE BE TECH CEOS AND SOCCER PLAYERS?
GIDDY
THAT'S A STRETCH.
YOU CAN'T, RIBBON! IT'S TOO EARLY FOR YOU!
THEY'LL ALL FALL HEAD OVER HEELS FOR MY CHARMS. ♡
SHE ISN'T LISTENING...
I MIGHT EVEN GET PROPOSALS ON THE SPOT! ♡
EEEK!
WHATEVER WILL I DO?
FWUMP
NOBODY'S GONNA DO THAT!
AND IF THEY DO, YOUR FATHER WON'T APPROVE OF THEM, PEPOH!
I KNOW, RIBBON. LET'S PLAY A GAME.
HE'S TRYING TO CHANGE THE TOPIC.
LET'S ALL PLAY HIDE-AND-SEEK!

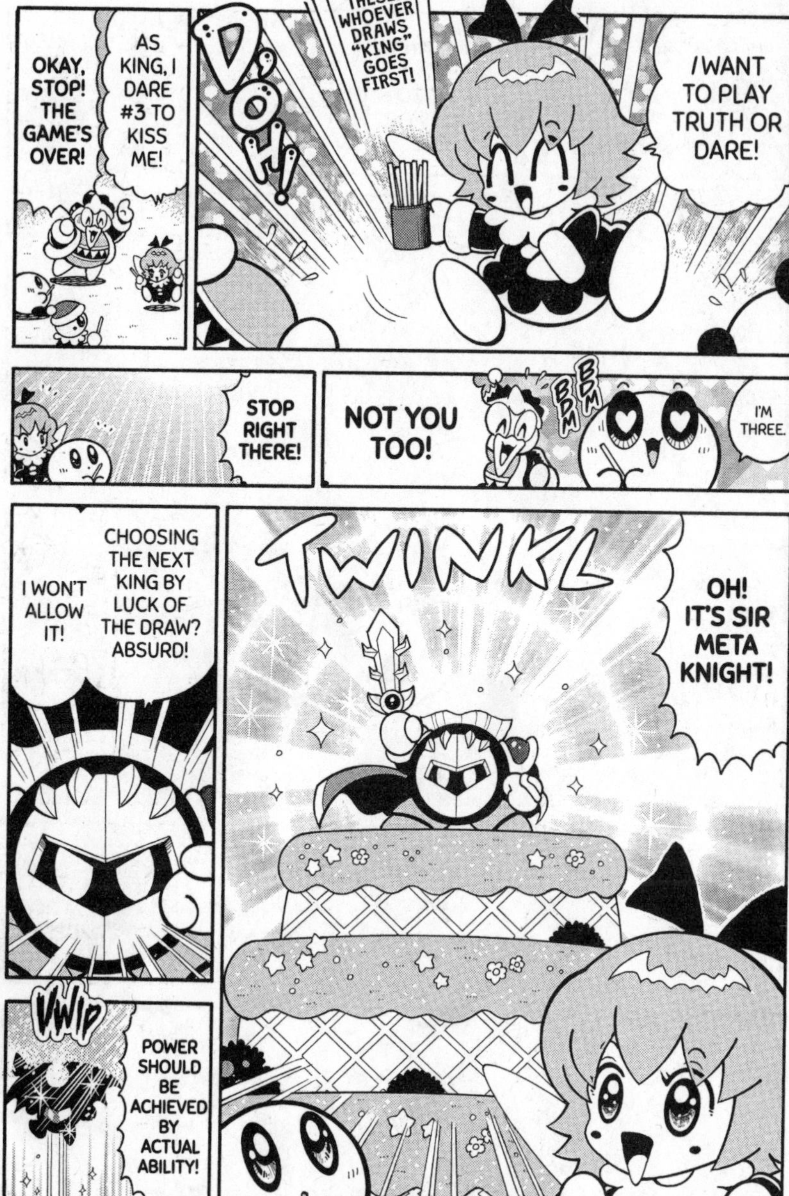
I WANT TO PLAY TRUTH OR DARE!
DRAW THESE. WHOEVER DRAWS "KING" GOES FIRST!
D'OH!
AS KING, I DARE #3 TO KISS ME!
OKAY, STOP! THE GAME'S OVER!
I'M THREE.
BDM BDM
NOT YOU TOO!
STOP RIGHT THERE!
TWINKL
OH! IT'S SIR META KNIGHT!
CHOOSING THE NEXT KING BY LUCK OF THE DRAW? ABSURD!
I WON'T ALLOW IT!
VWIP
POWER SHOULD BE ACHIEVED BY ACTUAL ABILITY!

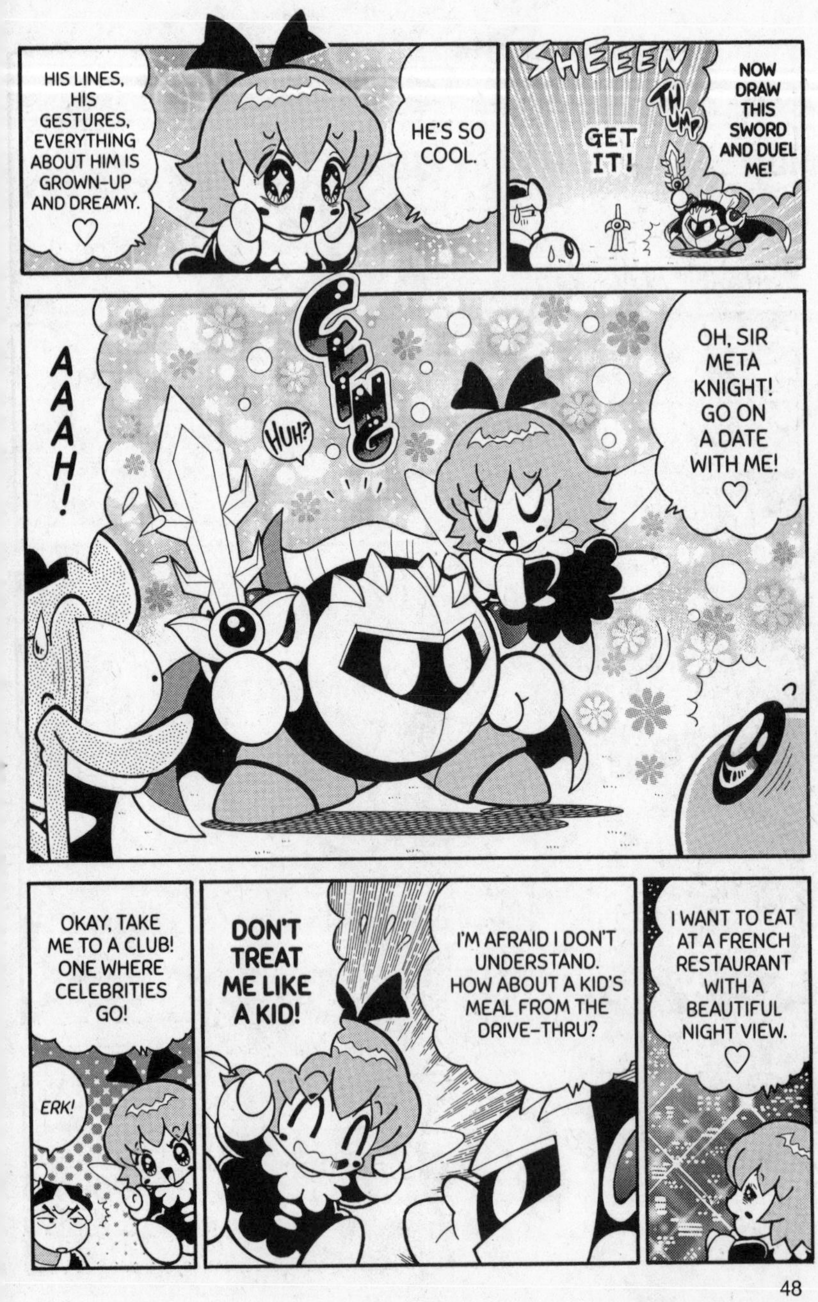
SHEEEN
NOW DRAW THIS SWORD AND DUEL ME!
THUMP
GET IT!
HE'S SO COOL.
HIS LINES, HIS GESTURES, EVERYTHING ABOUT HIM IS GROWN-UP AND DREAMY. ♡
OH, SIR META KNIGHT! GO ON A DATE WITH ME! ♡
CLING
HUH?
AAAAH!
I WANT TO EAT AT A FRENCH RESTAURANT WITH A BEAUTIFUL NIGHT VIEW. ♡
I'M AFRAID I DON'T UNDERSTAND. HOW ABOUT A KID'S MEAL FROM THE DRIVE-THRU?
DON'T TREAT ME LIKE A KID!
OKAY, TAKE ME TO A CLUB! ONE WHERE CELEBRITIES GO!
ERK!

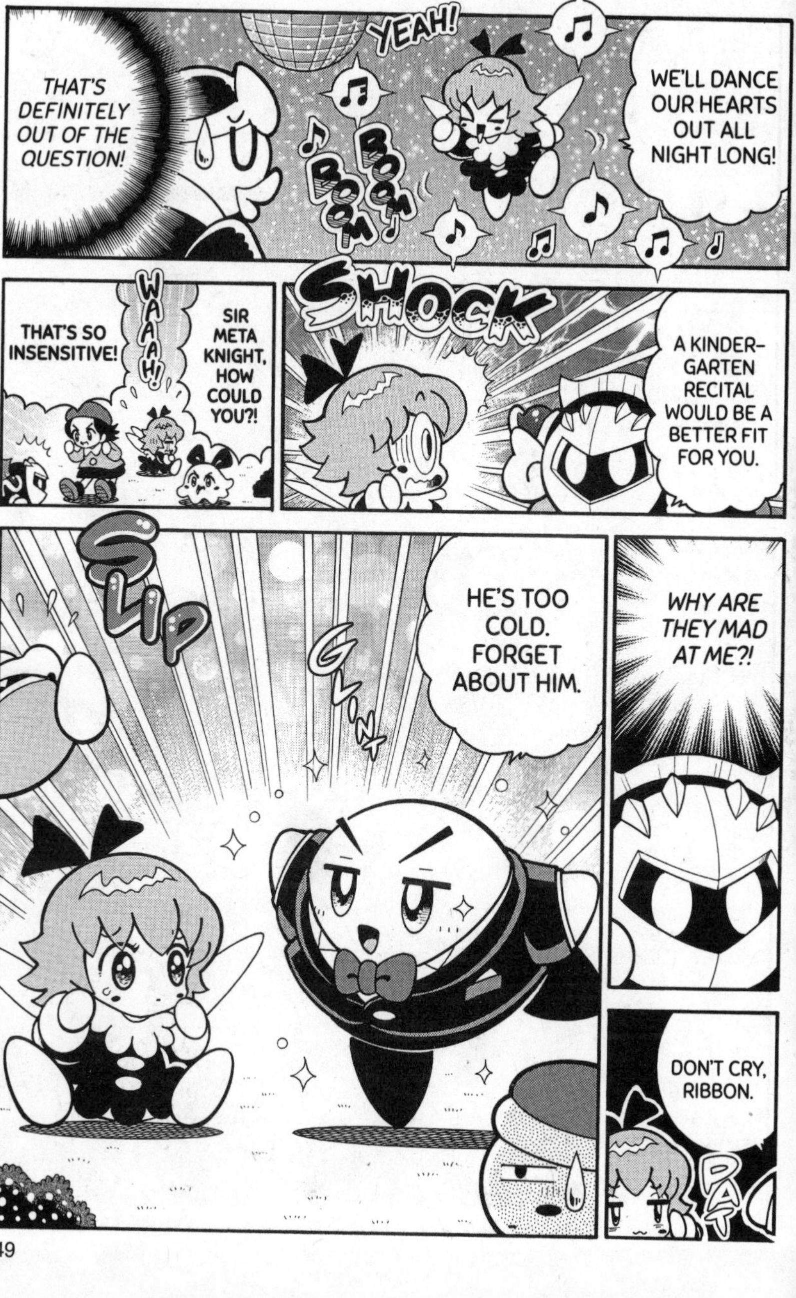
WE'LL DANCE OUR HEARTS OUT ALL NIGHT LONG!
YEAH!
BOOM BOOM
THAT'S DEFINITELY OUT OF THE QUESTION!
SHOCK
A KINDER-GARTEN RECITAL WOULD BE A BETTER FIT FOR YOU.
SIR META KNIGHT, HOW COULD YOU?!
WAAAAH!
THAT'S SO INSENSITIVE!
WHY ARE THEY MAD AT ME?!
DON'T CRY, RIBBON.
PAT
HE'S TOO COLD. FORGET ABOUT HIM.
SLIP
GLINT

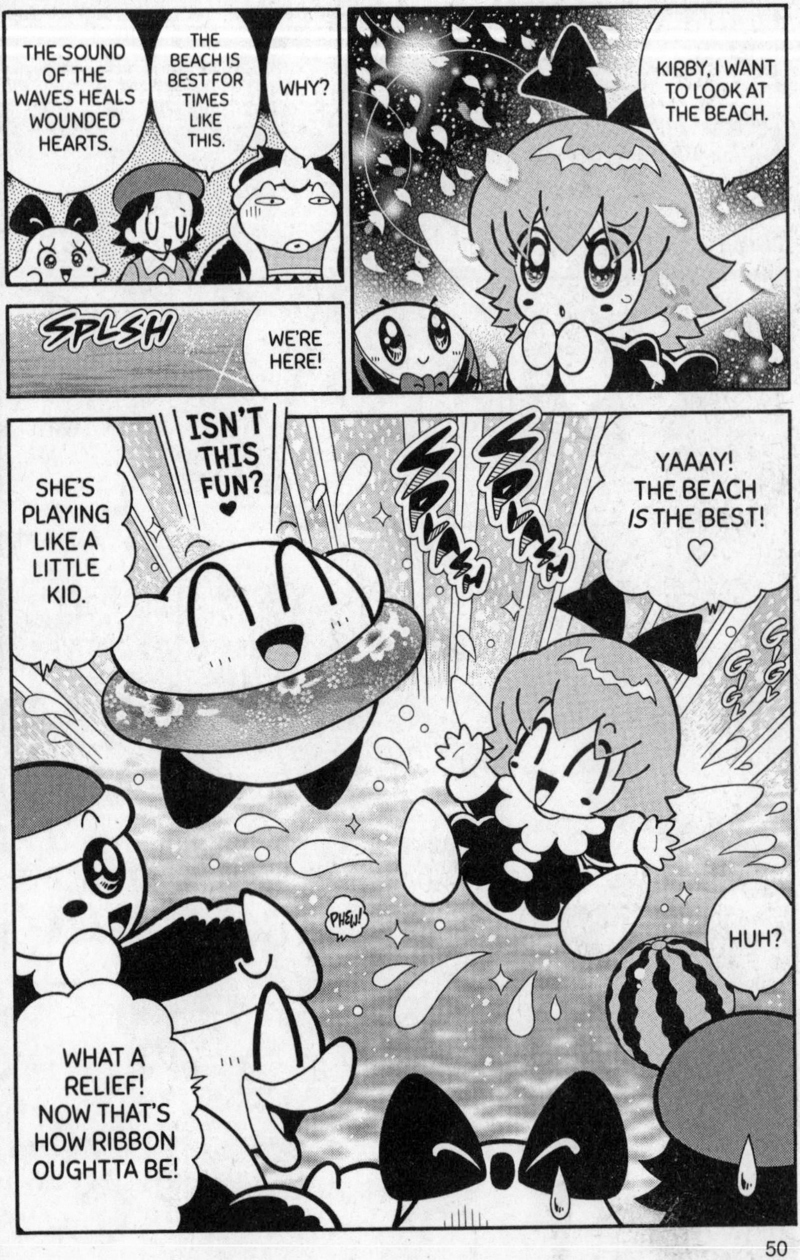
KIRBY, I WANT TO LOOK AT THE BEACH.
WHY?
THE BEACH IS BEST FOR TIMES LIKE THIS.
THE SOUND OF THE WAVES HEALS WOUNDED HEARTS.
WE'RE HERE!
SPLSH
YAAAY! THE BEACH *IS* THE BEST! ♡
ISN'T THIS FUN? ♥
SHE'S PLAYING LIKE A LITTLE KID.
HUH?
PHEW!
WHAT A RELIEF! NOW THAT'S HOW RIBBON OUGHTTA BE!

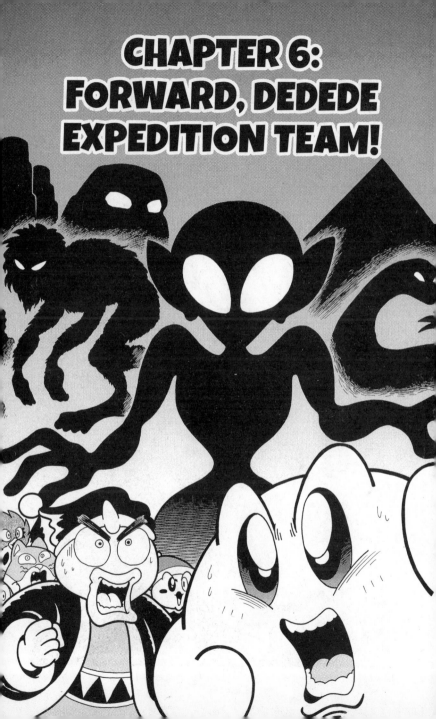

CHAPTER 6: FORWARD, DEDEDE EXPEDITION TEAM!

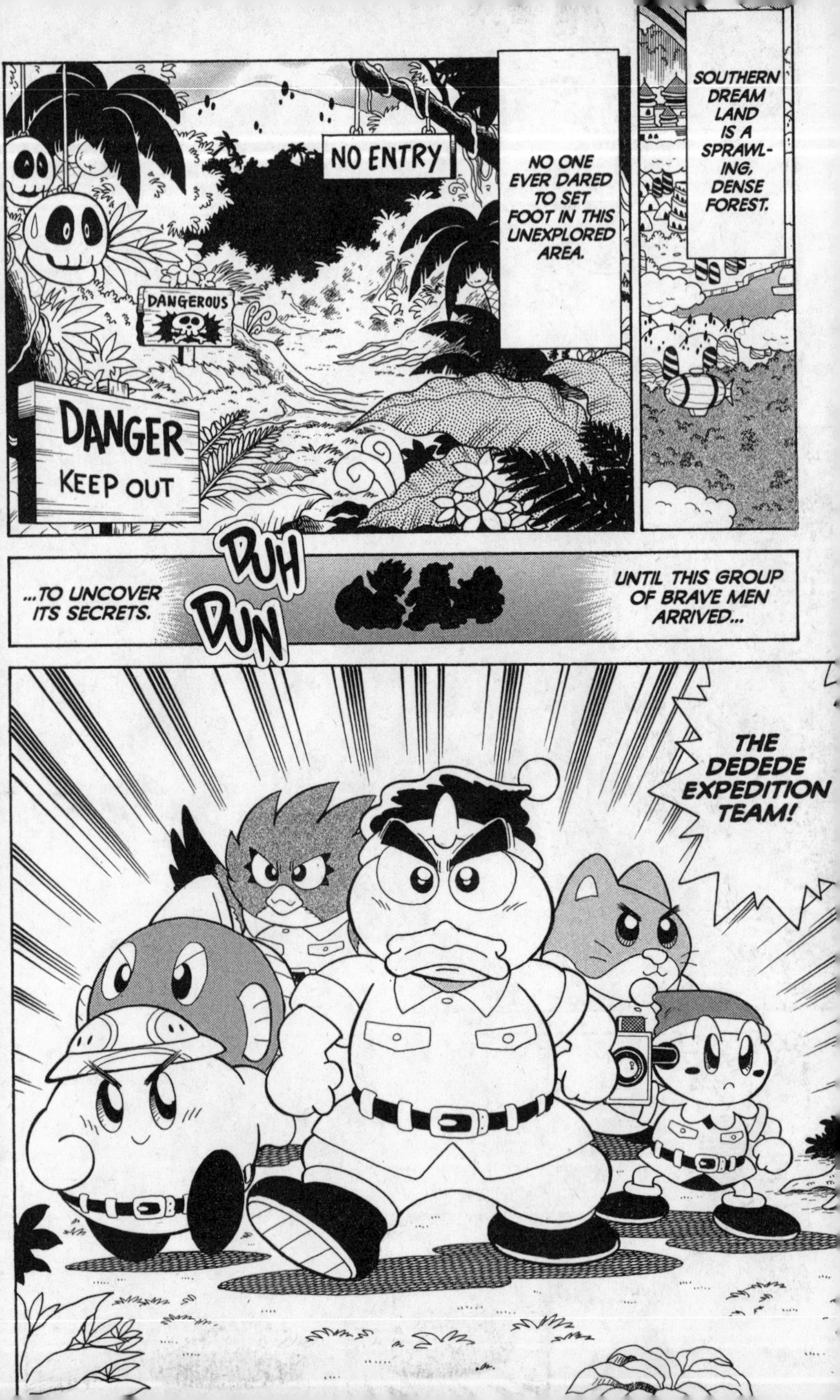
SOUTHERN DREAM LAND IS A SPRAWLING, DENSE FOREST.
NO ENTRY
NO ONE EVER DARED TO SET FOOT IN THIS UNEXPLORED AREA.
DANGEROUS
DANGER
KEEP OUT
UNTIL THIS GROUP OF BRAVE MEN ARRIVED...
DUH
DUN
...TO UNCOVER ITS SECRETS.
THE DEDEDE EXPEDITION TEAM!

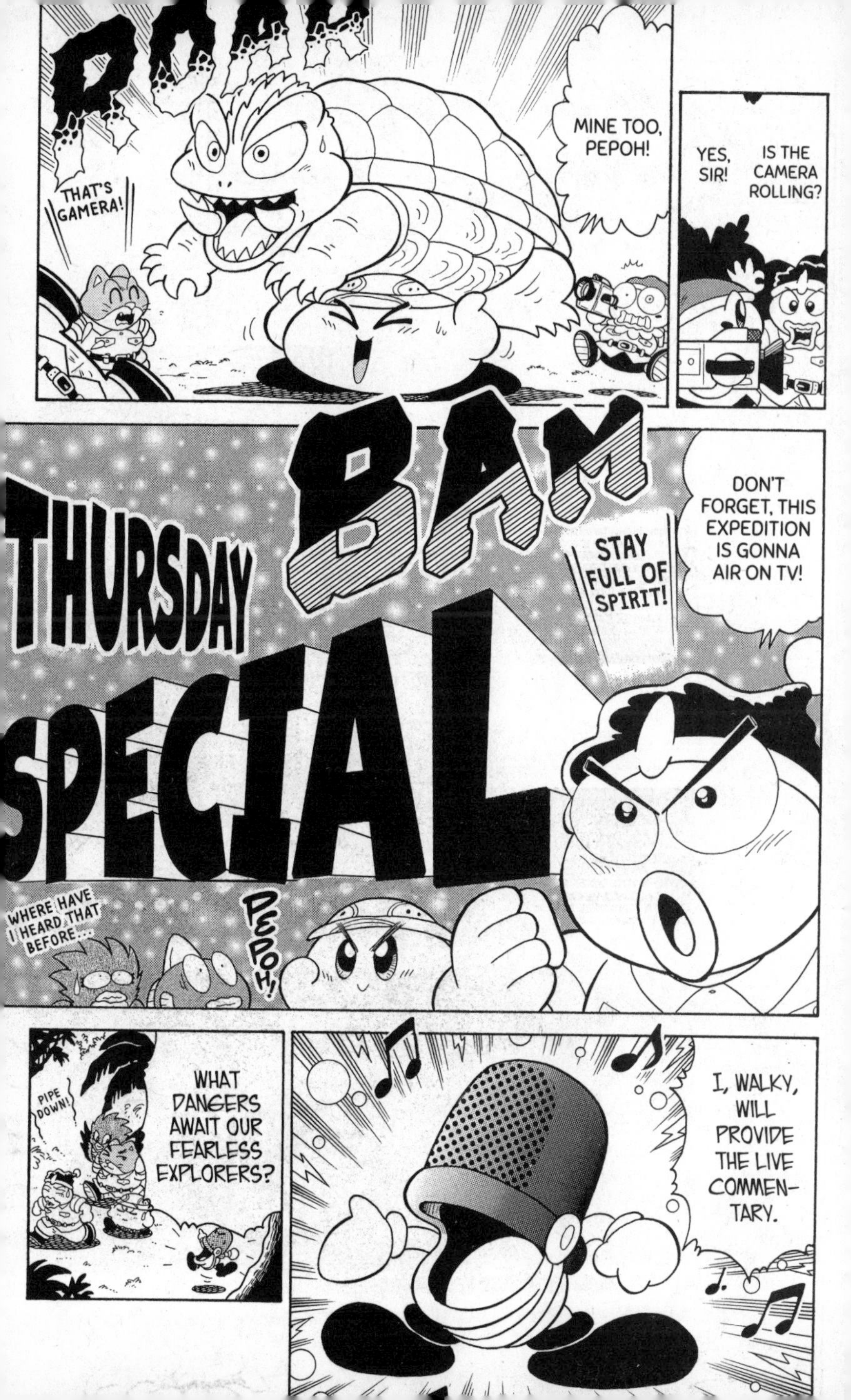
IS THE CAMERA ROLLING?
YES, SIR!
MINE TOO, PEPOH!
ROAR
THAT'S GAMERA!
DON'T FORGET, THIS EXPEDITION IS GONNA AIR ON TV!
STAY FULL OF SPIRIT!
BAM
THURSDAY SPECIAL
PEPOH!
WHERE HAVE I HEARD THAT BEFORE...
I, WALKY, WILL PROVIDE THE LIVE COMMEN-TARY.
WHAT DANGERS AWAIT OUR FEARLESS EXPLORERS?
PIPE DOWN!

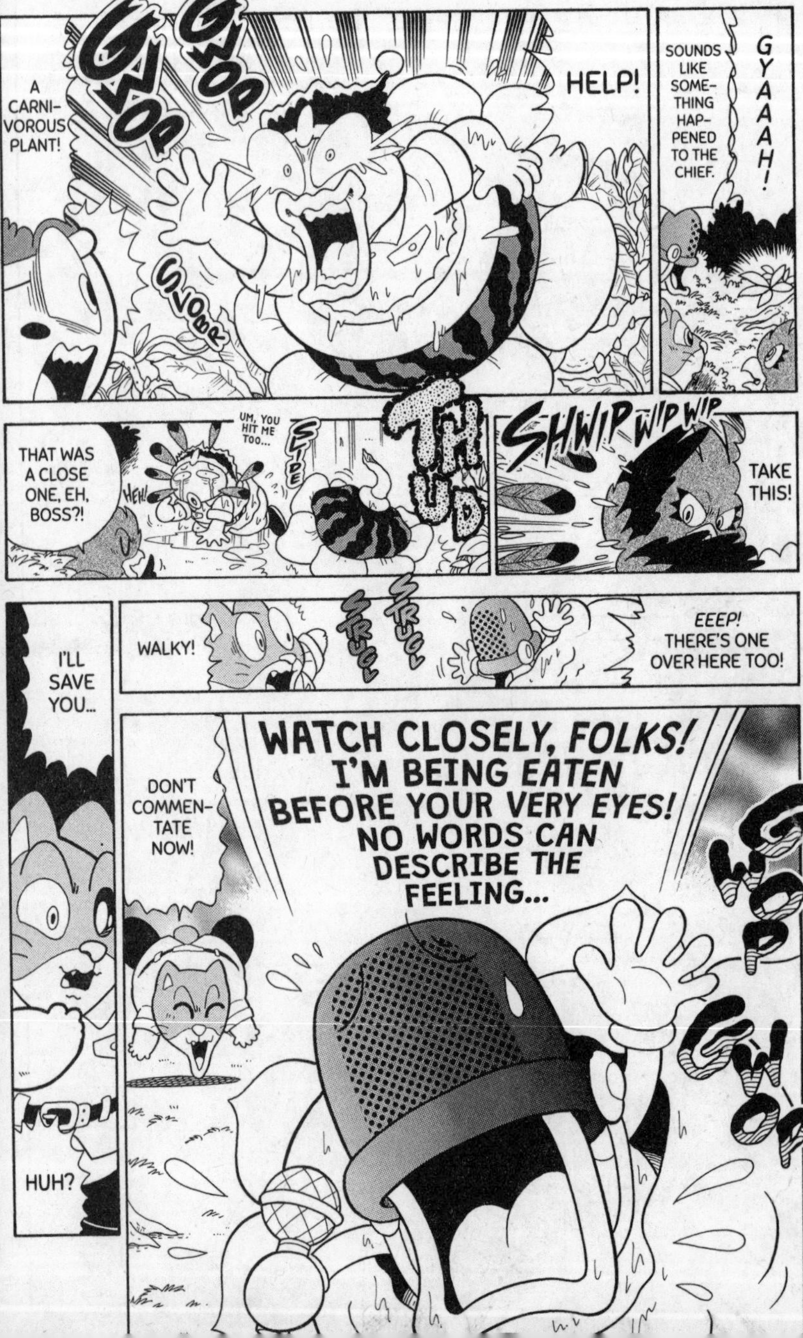
SOUNDS LIKE SOME-THING HAP-PENED TO THE CHIEF.
GYAAAAH!
HELP!
GWOA GWOA
A CARNI-VOROUS PLANT!
SHWIP WIP WIP
TAKE THIS!
THUD
SLIDE
UM, YOU HIT ME TOO...
HEH!
THAT WAS A CLOSE ONE, EH, BOSS?!
EEEP! THERE'S ONE OVER HERE TOO!
WALKY!
GWOA GWOA
WATCH CLOSELY, FOLKS! I'M BEING EATEN BEFORE YOUR VERY EYES! NO WORDS CAN DESCRIBE THE FEELING...
DON'T COMMEN-TATE NOW!
I'LL SAVE YOU...
HUH?

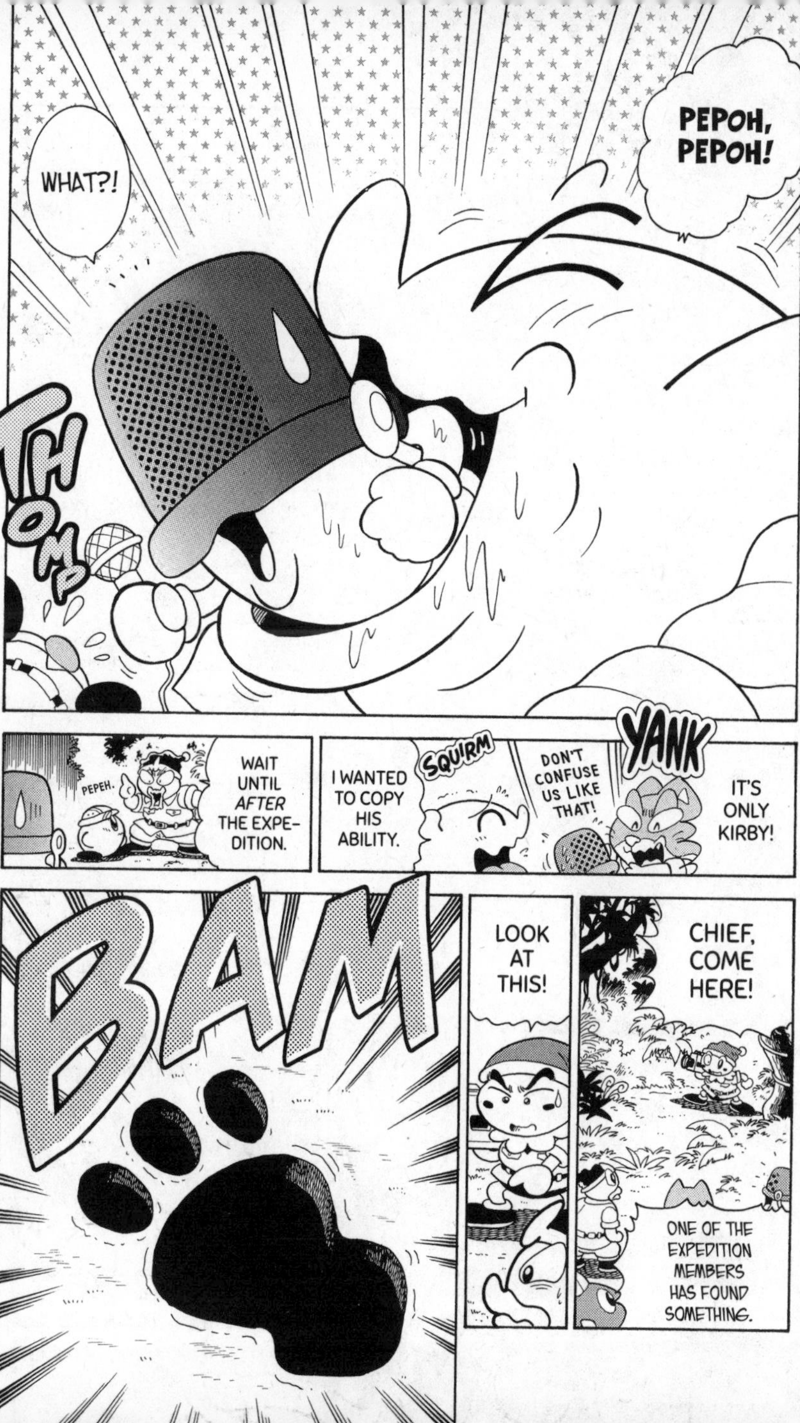
PEPOH, PEPOH!
WHAT?!
THOMP
YANK
IT'S ONLY KIRBY!
DON'T CONFUSE US LIKE THAT!
SQUIRM
I WANTED TO COPY HIS ABILITY.
WAIT UNTIL *AFTER* THE EXPEDITION.
PEPEH.
CHIEF, COME HERE!
ONE OF THE EXPEDITION MEMBERS HAS FOUND SOMETHING.
LOOK AT THIS!
BAM

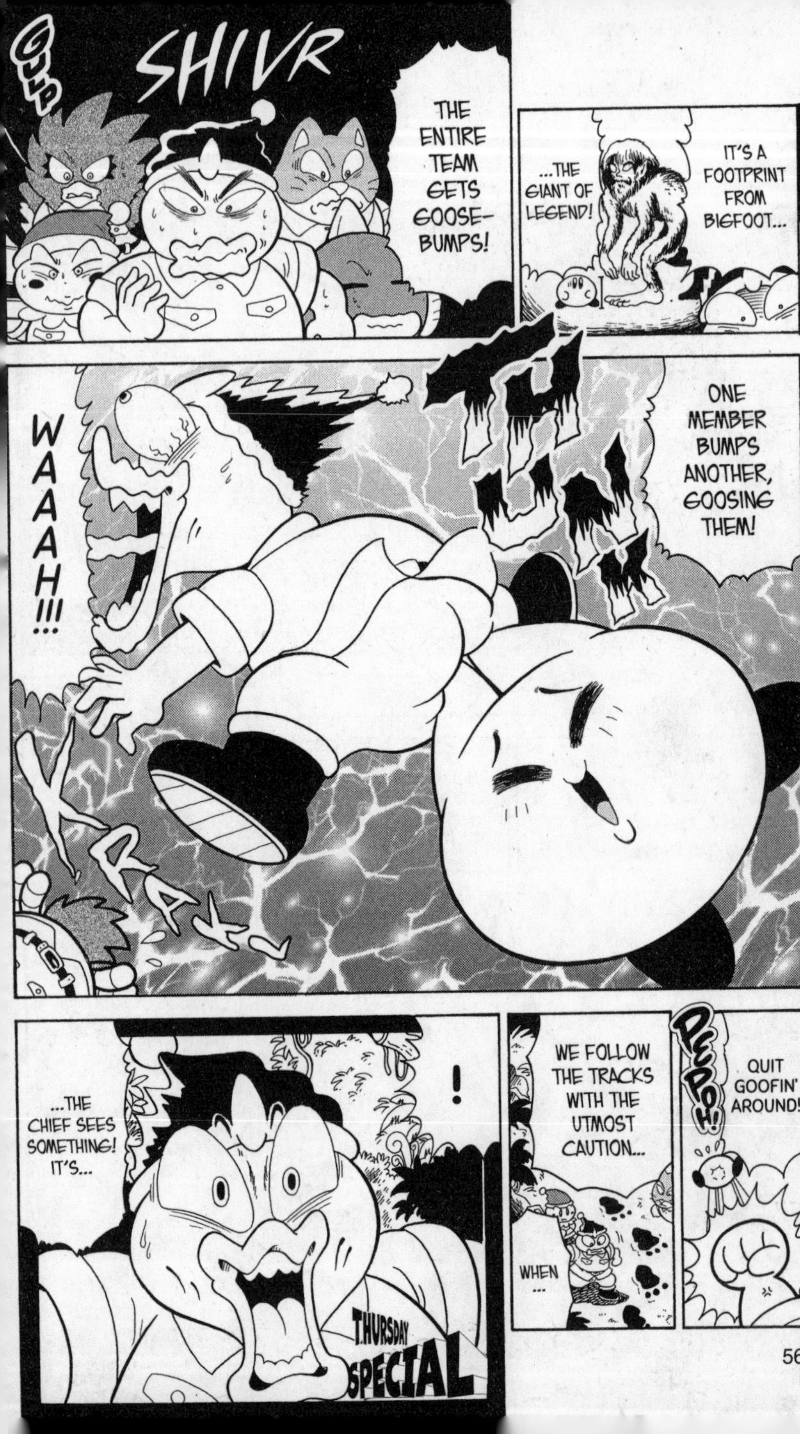
IT'S A FOOTPRINT FROM BIGFOOT...
...THE GIANT OF LEGEND!
SHIVR
GULP
THE ENTIRE TEAM GETS GOOSE-BUMPS!
ONE MEMBER BUMPS ANOTHER, GOOSING THEM!
THUMP
WAAAAH!!!
KRAK
QUIT GOOFIN' AROUND!
PEPOH!
WE FOLLOW THE TRACKS WITH THE UTMOST CAUTION...
WHEN ...
!
...THE CHIEF SEES SOMETHING! IT'S...
THURSDAY SPECIAL

AUTHOR'S COMMENT

AS A KID, I WAS ADDICTED TO *KAWAGUCHI EXPEDITION SERIES* ON TV. THE OVER-THE-TOP NARRATION AND THE EXPEDITION LEADER'S PASSION STILL STICK OUT IN MY MEMORY. AT THAT TIME, THE WORLD WAS STILL FULL OF WONDER AND MYSTERY.

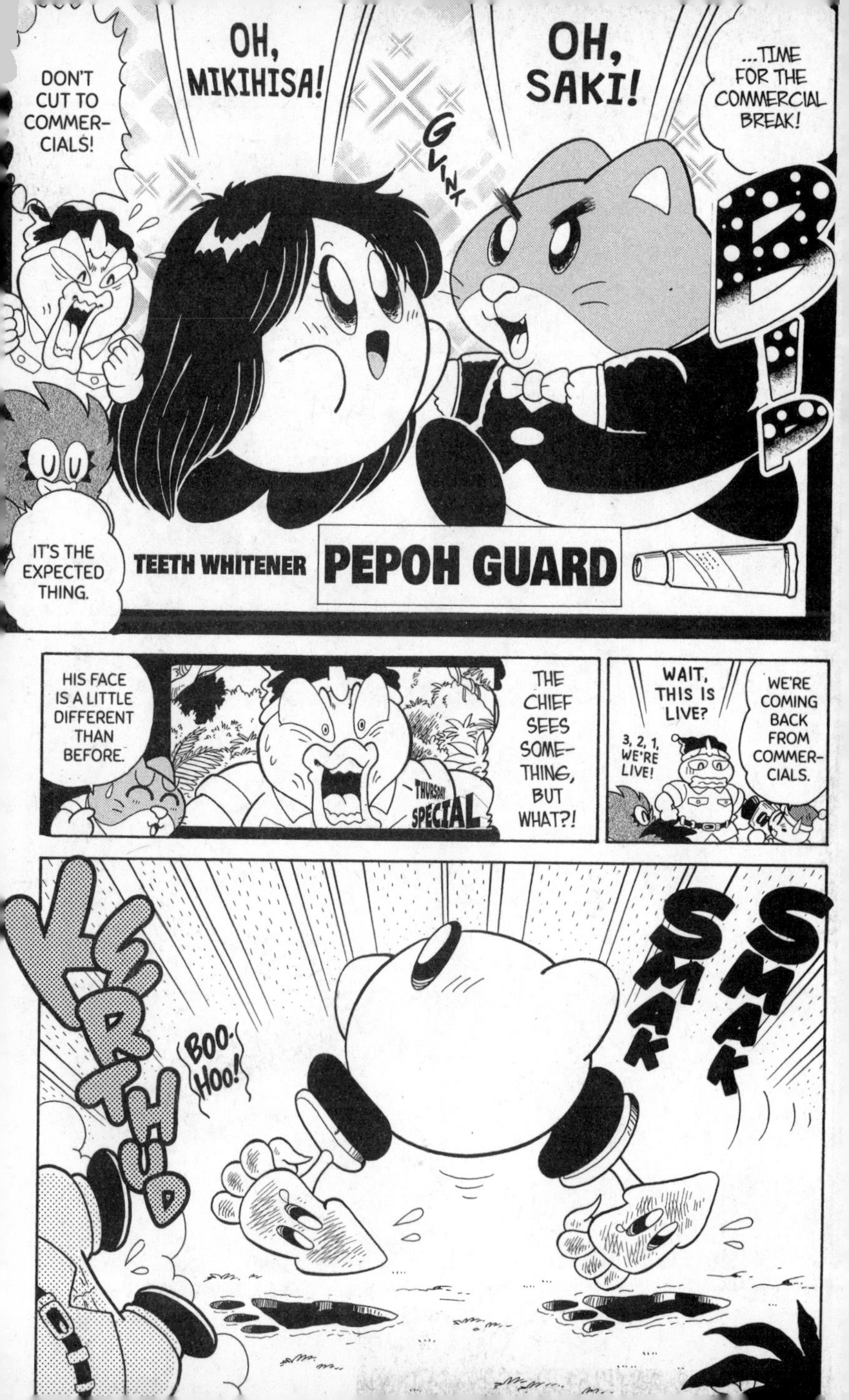
...TIME FOR THE COMMERCIAL BREAK!
OH, SAKI!
GLINT
OH, MIKIHISA!
DON'T CUT TO COMMERCIALS!
TEETH WHITENER
PEPOH GUARD
IT'S THE EXPECTED THING.
WE'RE COMING BACK FROM COMMERCIALS.
WAIT, THIS IS LIVE?
3, 2, 1, WE'RE LIVE!
THE CHIEF SEES SOMETHING, BUT WHAT?!
THURSDAY SPECIAL
HIS FACE IS A LITTLE DIFFERENT THAN BEFORE.
SMAK
SMAK
BOO-HOO!
KERTHUD

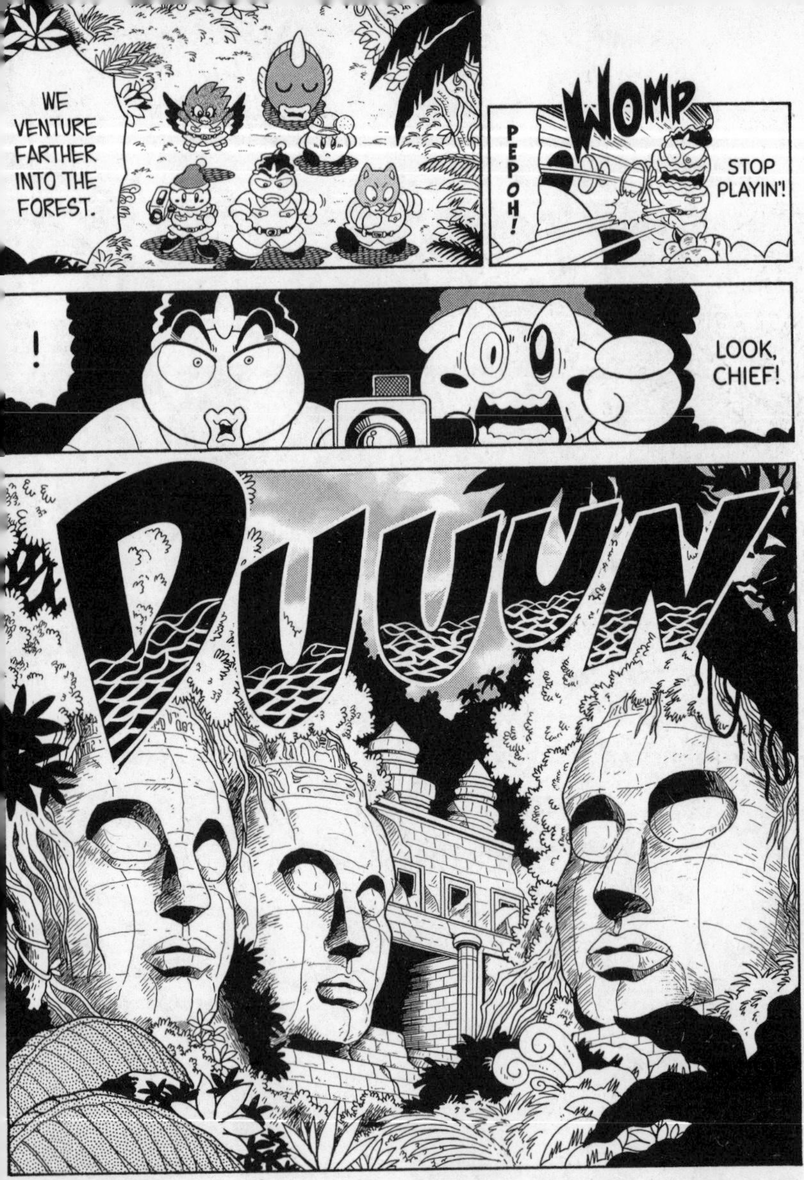
WOMP
PEPOH!
STOP PLAYIN'!
WE VENTURE FARTHER INTO THE FOREST.
LOOK, CHIEF!
!
DUUUN
ANCIENT RUINS!
AMAZIN'!

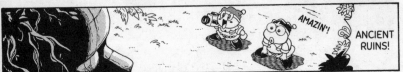

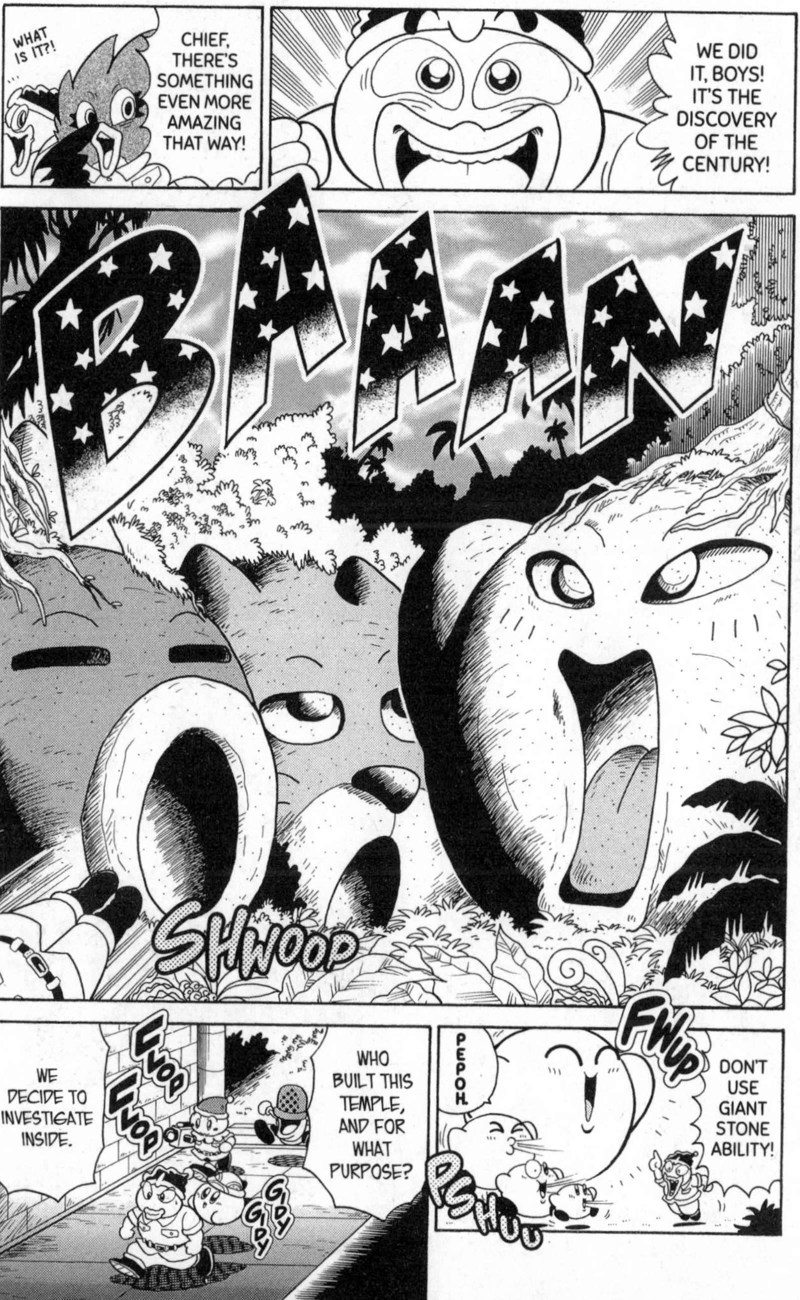
WE DID IT, BOYS! IT'S THE DISCOVERY OF THE CENTURY!
CHIEF, THERE'S SOMETHING EVEN MORE AMAZING THAT WAY!
WHAT IS IT?!
...
BAAAN
SHWOOP
FWUP
DON'T USE GIANT STONE ABILITY!
PEPOH
PSHUU
WHO BUILT THIS TEMPLE, AND FOR WHAT PURPOSE?
CLOP CLOP
WE DECIDE TO INVESTIGATE INSIDE.
GIDY GIDY

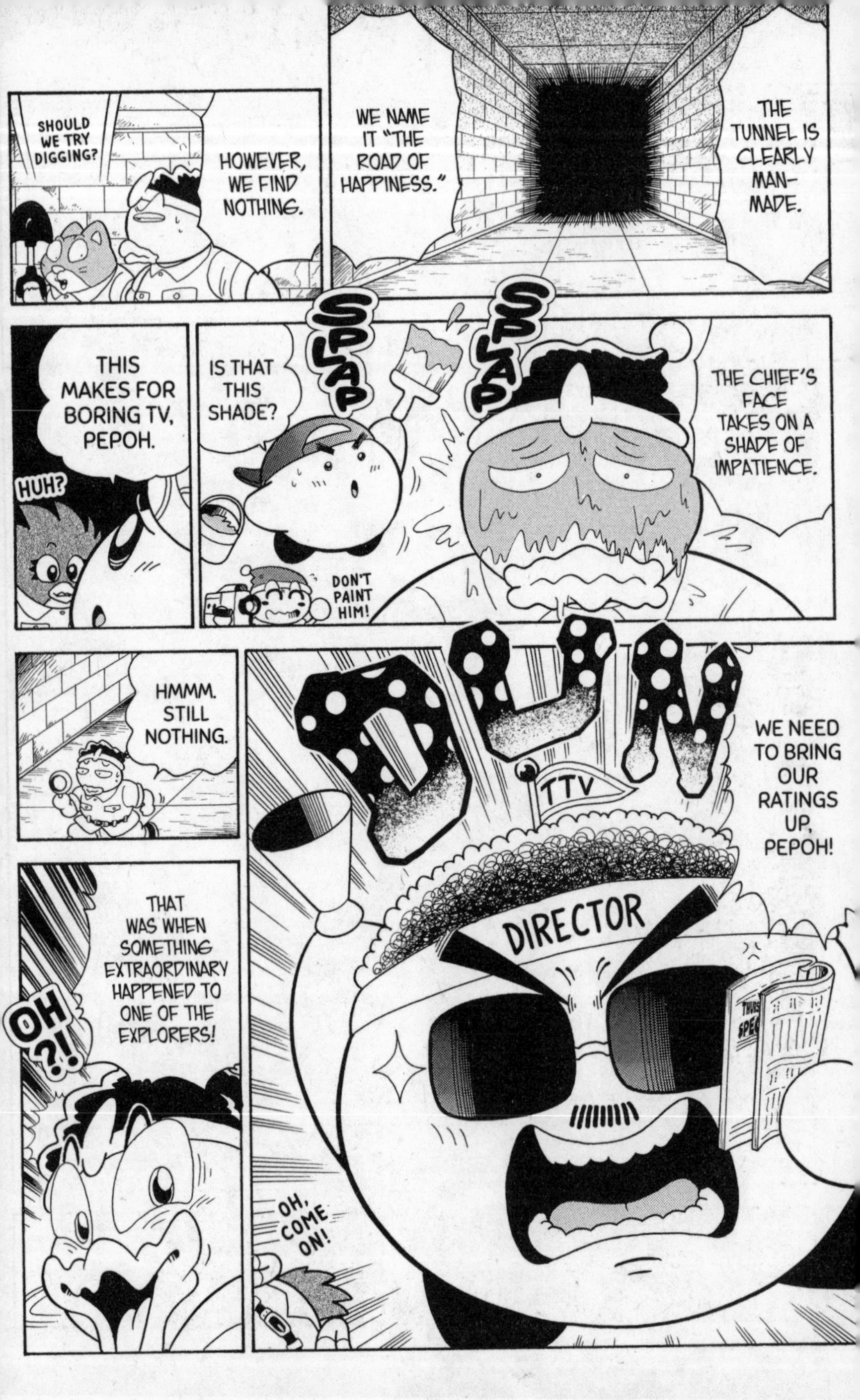
THE TUNNEL IS CLEARLY MAN-MADE.
WE NAME IT "THE ROAD OF HAPPINESS."
HOWEVER, WE FIND NOTHING.
SHOULD WE TRY DIGGING?
THE CHIEF'S FACE TAKES ON A SHADE OF IMPATIENCE.
SPLAP
SPLAP
IS THAT THIS SHADE?
DON'T PAINT HIM!
THIS MAKES FOR BORING TV, PEPOH.
HUH?
DUN
TTV
WE NEED TO BRING OUR RATINGS UP, PEPOH!
DIRECTOR
OH, COME ON!
HMMM. STILL NOTHING.
THAT WAS WHEN SOMETHING EXTRAORDINARY HAPPENED TO ONE OF THE EXPLORERS!
OH?!

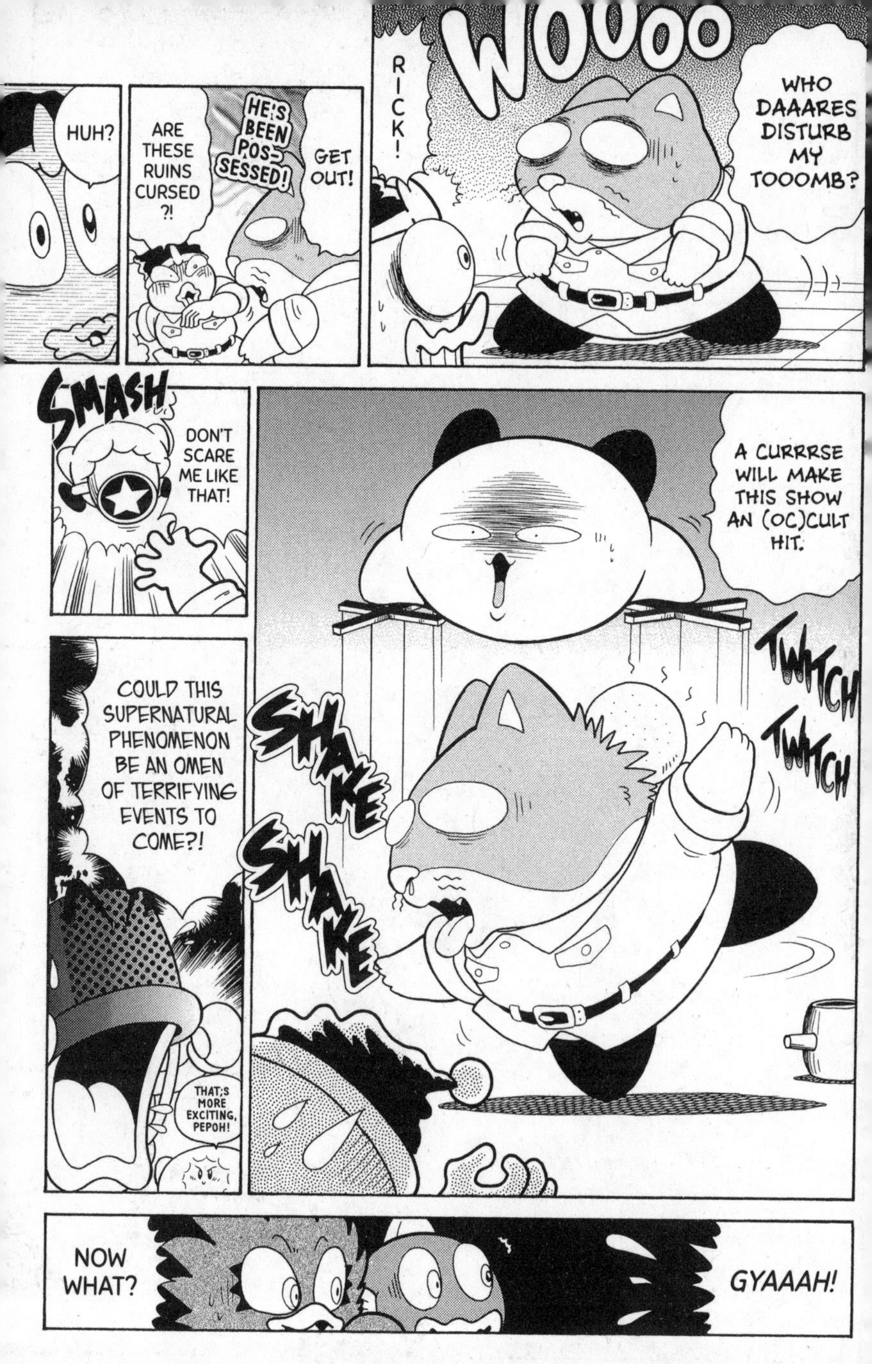
WOOOO
WHO DAAARES DISTURB MY TOOOMB?
RICK!
GET OUT!
HE'S BEEN POS-SESSED!
ARE THESE RUINS CURSED?!
HUH?
A CURRRSE WILL MAKE THIS SHOW AN (OC)CULT HIT.
TWITCH
TWITCH
SHAKE
SHAKE
SMASH
DON'T SCARE ME LIKE THAT!
COULD THIS SUPERNATURAL PHENOMENON BE AN OMEN OF TERRIFYING EVENTS TO COME?!
THAT;S MORE EXCITING, PEPOH!
GYAAAH!
NOW WHAT?

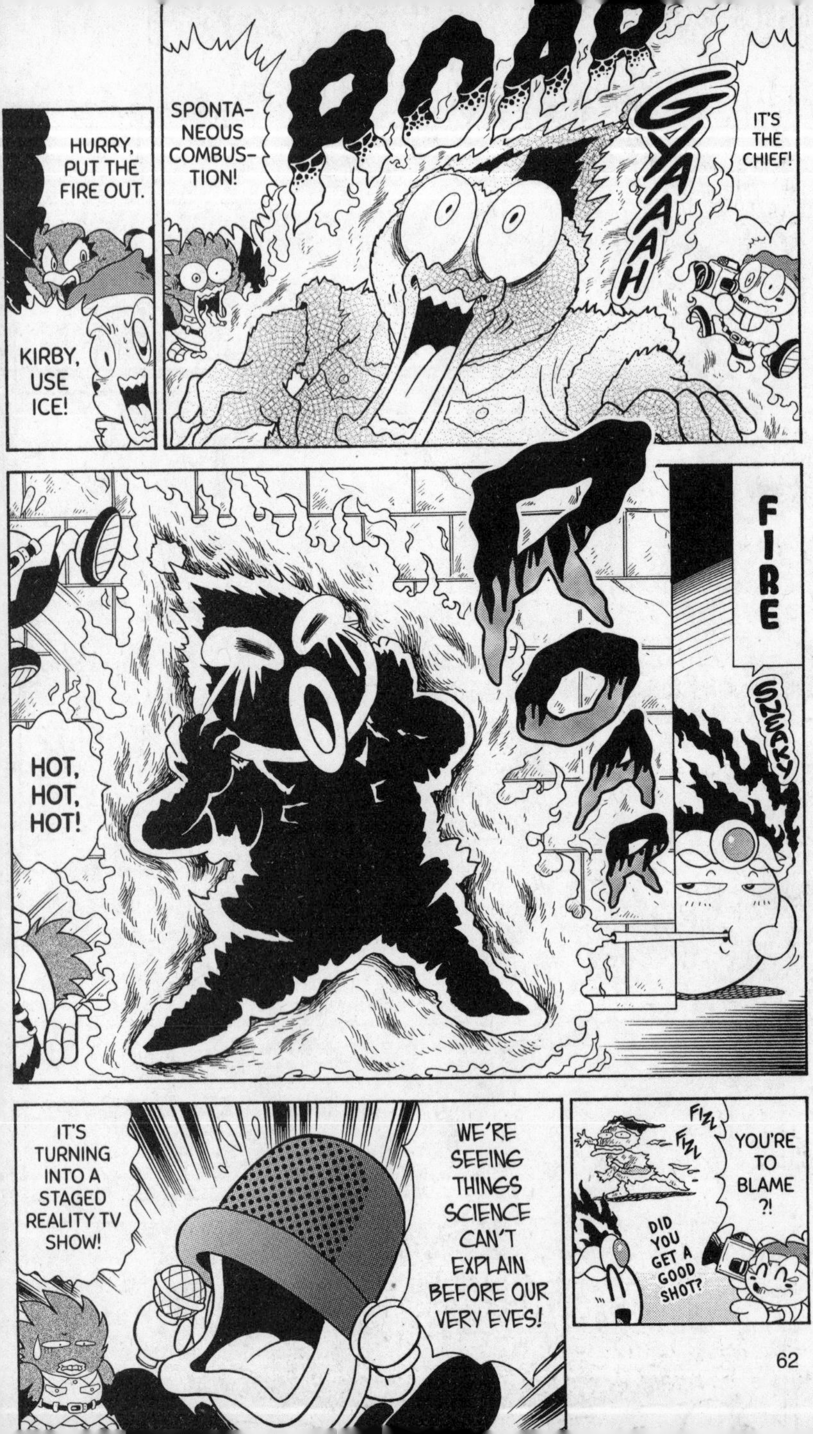
ROAR
GYAAAH
IT'S THE CHIEF!
SPONTANEOUS COMBUSTION!
HURRY, PUT THE FIRE OUT.
KIRBY, USE ICE!
FIRE
SNEAKY
ROAR
HOT, HOT, HOT!
YOU'RE TO BLAME?!
FIZZ
FIZZ
DID YOU GET A GOOD SHOT?
WE'RE SEEING THINGS SCIENCE CAN'T EXPLAIN BEFORE OUR VERY EYES!
IT'S TURNING INTO A STAGED REALITY TV SHOW!

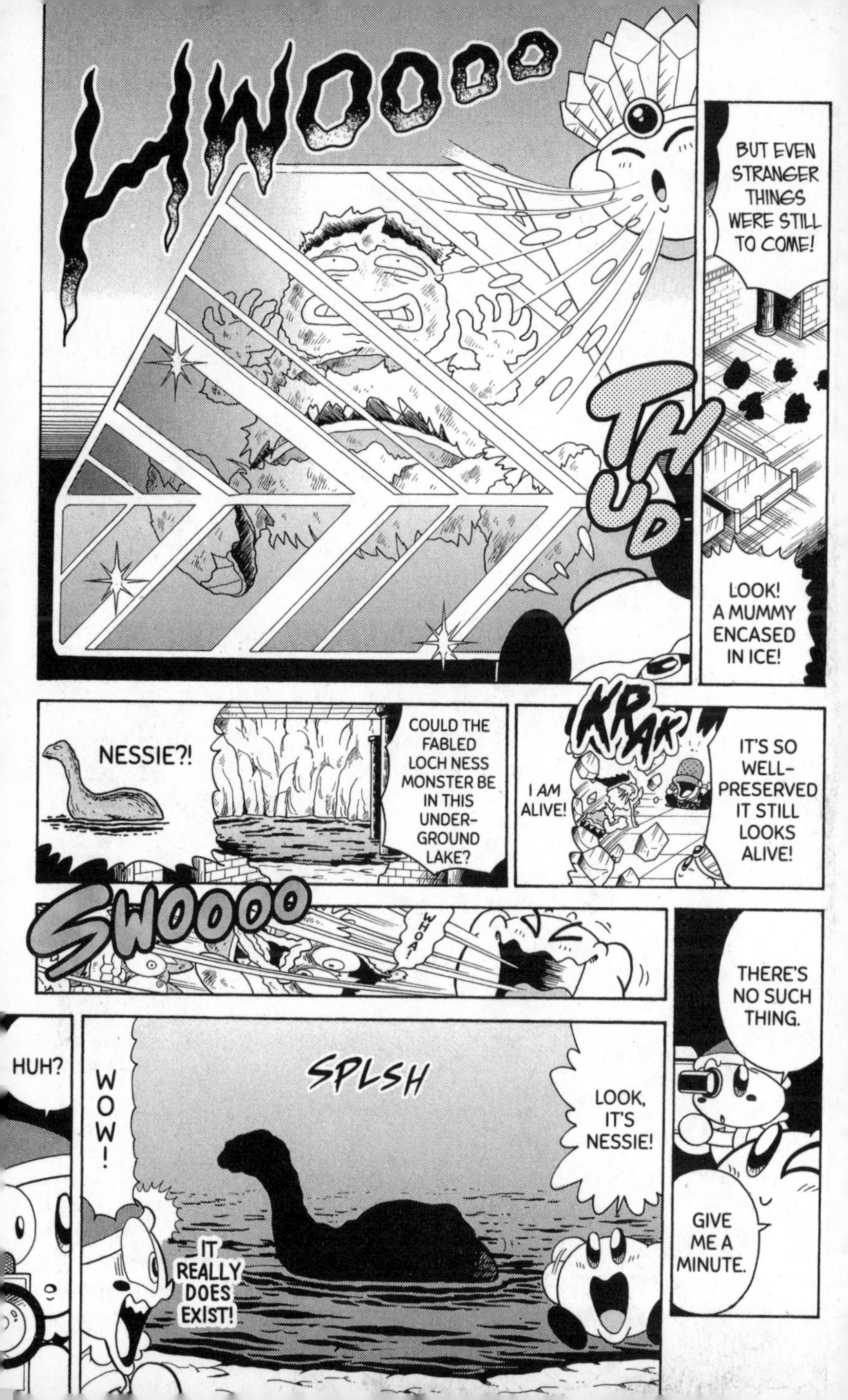

BUT EVEN STRANGER THINGS WERE STILL TO COME!
LOOK! A MUMMY ENCASED IN ICE!
HWOOOO
THUD
KRAK
IT'S SO WELL-PRESERVED IT STILL LOOKS ALIVE!
I AM ALIVE!
COULD THE FABLED LOCH NESS MONSTER BE IN THIS UNDERGROUND LAKE?
NESSIE?!
THERE'S NO SUCH THING.
GIVE ME A MINUTE.
SWOOOO
WHOA!
LOOK, IT'S NESSIE!
SPLSH
WOW!
IT REALLY DOES EXIST!
HUH?

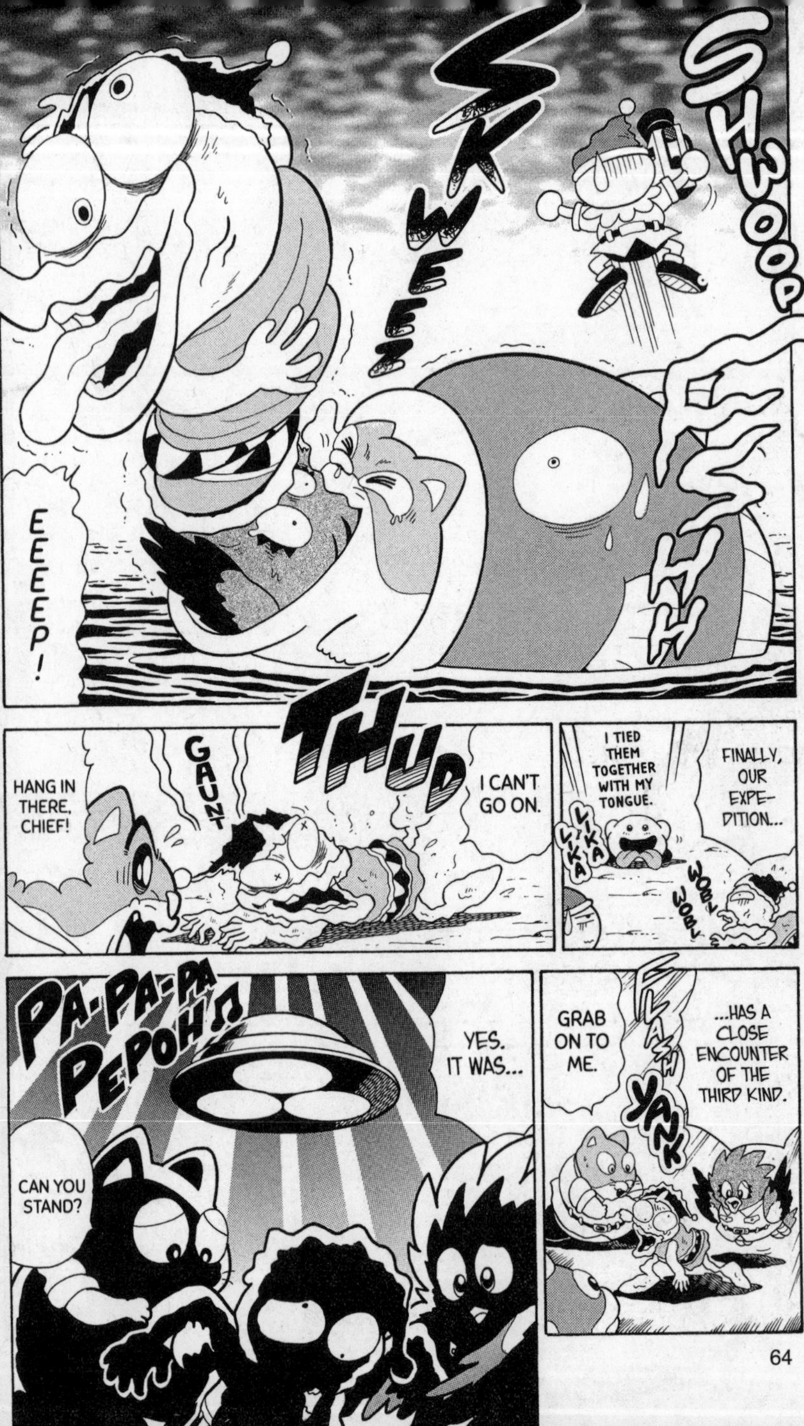
SHWOOP
SKWEEZ
FSHHH
EEEEEP!
FINALLY, OUR EXPEDITION...
I TIED THEM TOGETHER WITH MY TONGUE.
LIKA LIKA LIKA
WOBN WOBN
I CAN'T GO ON.
THUD
GAUNT
HANG IN THERE, CHIEF!
...HAS A CLOSE ENCOUNTER OF THE THIRD KIND.
FLASH
YANK
GRAB ON TO ME.
YES. IT WAS...
PA-PA-PA PEPOH♫
CAN YOU STAND?

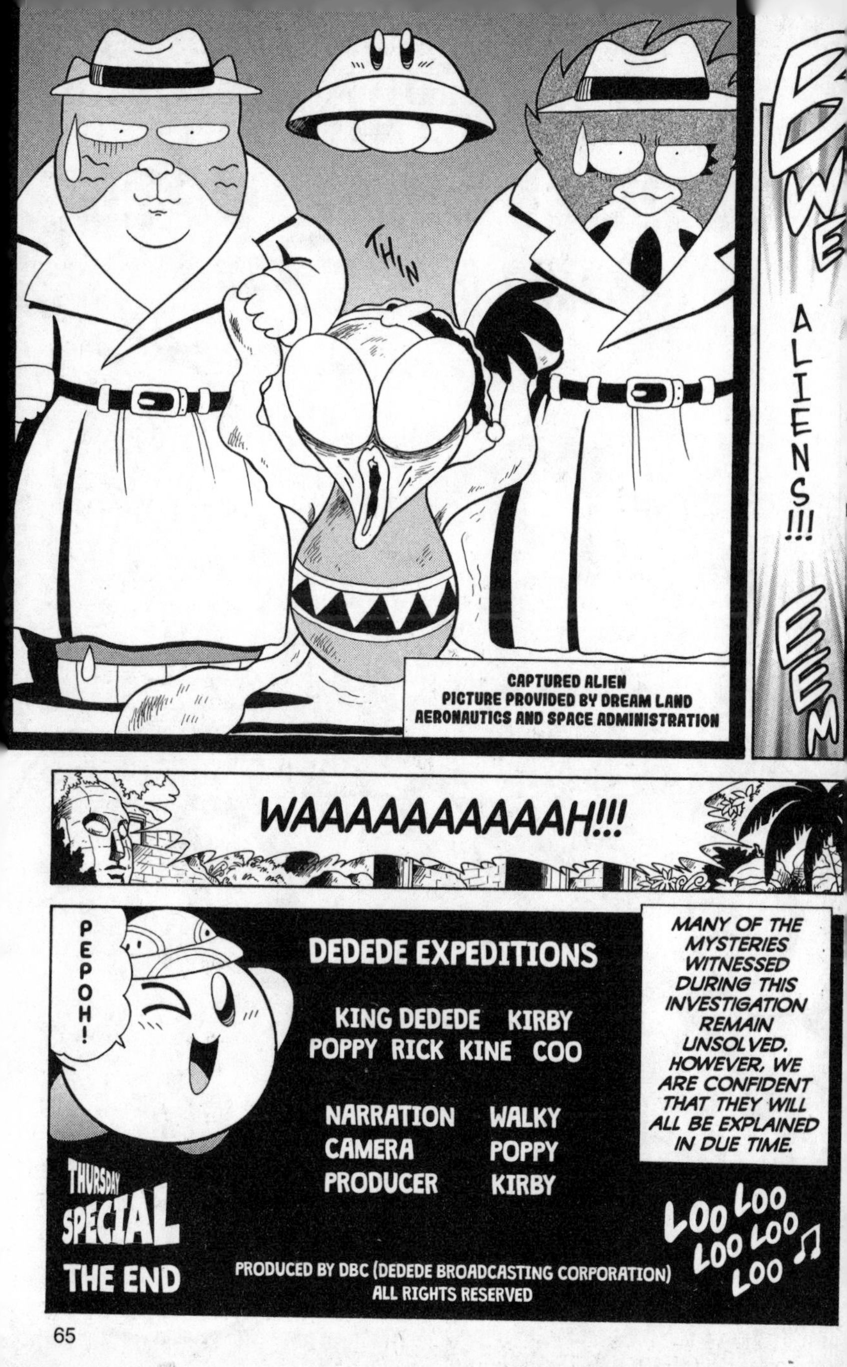
BWE
ALIENS!!!
EEM
THIN
CAPTURED ALIEN
PICTURE PROVIDED BY DREAM LAND
AERONAUTICS AND SPACE ADMINISTRATION
WAAAAAAAAAAH!!!
MANY OF THE MYSTERIES WITNESSED DURING THIS INVESTIGATION REMAIN UNSOLVED. HOWEVER, WE ARE CONFIDENT THAT THEY WILL ALL BE EXPLAINED IN DUE TIME.
DEDEDE EXPEDITIONS
KING DEDEDE KIRBY
POPPY RICK KINE COO
NARRATION WALKY
CAMERA POPPY
PRODUCER KIRBY
PRODUCED BY DBC (DEDEDE BROADCASTING CORPORATION)
ALL RIGHTS RESERVED
LOO LOO LOO LOO LOO ♫
PEPOH!
THURSDAY SPECIAL
THE END

CHAPTER 7: SUPER POWER-UP?! OLD KIRBY!

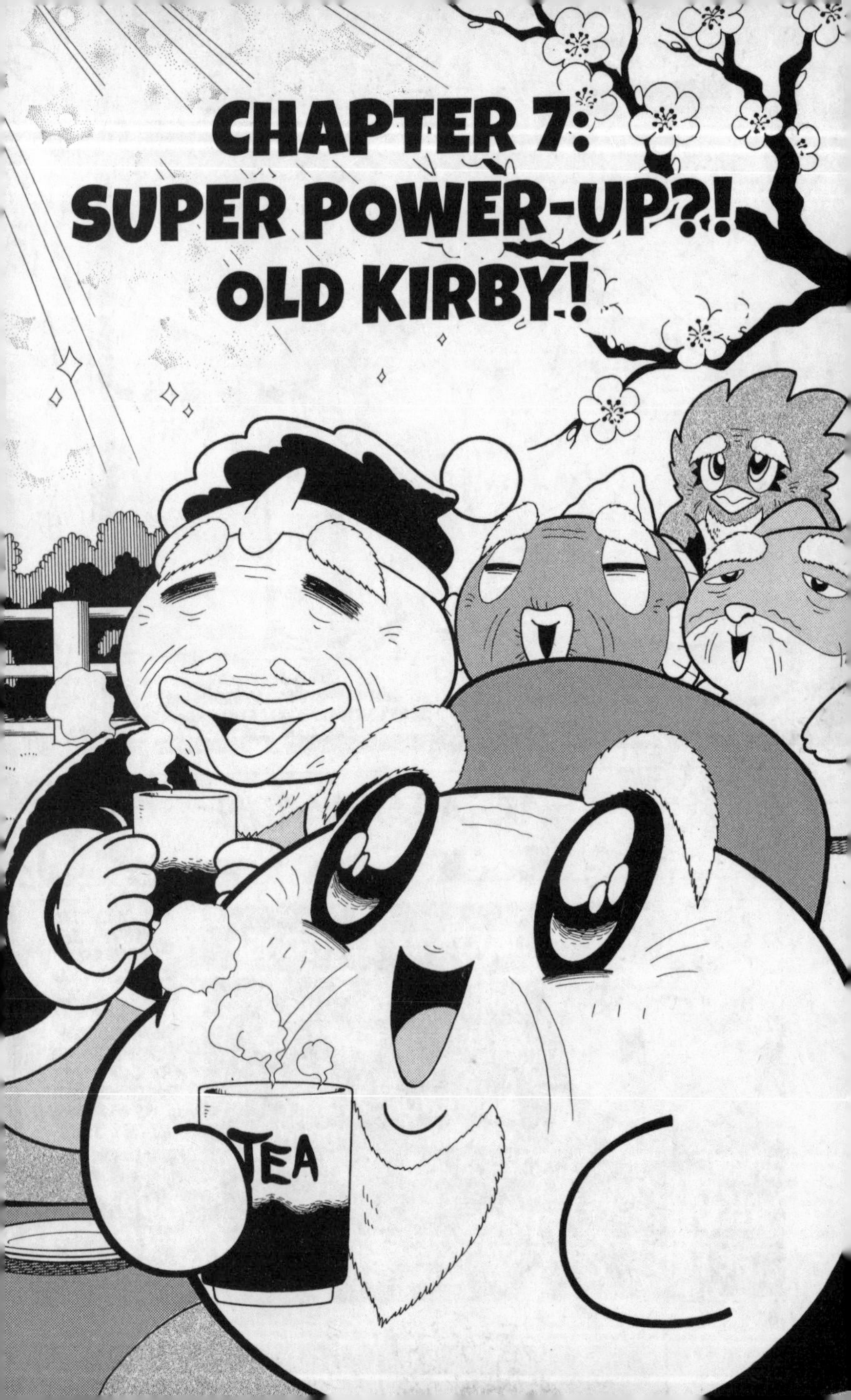
TEA

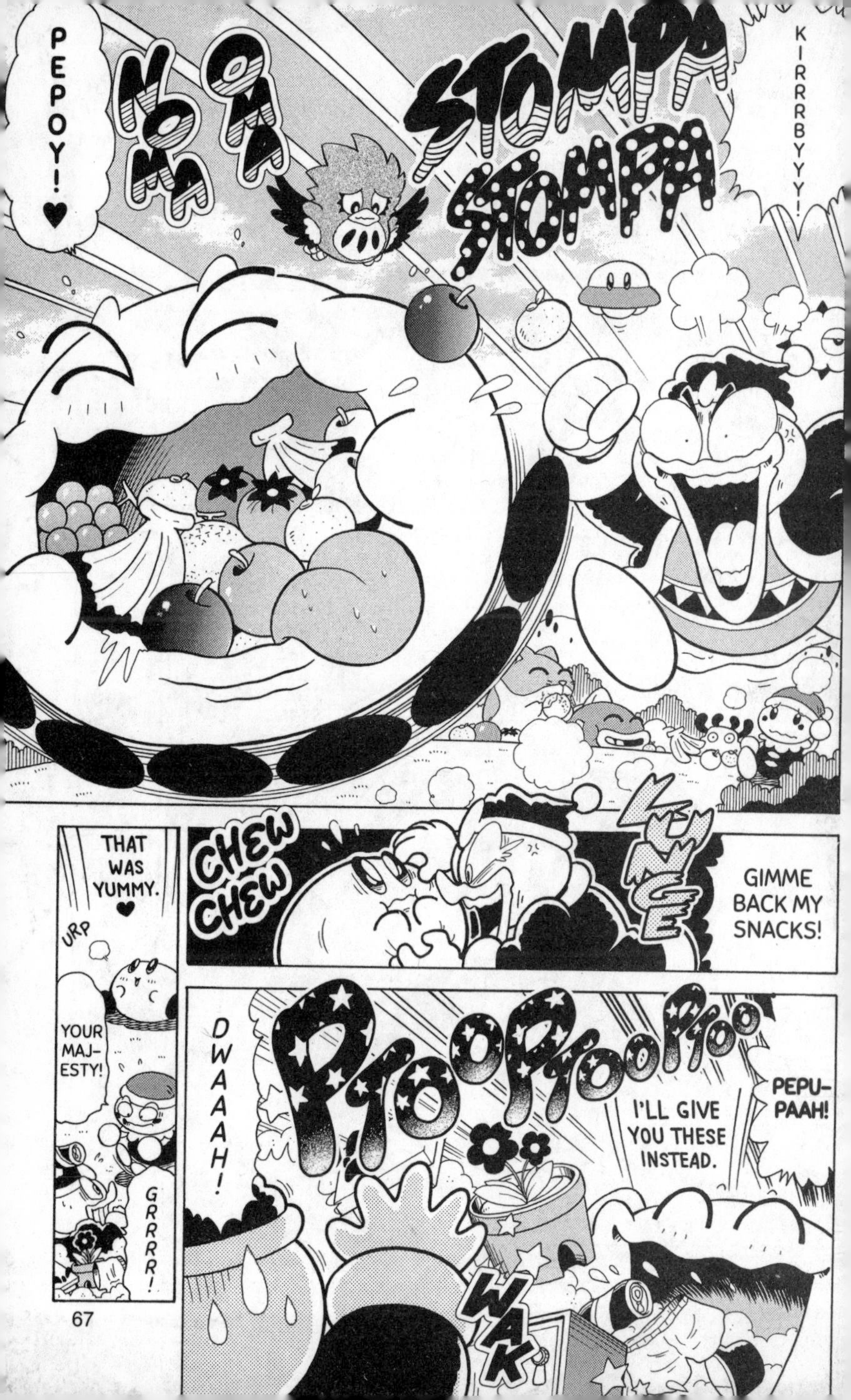
KIRRRBYYY!
STOMPA STOMPA
OMA NOMA
PEPOY! ♥
GIMME BACK MY SNACKS!
LUNGE
CHEW CHEW
PEPU-PAAH!
I'LL GIVE YOU THESE INSTEAD.
PYOOPYOOPYOO
DWAAAAH!
WAK
THAT WAS YUMMY. ♥
URP
YOUR MAJ-ESTY!
GRRRR!

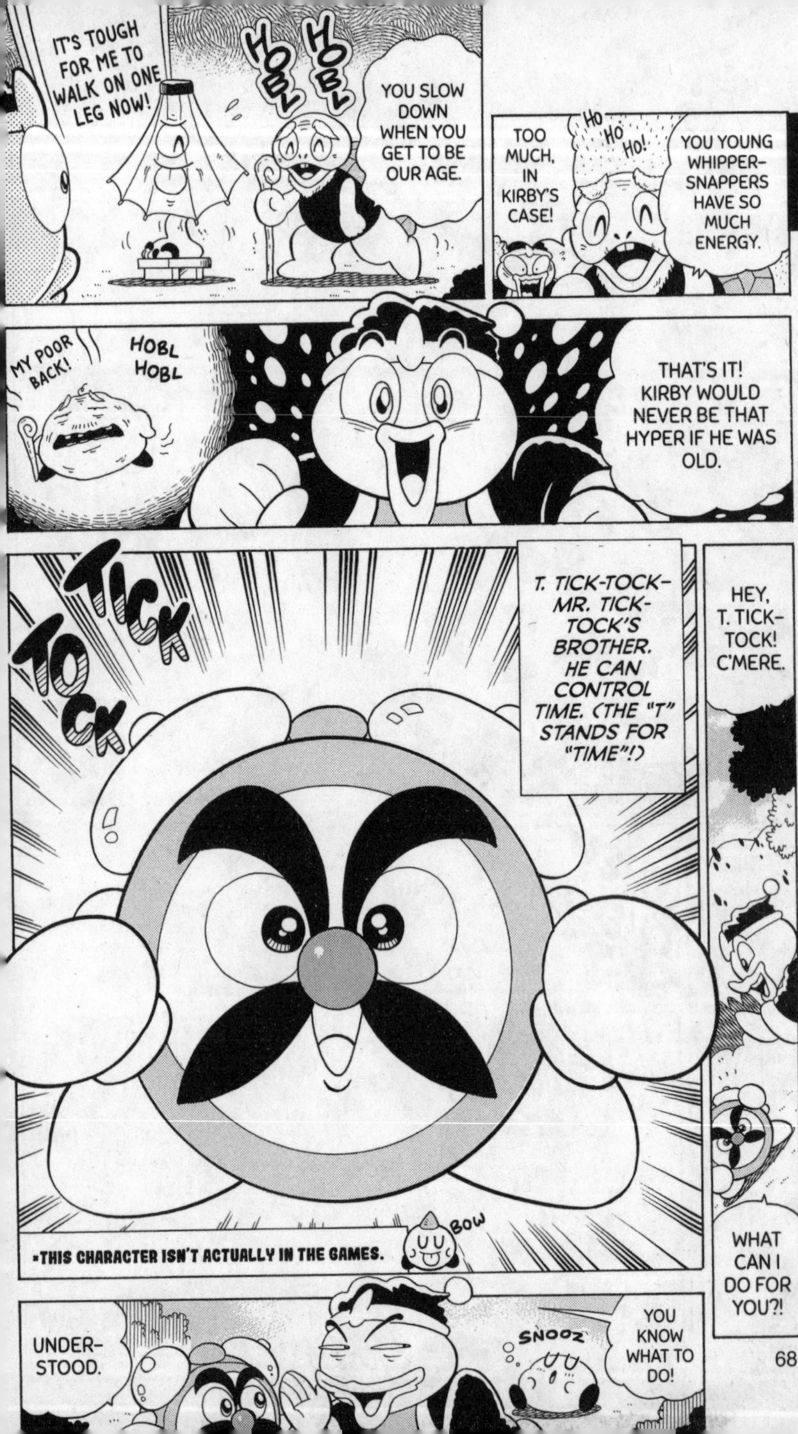
YOU YOUNG WHIPPER-SNAPPERS HAVE SO MUCH ENERGY.
HO HO HO!
TOO MUCH, IN KIRBY'S CASE!
HOBL HOBL
YOU SLOW DOWN WHEN YOU GET TO BE OUR AGE.
IT'S TOUGH FOR ME TO WALK ON ONE LEG NOW!
THAT'S IT! KIRBY WOULD NEVER BE THAT HYPER IF HE WAS OLD.
HOBL HOBL
MY POOR BACK!
HEY, T. TICK-TOCK! C'MERE.
WHAT CAN I DO FOR YOU?!
T. TICK-TOCK— MR. TICK-TOCK'S BROTHER. HE CAN CONTROL TIME. (THE "T" STANDS FOR "TIME"!)
TICK TOCK
BOW
*THIS CHARACTER ISN'T ACTUALLY IN THE GAMES.
YOU KNOW WHAT TO DO!
SNOOZ
UNDER-STOOD.

AUTHOR'S COMMENT

I'VE GOTTEN ON IN AGE TOO. I'LL PROBABLY BE AN OLD GEEZER BEFORE I KNOW IT. STAIRS ARE SERIOUSLY TOUGH FOR ME LATELY. NO CHOICE BUT TO WORK ON GETTING FIT!

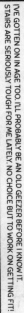

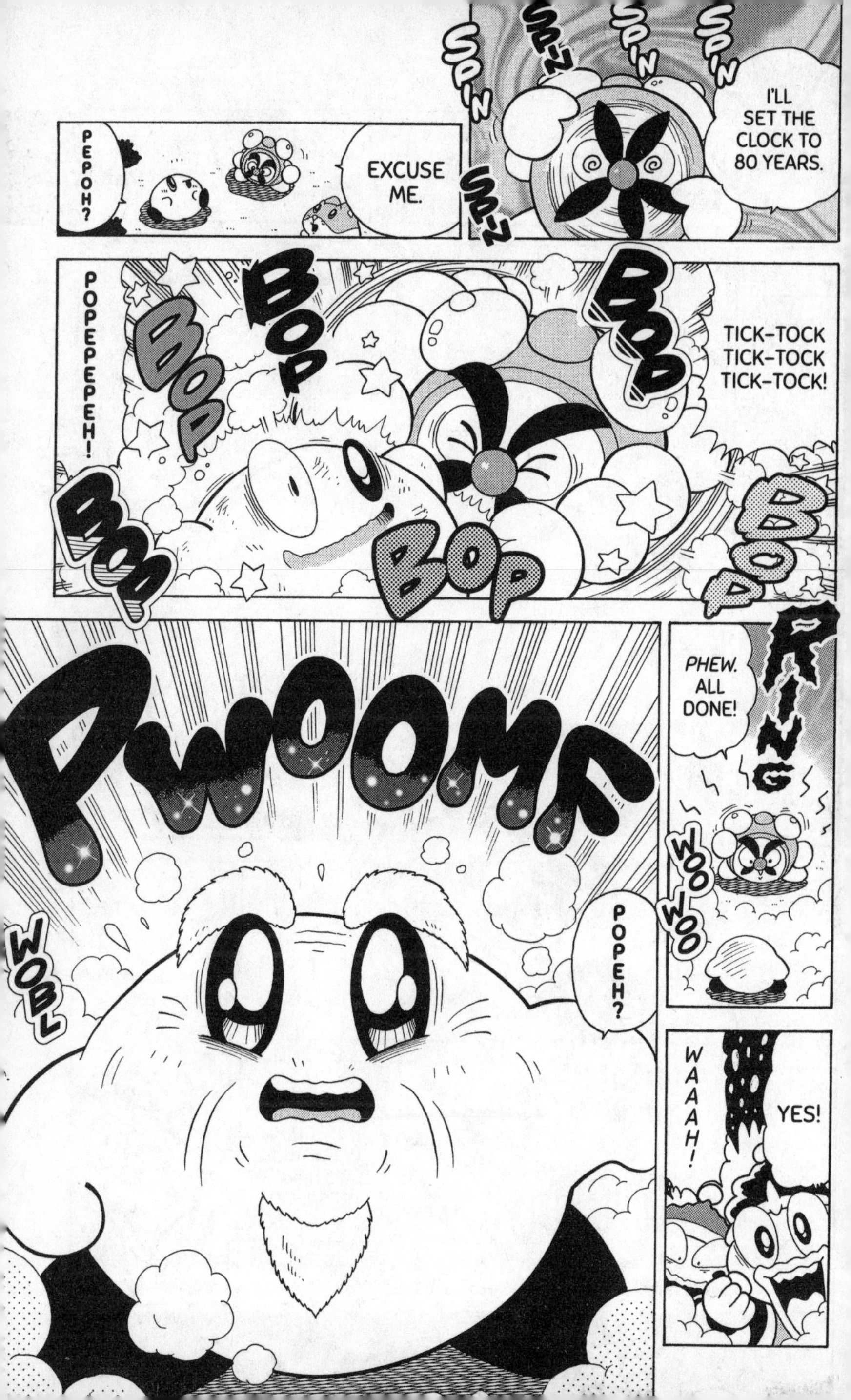

SPIN
SPIN
SPIN
SPIN
SPIN
I'LL SET THE CLOCK TO 80 YEARS.
EXCUSE ME.
PEPOH?
TICK-TOCK TICK-TOCK TICK-TOCK!
BOP
BOP
BOP
BOP
BOP
BOP
POPEPEPEH!
PHEW. ALL DONE!
RING
WOO WOO
YES!
WAAAAH!
PWOOMF
POPEH?
WOBL

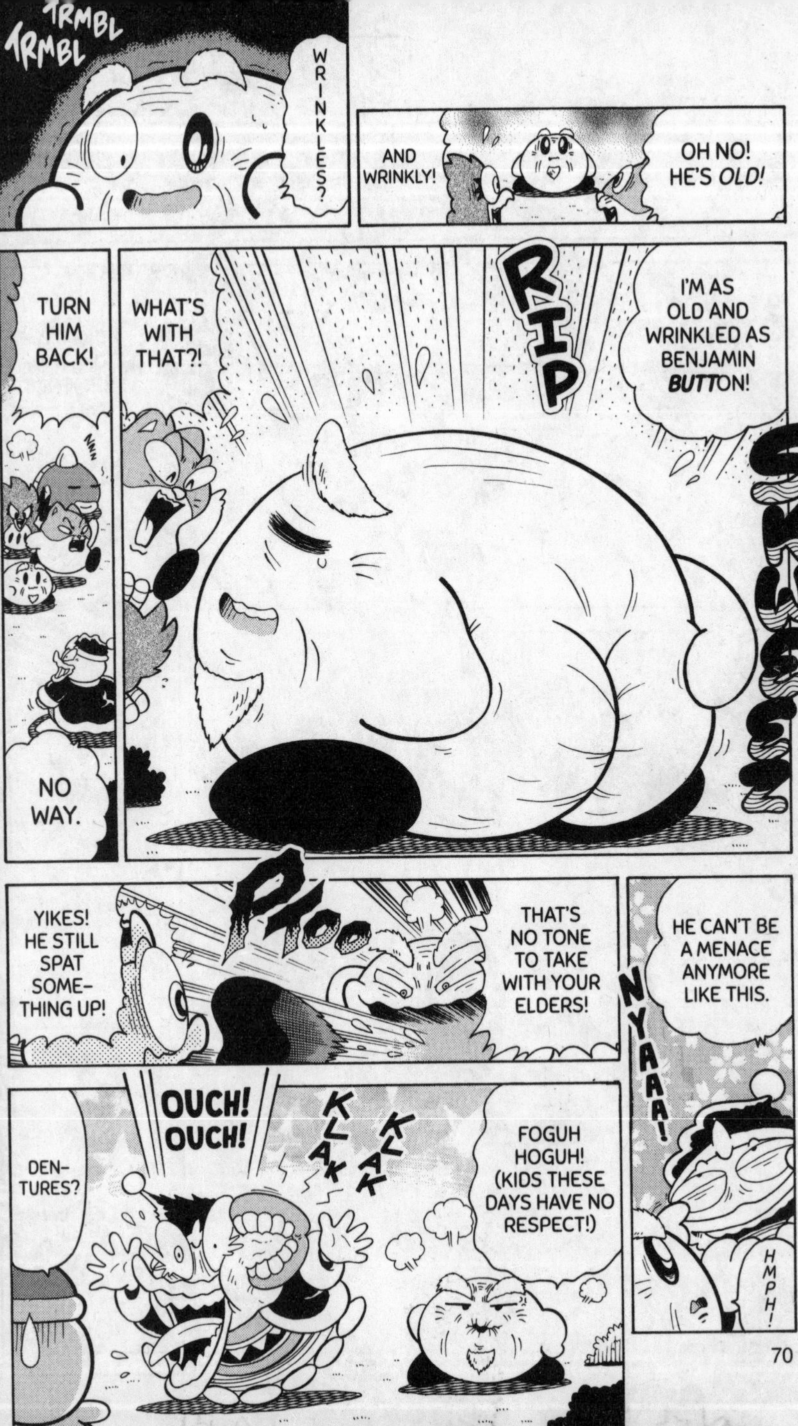
OH NO!
HE'S *OLD!*
AND WRINKLY!
TRMBL TRMBL
WRINKLES?
RIP
I'M AS OLD AND WRINKLED AS BENJAMIN ***BUTT***ON!
SKWEEN
WHAT'S WITH THAT?!
TURN HIM BACK!
NNN
NO WAY.
HE CAN'T BE A MENACE ANYMORE LIKE THIS.
NYAAA!
HMPH!
THAT'S NO TONE TO TAKE WITH YOUR ELDERS!
PHOO
YIKES! HE STILL SPAT SOME-THING UP!
FOGUH HOGUH! (KIDS THESE DAYS HAVE NO RESPECT!)
KLAK KLAK
KLAK
OUCH! OUCH!
DEN-TURES?

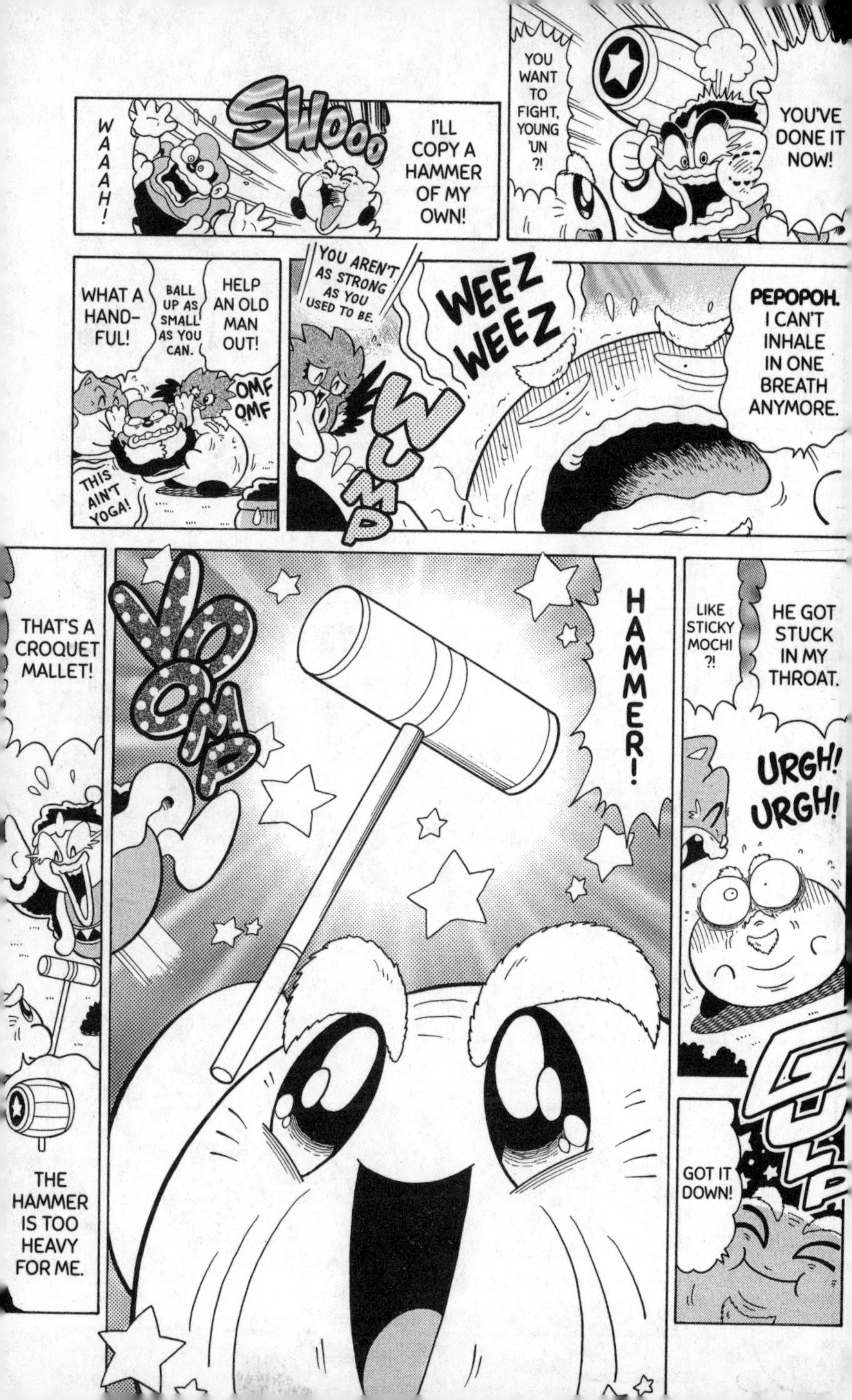
YOU'VE DONE IT NOW!
YOU WANT TO FIGHT, YOUNG 'UN?!
I'LL COPY A HAMMER OF MY OWN!
SWOOO
WAAAAH!
PEPOPOH. I CAN'T INHALE IN ONE BREATH ANYMORE.
WEEZ WEEZ
YOU AREN'T AS STRONG AS YOU USED TO BE.
WUMP
HELP AN OLD MAN OUT!
BALL UP AS SMALL AS YOU CAN.
WHAT A HANDFUL!
OMF OMF
THIS AIN'T YOGA!
HE GOT STUCK IN MY THROAT.
LIKE STICKY MOCHI?!
URGH! URGH!
GOT IT DOWN!
HAMMER!
THAT'S A CROQUET MALLET!
THE HAMMER IS TOO HEAVY FOR ME.

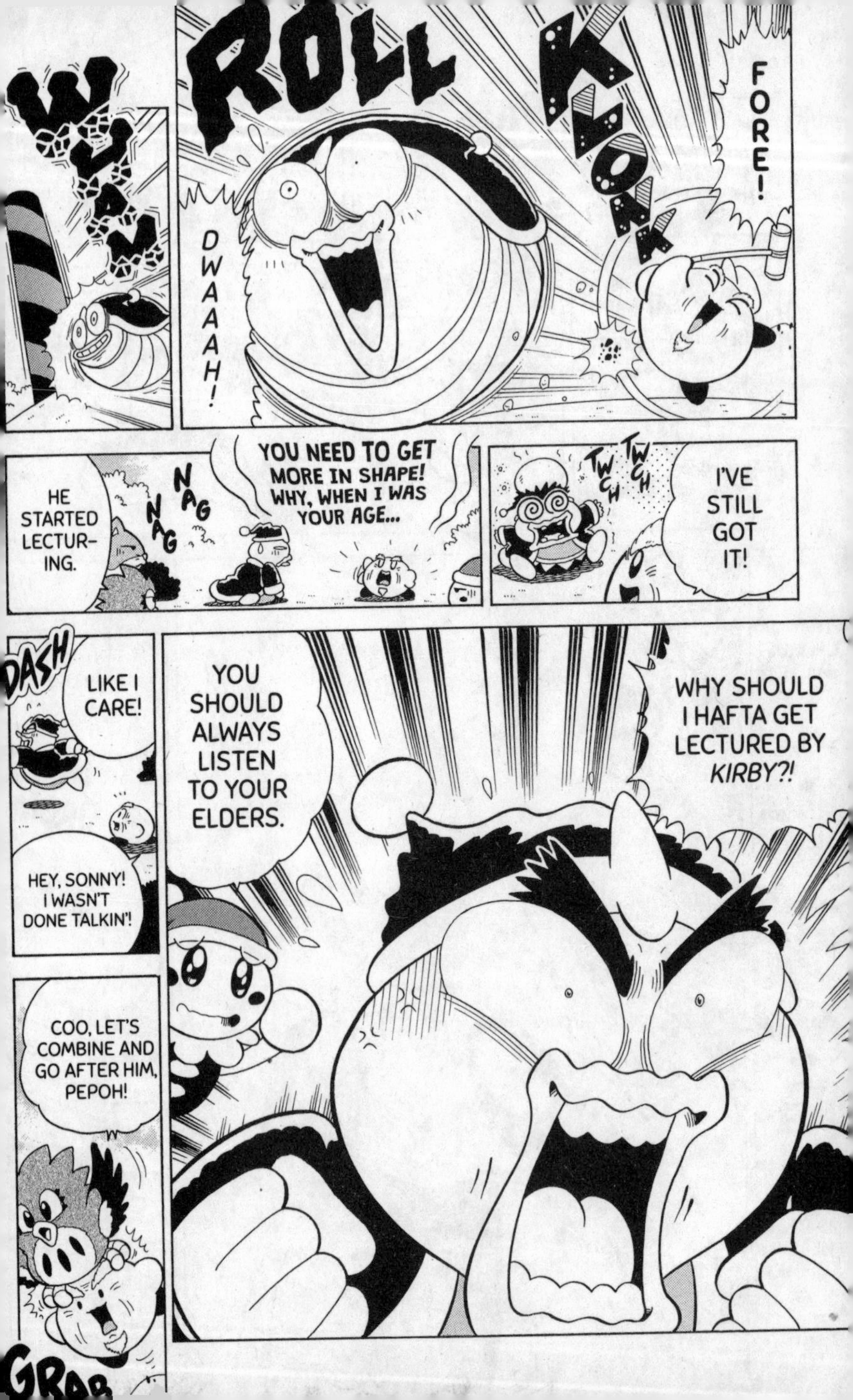
FORE!
KLONK
ROLL
DWAAAAH!
WHAM
I'VE STILL GOT IT!
TWCH TWCH
YOU NEED TO GET MORE IN SHAPE! WHY, WHEN I WAS YOUR AGE...
NAG NAG
HE STARTED LECTURING.
WHY SHOULD I HAFTA GET LECTURED BY *KIRBY?!*
YOU SHOULD ALWAYS LISTEN TO YOUR ELDERS.
DASH
LIKE I CARE!
HEY, SONNY! I WASN'T DONE TALKIN'!
COO, LET'S COMBINE AND GO AFTER HIM, PEPOH!
GRAB

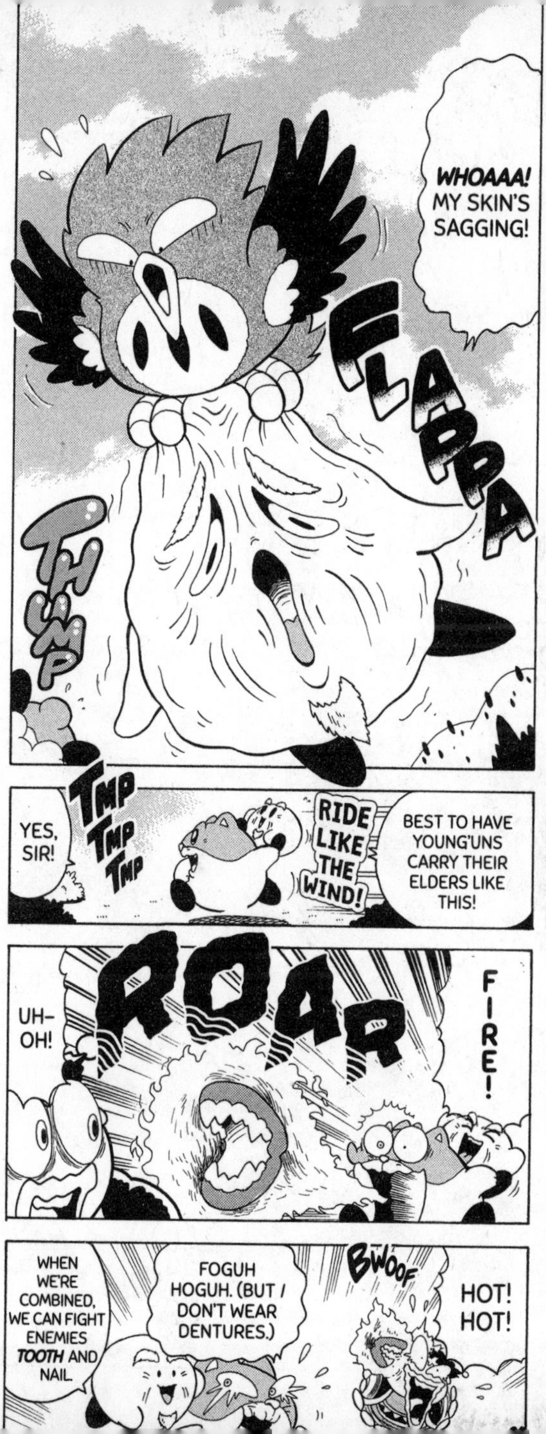
WHOAAA! MY SKIN'S SAGGING!
FLABBA
THUMP
BEST TO HAVE YOUNG'UNS CARRY THEIR ELDERS LIKE THIS!
RIDE LIKE THE WIND!
TMP TMP TMP
YES, SIR!
FIRE!
ROAR
UH-OH!
HOT! HOT!
BWOOF
FOGUH HOGUH. (BUT I DON'T WEAR DENTURES.)
WHEN WE'RE COMBINED, WE CAN FIGHT ENEMIES TOOTH AND NAIL.

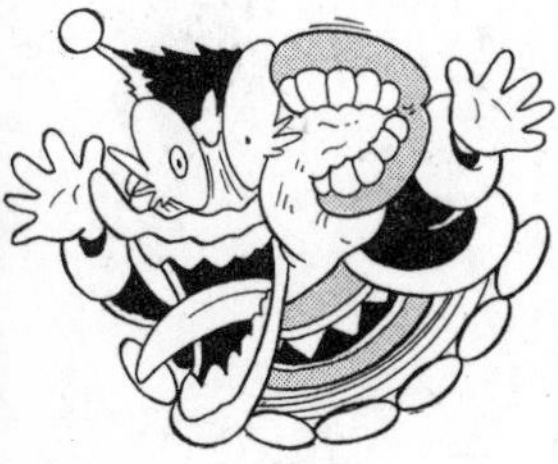

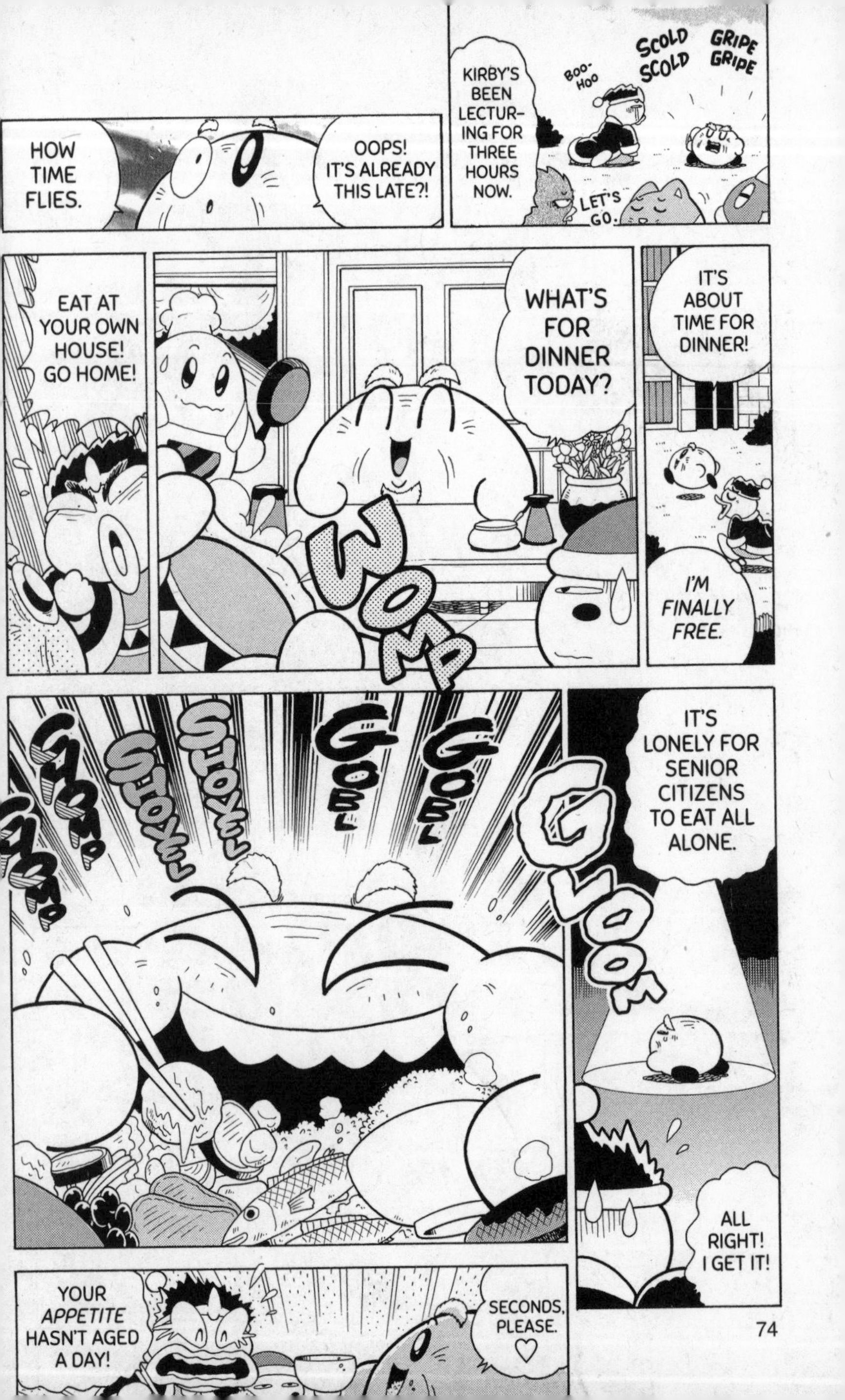
KIRBY'S BEEN LECTURING FOR THREE HOURS NOW.
SCOLD SCOLD
GRIPE GRIPE
BOO-HOO
LET'S GO.
OOPS! IT'S ALREADY THIS LATE?!
HOW TIME FLIES.
IT'S ABOUT TIME FOR DINNER!
I'M FINALLY FREE.
WHAT'S FOR DINNER TODAY?
WOMP
EAT AT YOUR OWN HOUSE! GO HOME!
IT'S LONELY FOR SENIOR CITIZENS TO EAT ALL ALONE.
GLOOOM
ALL RIGHT! I GET IT!
GOBBL GOBBL
SHOVEL SHOVEL
CHOMP CHOMP
SECONDS, PLEASE. ♡
YOUR APPETITE HASN'T AGED A DAY!

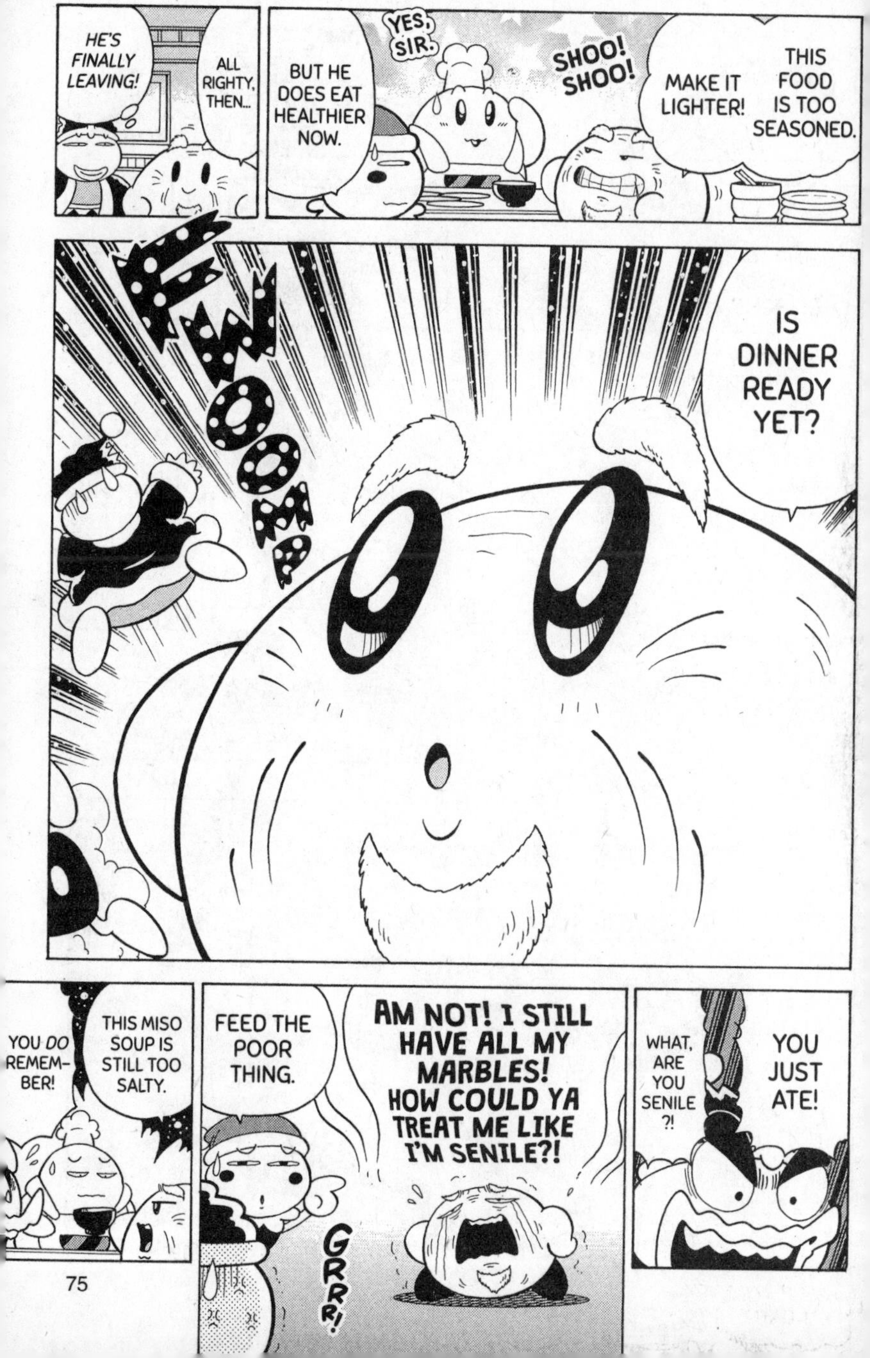
THIS FOOD IS TOO SEASONED.
MAKE IT LIGHTER!
SHOO! SHOO!
YES, SIR.
BUT HE DOES EAT HEALTHIER NOW.
ALL RIGHTY, THEN...
HE'S FINALLY LEAVING!
IS DINNER READY YET?
YOU JUST ATE!
WHAT, ARE YOU SENILE ?!
AM NOT! I STILL HAVE ALL MY MARBLES! HOW COULD YA TREAT ME LIKE I'M SENILE?!
FEED THE POOR THING.
GRRR!
THIS MISO SOUP IS STILL TOO SALTY.
YOU *DO* REMEMBER!

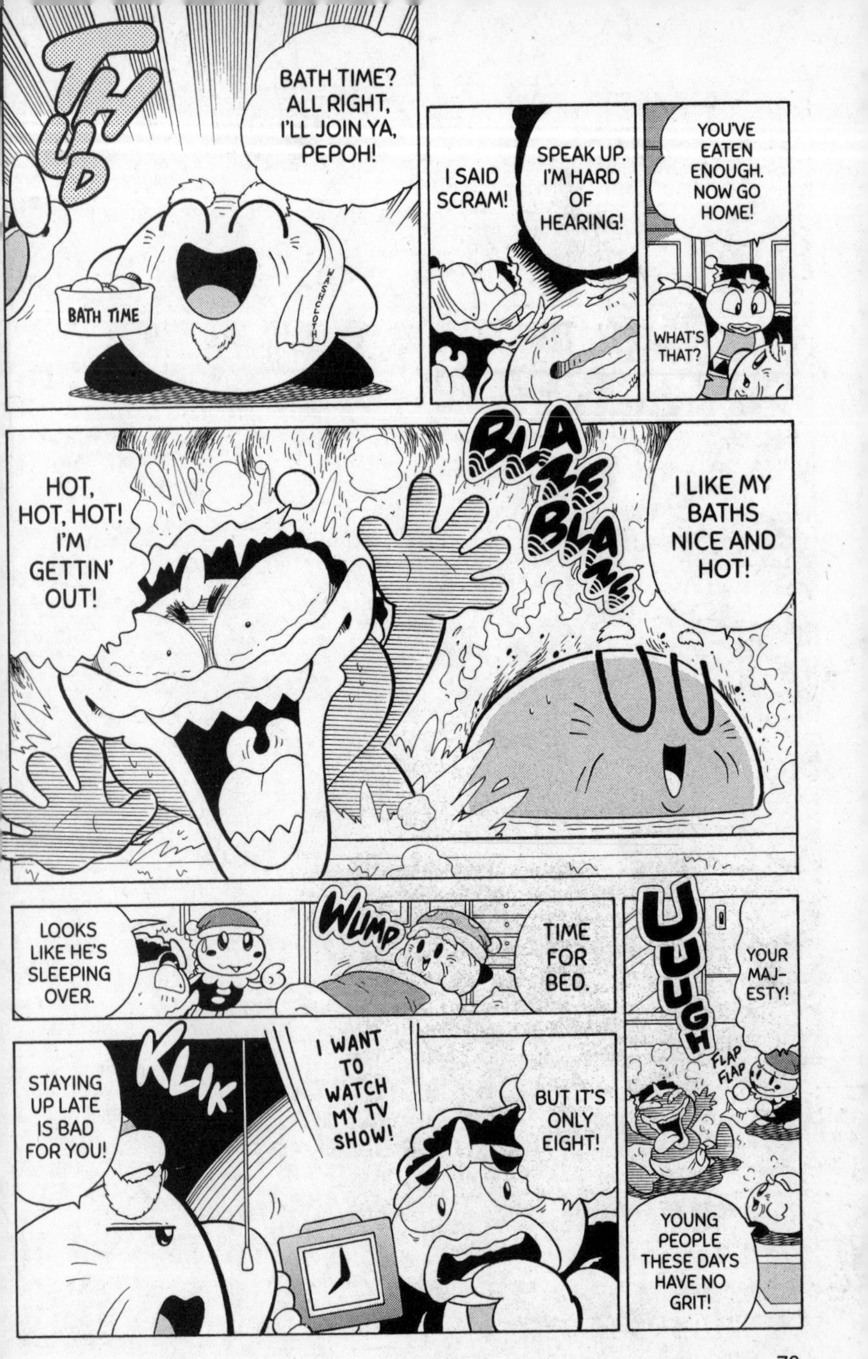
YOU'VE EATEN ENOUGH. NOW GO HOME!
WHAT'S THAT?
SPEAK UP. I'M HARD OF HEARING!
I SAID SCRAM!
THUD
BATH TIME? ALL RIGHT, I'LL JOIN YA, PEPOH!
BATH TIME
WASHCLOTH
I LIKE MY BATHS NICE AND HOT!
BLAZE BLAZE
HOT, HOT, HOT! I'M GETTIN' OUT!
UUUGH
YOUR MAJ-ESTY!
FLAP FLAP
YOUNG PEOPLE THESE DAYS HAVE NO GRIT!
TIME FOR BED.
WUMP
LOOKS LIKE HE'S SLEEPING OVER.
BUT IT'S ONLY EIGHT!
I WANT TO WATCH MY TV SHOW!
KLIK
STAYING UP LATE IS BAD FOR YOU!

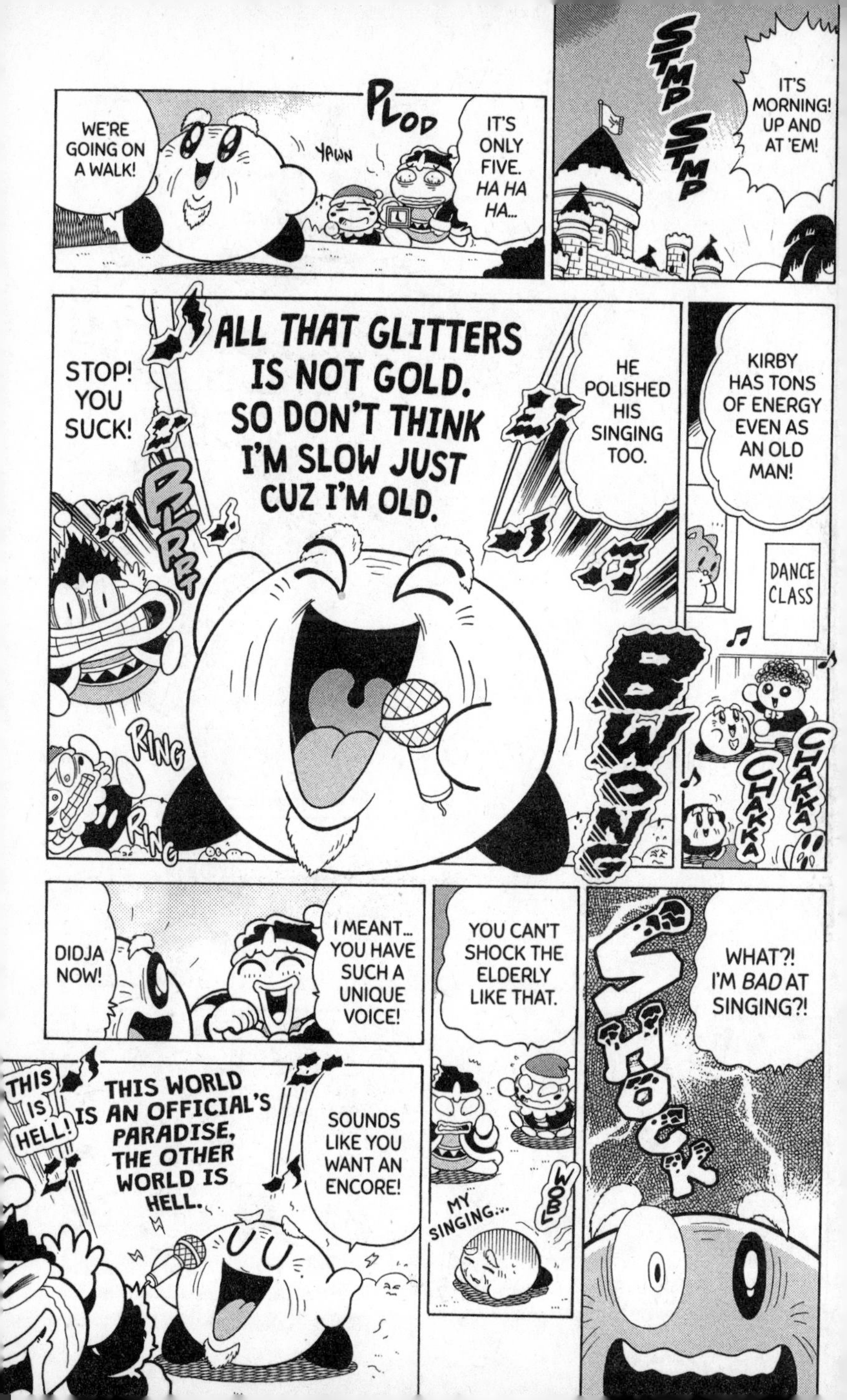
STMP STMP
IT'S MORNING! UP AND AT 'EM!
PLOD
IT'S ONLY FIVE. HA HA HA...
YAWN
WE'RE GOING ON A WALK!
KIRBY HAS TONS OF ENERGY EVEN AS AN OLD MAN!
DANCE CLASS
CHAKKA CHAKKA
HE POLISHED HIS SINGING TOO.
ALL THAT GLITTERS IS NOT GOLD. SO DON'T THINK I'M SLOW JUST CUZ I'M OLD.
BWOW
STOP! YOU SUCK!
BLRRT
RING RING
SHOCK
WHAT?! I'M BAD AT SINGING?!
YOU CAN'T SHOCK THE ELDERLY LIKE THAT.
I MEANT... YOU HAVE SUCH A UNIQUE VOICE!
DIDJA NOW!
MY SINGING...
WOBL
SOUNDS LIKE YOU WANT AN ENCORE!
THIS WORLD IS AN OFFICIAL'S PARADISE, THE OTHER WORLD IS HELL.
THIS IS HELL!

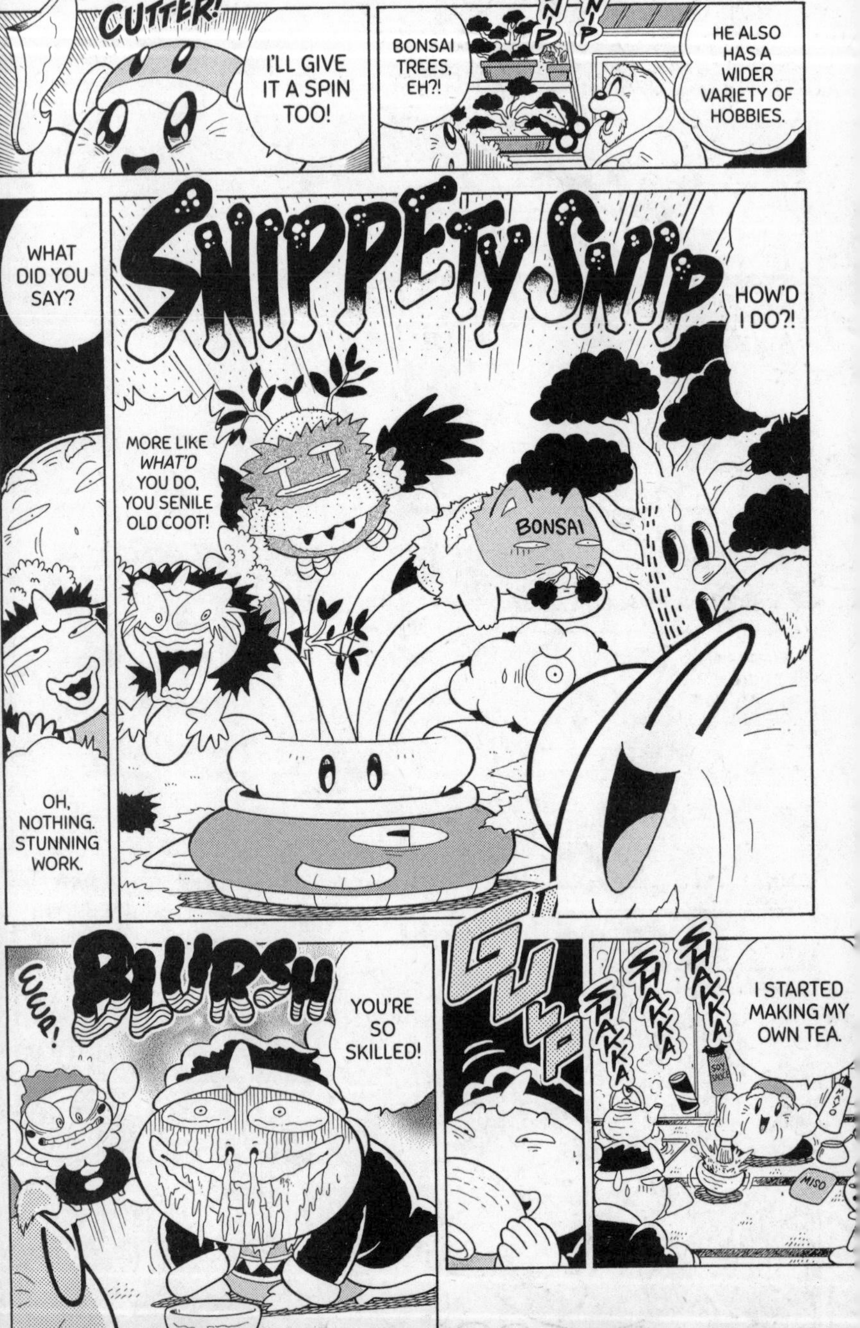
SNIP
SNIP
HE ALSO HAS A WIDER VARIETY OF HOBBIES.
BONSAI TREES, EH?!
CUTTER!
I'LL GIVE IT A SPIN TOO!
SNIPPETY SNIP
HOW'D I DO?!
MORE LIKE *WHAT'D* YOU DO, YOU SENILE OLD COOT!
BONSAI
WHAT DID YOU SAY?
OH, NOTHING. STUNNING WORK.
SHAKKA
SHAKKA
SHAKKA
I STARTED MAKING MY OWN TEA.
SOY SAUCE
MAYO
MISO
GULP
YOU'RE SO SKILLED!
BLURSH

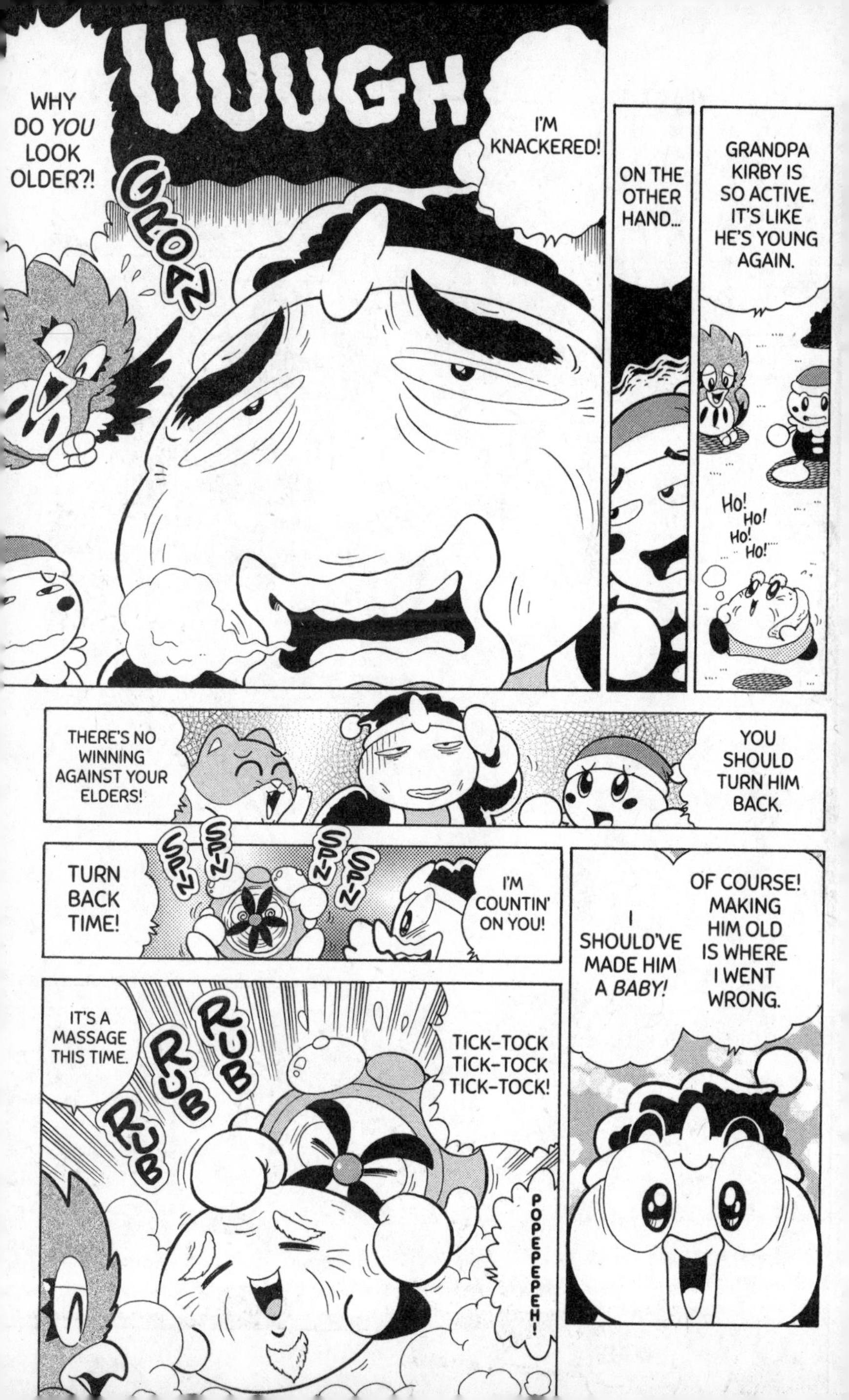
GRANDPA KIRBY IS SO ACTIVE. IT'S LIKE HE'S YOUNG AGAIN.
Ho! Ho! Ho! Ho!
ON THE OTHER HAND...
UUUGH
I'M KNACKERED!
GROAN
WHY DO *YOU* LOOK OLDER?!
YOU SHOULD TURN HIM BACK.
THERE'S NO WINNING AGAINST YOUR ELDERS!
OF COURSE! MAKING HIM OLD IS WHERE I WENT WRONG.
I SHOULD'VE MADE HIM A *BABY!*
I'M COUNTIN' ON YOU!
SPIN SPIN SPIN SPIN
TURN BACK TIME!
TICK-TOCK TICK-TOCK TICK-TOCK!
RUB RUB RUB
IT'S A MASSAGE THIS TIME.
POPEPEPEPEH!

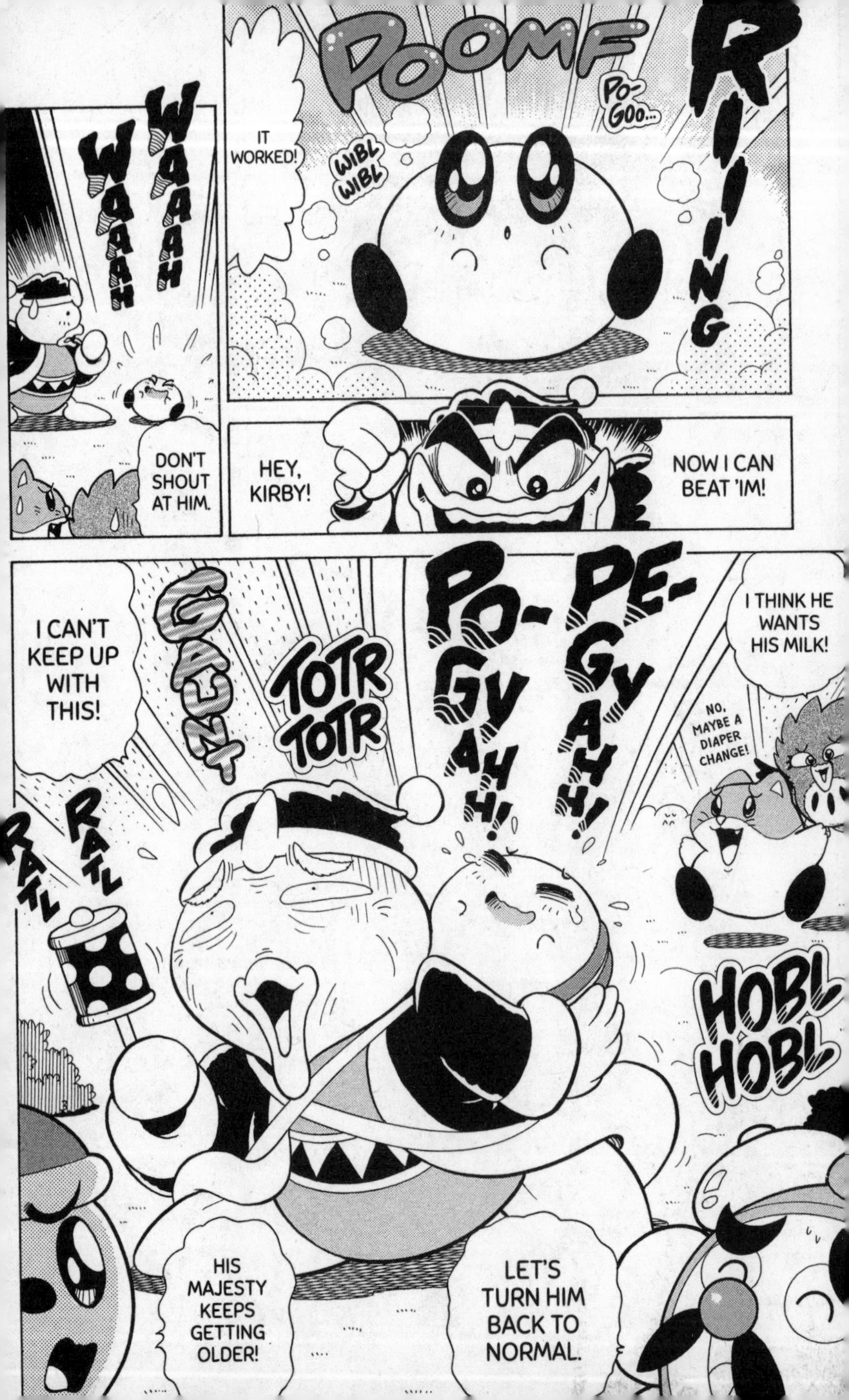
RIIIING
POOMF
PO-GOO...
WIBL WIBL
IT WORKED!
NOW I CAN BEAT 'IM!
HEY, KIRBY!
WAAAAH
WAAAAH
DON'T SHOUT AT HIM.
I THINK HE WANTS HIS MILK!
NO, MAYBE A DIAPER CHANGE!
PE-GYAHH!
PO-GYAHH!
TOTR TOTR
GAUNT
I CAN'T KEEP UP WITH THIS!
RATL RATL
HOBL HOBL
LET'S TURN HIM BACK TO NORMAL.
HIS MAJESTY KEEPS GETTING OLDER!

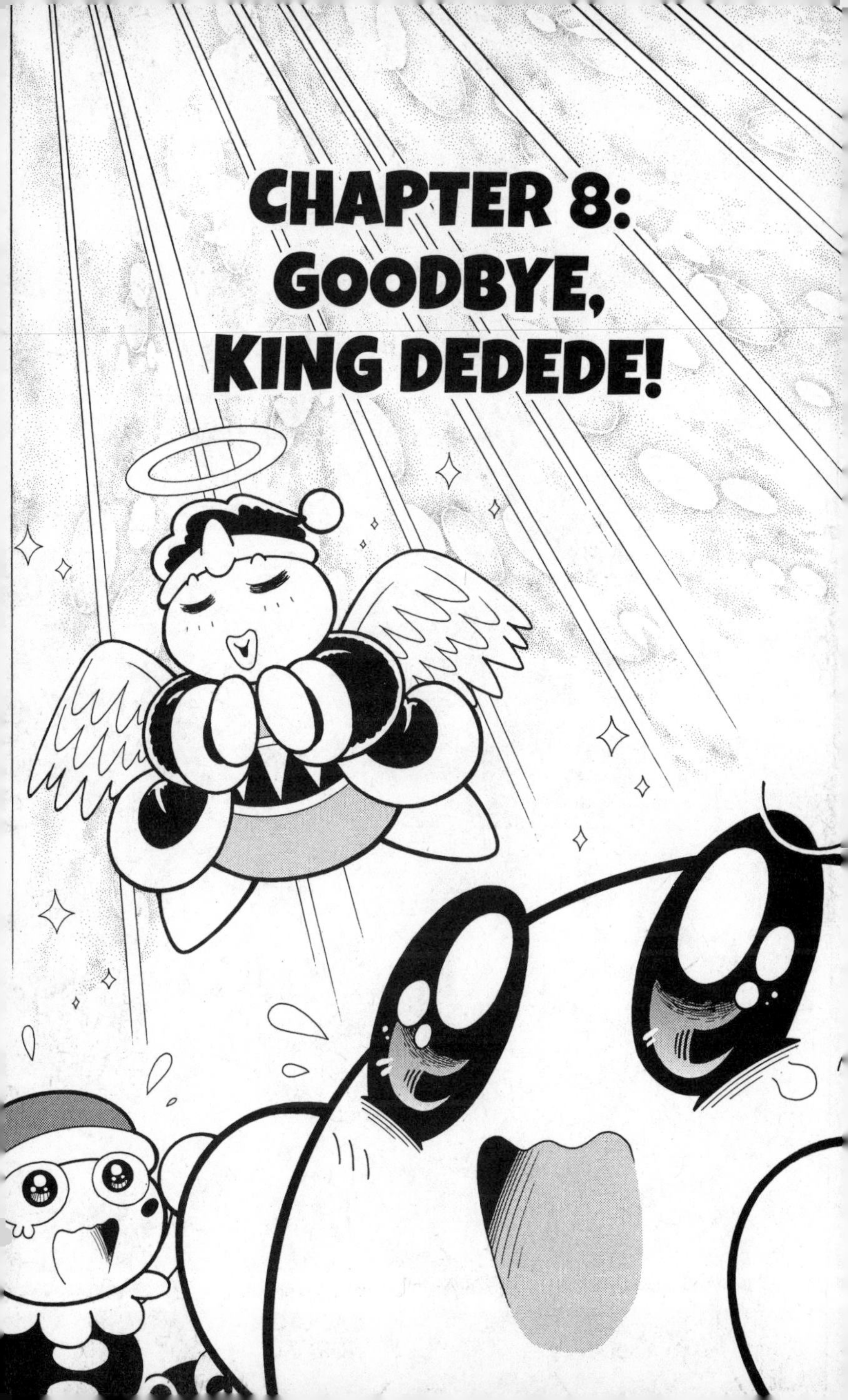
CHAPTER 8:
GOODBYE,
KING DEDEDE!

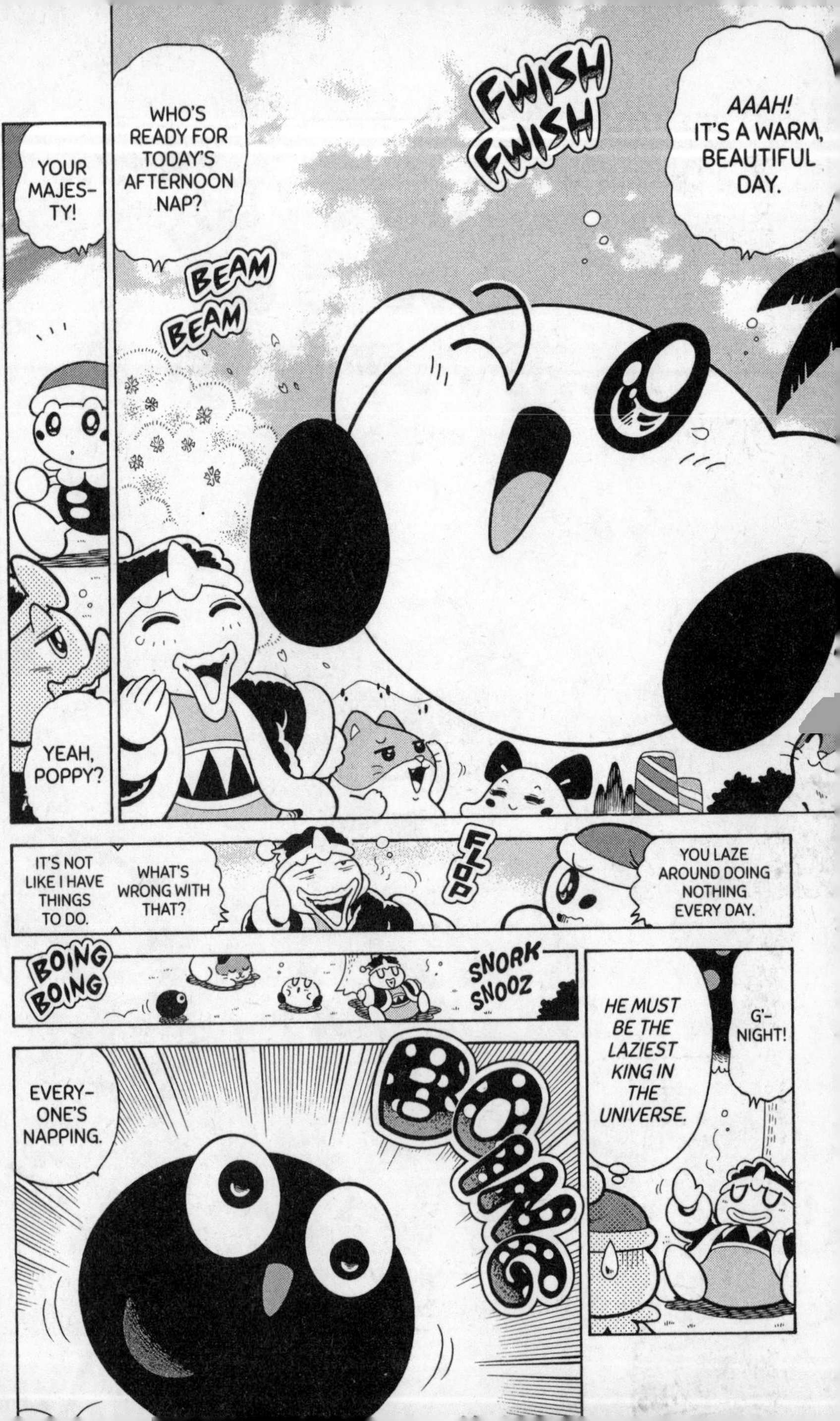
AAAH! IT'S A WARM, BEAUTIFUL DAY.
FWISH FWISH
WHO'S READY FOR TODAY'S AFTERNOON NAP?
BEAM BEAM
YOUR MAJES-TY!
YEAH, POPPY?
YOU LAZE AROUND DOING NOTHING EVERY DAY.
FLOP
WHAT'S WRONG WITH THAT?
IT'S NOT LIKE I HAVE THINGS TO DO.
G'-NIGHT!
HE MUST BE THE LAZIEST KING IN THE UNIVERSE.
SNORK-SNOOZ
BOING BOING
BOING
EVERY-ONE'S NAPPING.

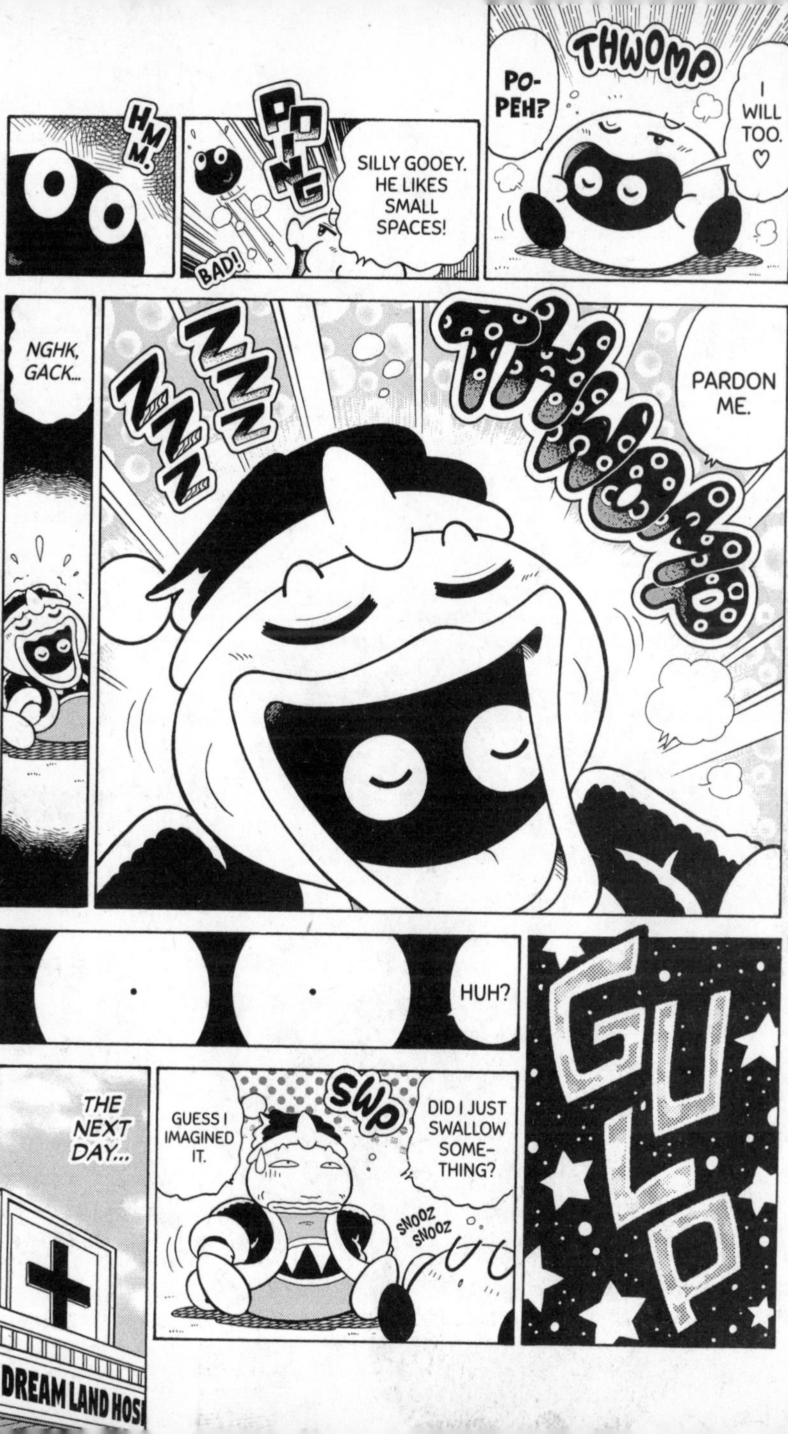

PO-PEH?
THWOMP
I WILL TOO. ♥
POING
SILLY GOOEY. HE LIKES SMALL SPACES!
BAD!
HMM.
PARDON ME.
THWOMP
ZZZ
NGHK, GACK...
GULP
HUH?
DID I JUST SWALLOW SOME-THING?
SWP
GUESS I IMAGINED IT.
SNOOZ SNOOZ
THE NEXT DAY...
DREAM LAND HOS

AUTHOR'S COMMENT

I'M A LAZY, IDLE PERSON. IF I DIDN'T HAVE AN EDITOR AND DEADLINES, I COULD NEVER HAVE LEFT BEHIND THIS LARGE OF A BODY OF WORK. IT WAS TOUGH AT THE TIME, BUT LOOKING BACK AT IT NOW, EVERY DAY WAS FULFILLING. (I DIDN'T GET TO DO ANY GOOFING AROUND, THOUGH...)

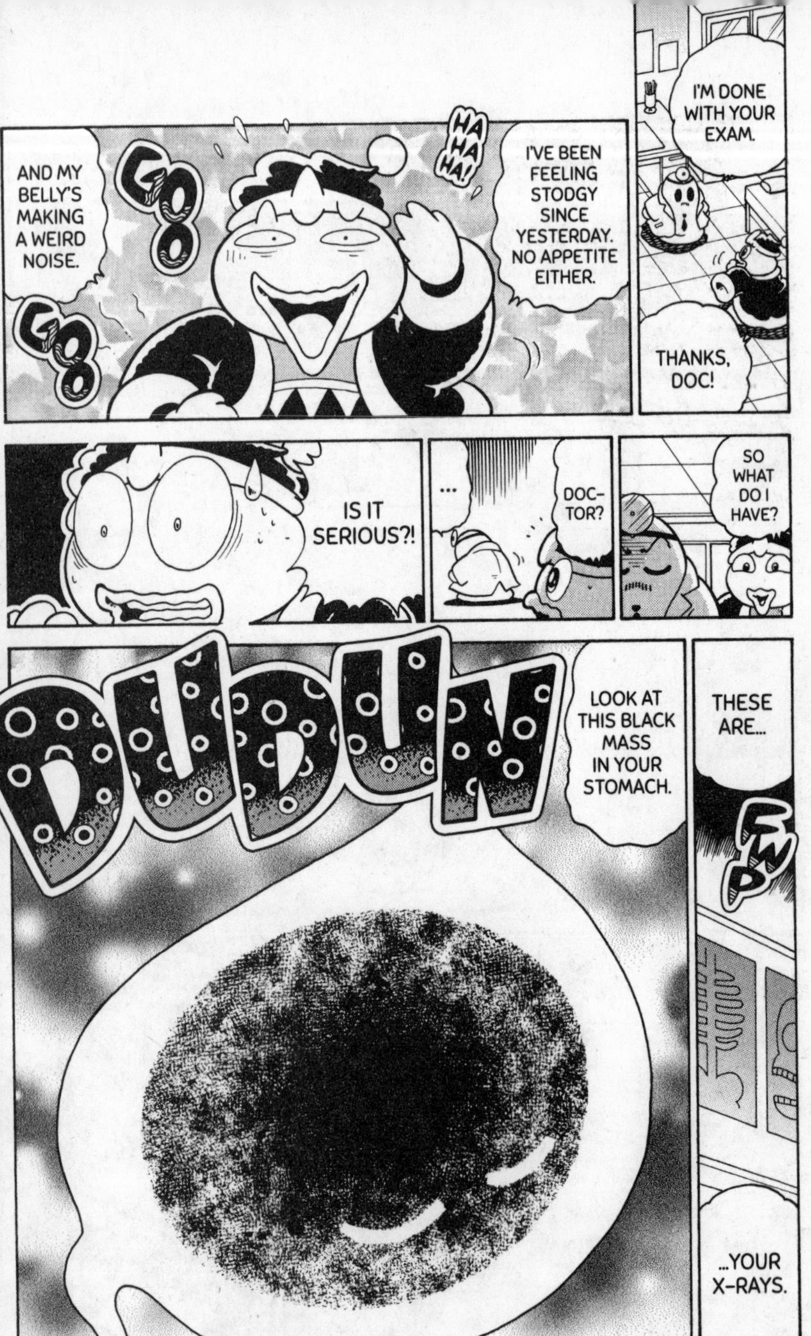
I'M DONE WITH YOUR EXAM.
THANKS, DOC!
HA HA HA!
I'VE BEEN FEELING STODGY SINCE YESTERDAY. NO APPETITE EITHER.
GOO
GOO
AND MY BELLY'S MAKING A WEIRD NOISE.
SO WHAT DO I HAVE?
DOC-TOR?
...
IS IT SERIOUS?!
THESE ARE...
FWP
...YOUR X-RAYS.
LOOK AT THIS BLACK MASS IN YOUR STOMACH.
DUDUN

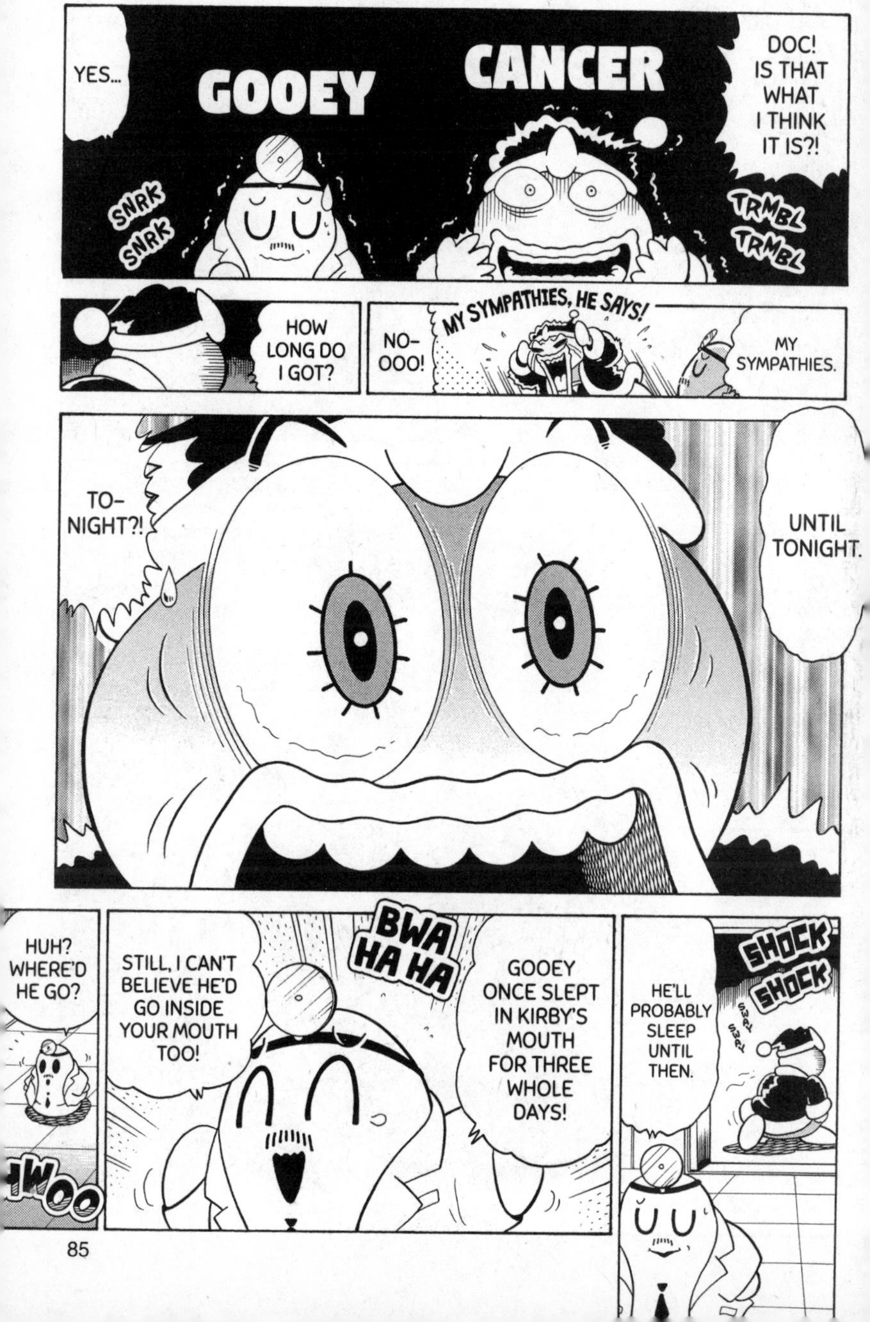
DOC! IS THAT WHAT I THINK IT IS?!
TRMBL TRMBL
YES...
GOOEY CANCER
SNRK SNRK
MY SYMPATHIES.
MY SYMPATHIES, HE SAYS!
NO-OOO!
HOW LONG DO I GOT?
UNTIL TONIGHT.
TO-NIGHT?!
SHOCK SHOCK
SWAY SWAY
HE'LL PROBABLY SLEEP UNTIL THEN.
BWA HA HA
GOOEY ONCE SLEPT IN KIRBY'S MOUTH FOR THREE WHOLE DAYS!
STILL, I CAN'T BELIEVE HE'D GO INSIDE YOUR MOUTH TOO!
HUH? WHERE'D HE GO?
WOO

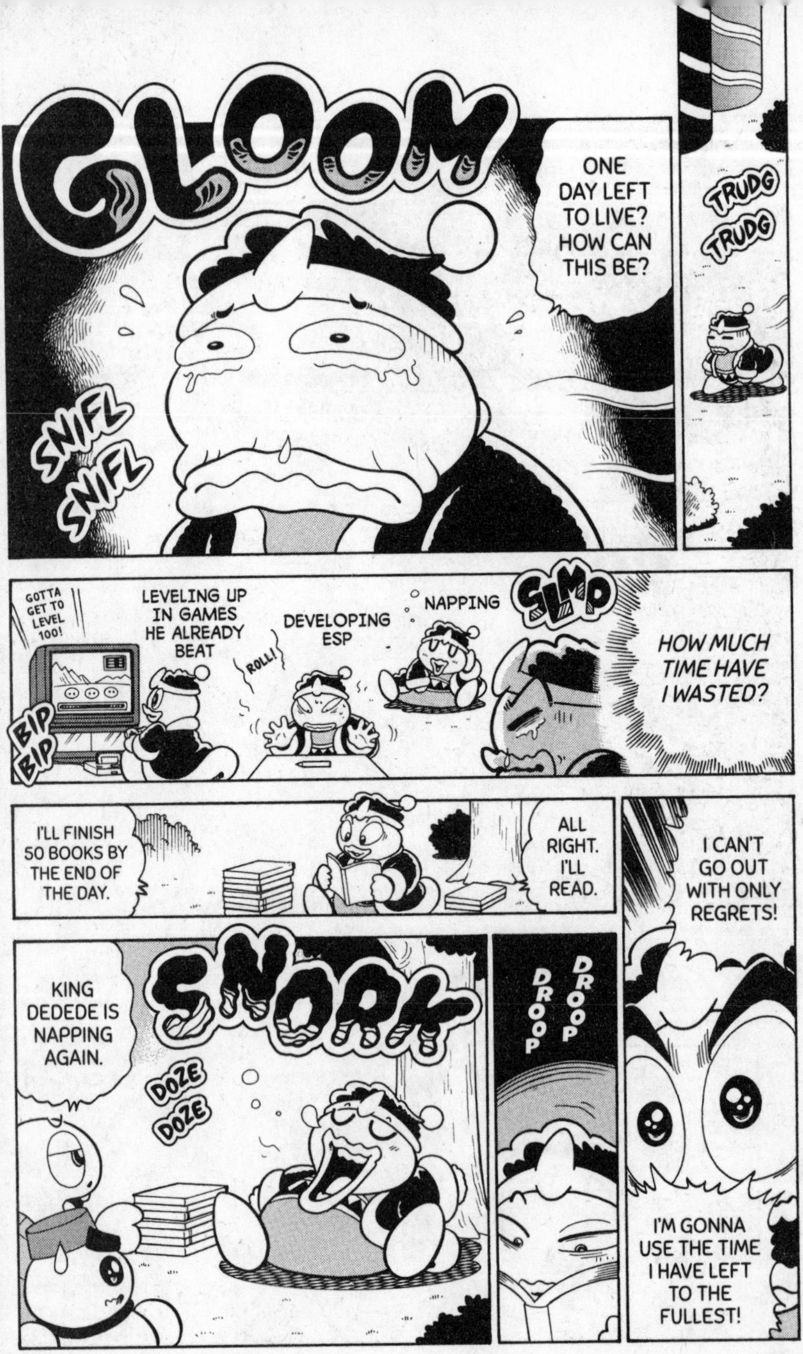
TRUDG
TRUDG
ONE DAY LEFT TO LIVE? HOW CAN THIS BE?
GLOOM
SNIFL
SNIFL
HOW MUCH TIME HAVE I WASTED?
SLMP
NAPPING
DEVELOPING ESP
ROLL!
LEVELING UP IN GAMES HE ALREADY BEAT
GOTTA GET TO LEVEL 100!
BIP
BIP
I CAN'T GO OUT WITH ONLY REGRETS!
I'M GONNA USE THE TIME I HAVE LEFT TO THE FULLEST!
ALL RIGHT. I'LL READ.
I'LL FINISH 50 BOOKS BY THE END OF THE DAY.
DROOP
DROOP
SNORK
KING DEDEDE IS NAPPING AGAIN.
DOZE
DOZE

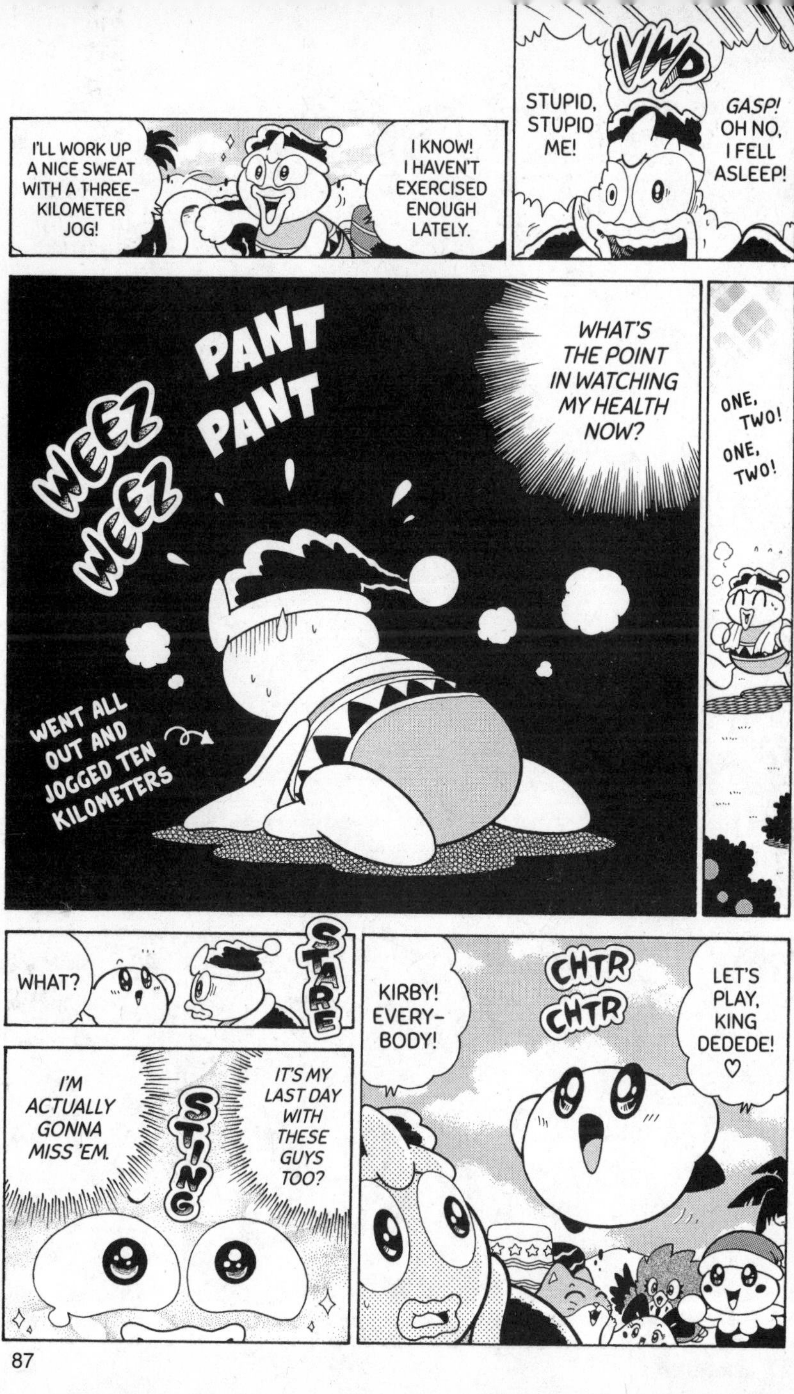
VWD
GASP! OH NO, I FELL ASLEEP!
STUPID, STUPID ME!
I KNOW! I HAVEN'T EXERCISED ENOUGH LATELY.
I'LL WORK UP A NICE SWEAT WITH A THREE-KILOMETER JOG!
ONE, TWO! ONE, TWO!
WHAT'S THE POINT IN WATCHING MY HEALTH NOW?
PANT PANT
WEEZ WEEZ
WENT ALL OUT AND JOGGED TEN KILOMETERS
LET'S PLAY, KING DEDEDE! ♡
CHTR CHTR
KIRBY! EVERY-BODY!
STARE
WHAT?
IT'S MY LAST DAY WITH THESE GUYS TOO?
STING
I'M ACTUALLY GONNA MISS 'EM.

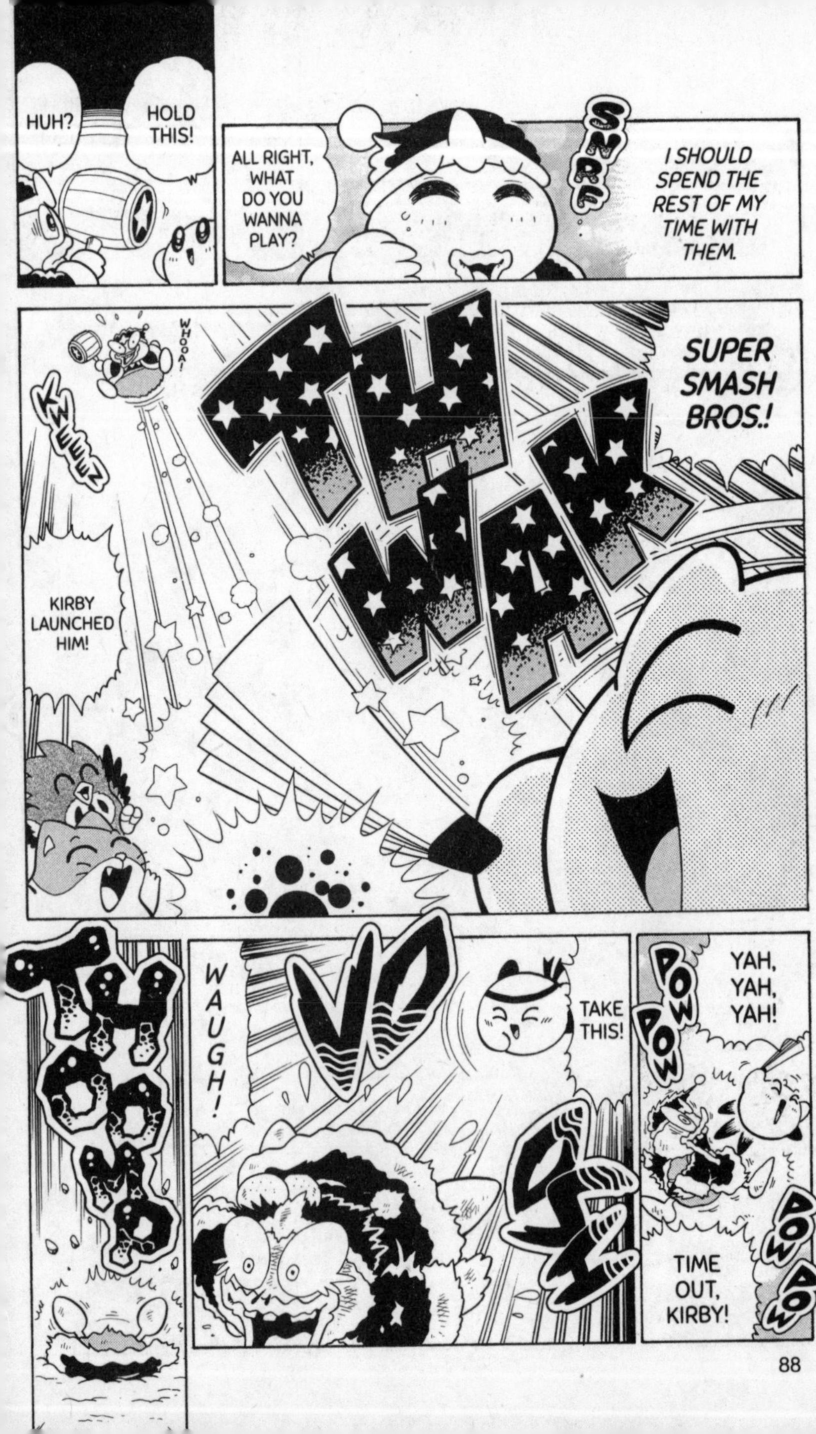
SNRF
I SHOULD SPEND THE REST OF MY TIME WITH THEM.
ALL RIGHT, WHAT DO YOU WANNA PLAY?
HOLD THIS!
HUH?
SUPER SMASH BROS.!
THWAK
WHOOA!
KWEEN
KIRBY LAUNCHED HIM!
YAH, YAH, YAH!
POW POW
POW POW
TIME OUT, KIRBY!
TAKE THIS!
WAUGH!
THOOMP

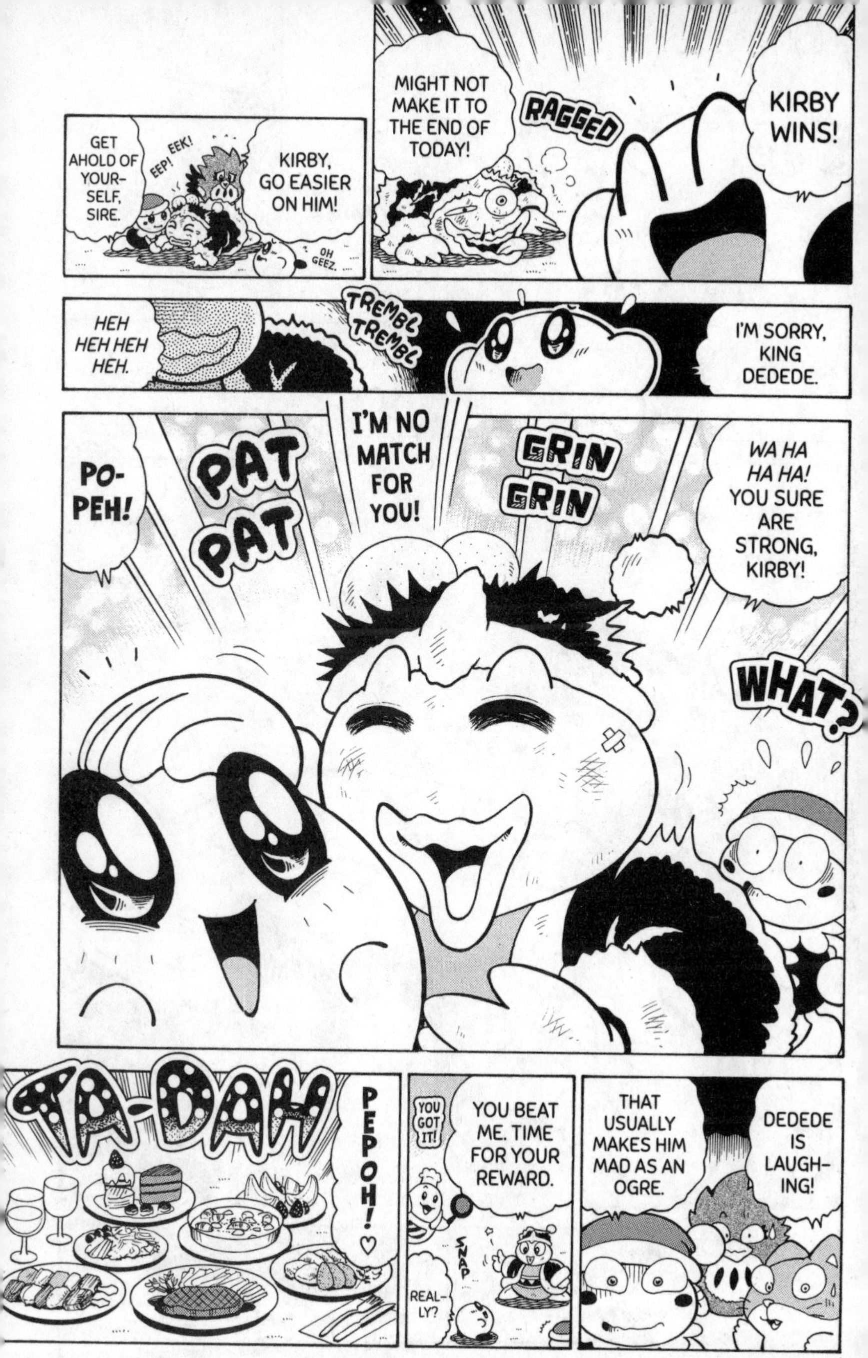
KIRBY WINS!
RAGGED
MIGHT NOT MAKE IT TO THE END OF TODAY!
KIRBY, GO EASIER ON HIM!
EEK! EEP!
GET AHOLD OF YOUR-SELF, SIRE.
OH GEEZ.
I'M SORRY, KING DEDEDE.
TREMBL TREMBL
HEH HEH HEH HEH.
WA HA HA HA! YOU SURE ARE STRONG, KIRBY!
GRIN GRIN
I'M NO MATCH FOR YOU!
PAT PAT
PO-PEH!
WHAT?
DEDEDE IS LAUGH-ING!
THAT USUALLY MAKES HIM MAD AS AN OGRE.
YOU BEAT ME. TIME FOR YOUR REWARD.
YOU GOT IT!
SNAP
REAL-LY?
PEPOH! ♡
TA-DAH

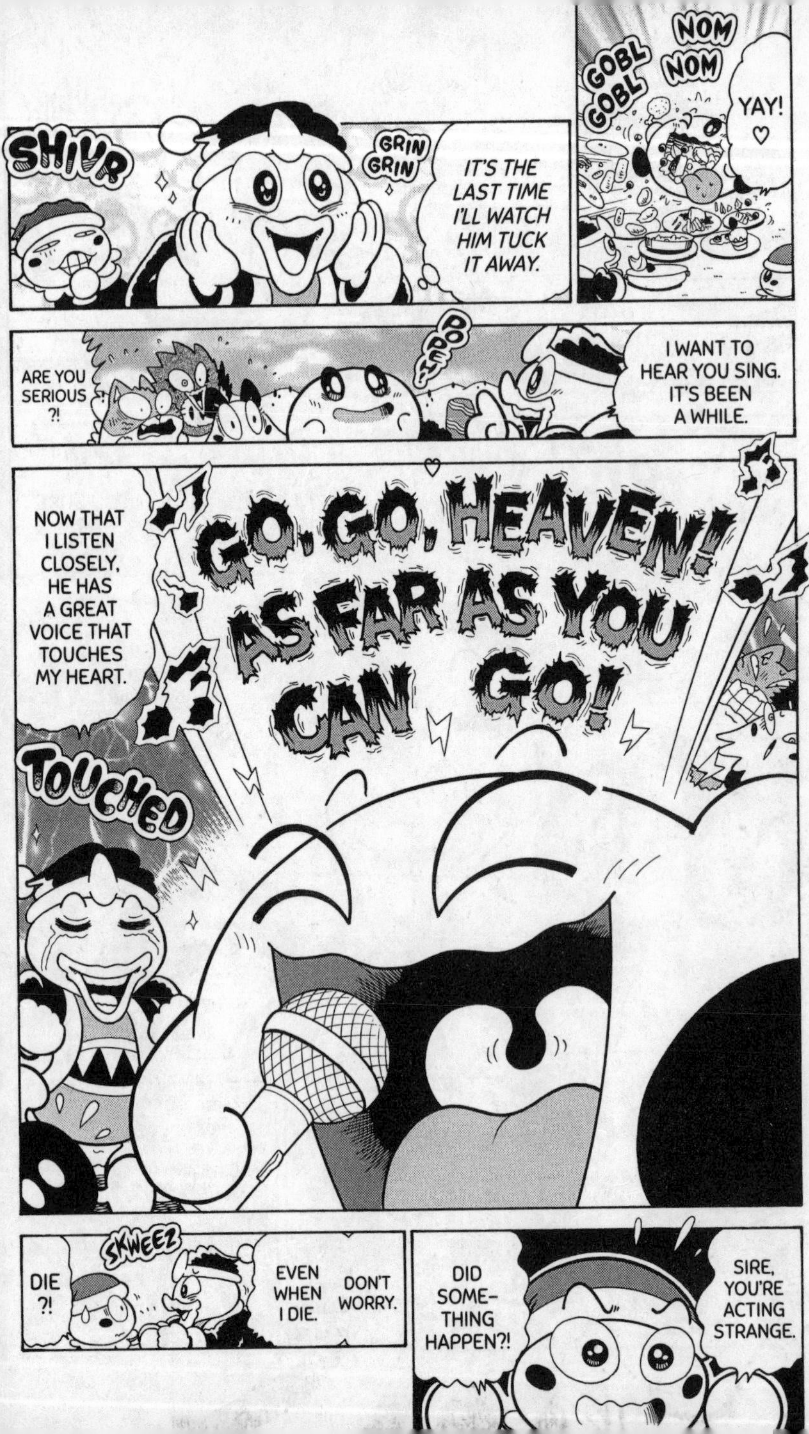
GOBL GOBL
NOM NOM
YAY! ♥
IT'S THE LAST TIME I'LL WATCH HIM TUCK IT AWAY.
GRIN GRIN
SHIVR
I WANT TO HEAR YOU SING. IT'S BEEN A WHILE.
DOE?!
ARE YOU SERIOUS ?!
GO, GO, HEAVEN! AS FAR AS YOU CAN GO!
NOW THAT I LISTEN CLOSELY, HE HAS A GREAT VOICE THAT TOUCHES MY HEART.
TOUCHED
SIRE, YOU'RE ACTING STRANGE.
DID SOME-THING HAPPEN?!
DON'T WORRY.
EVEN WHEN I DIE.
SKWEEZ
DIE ?!

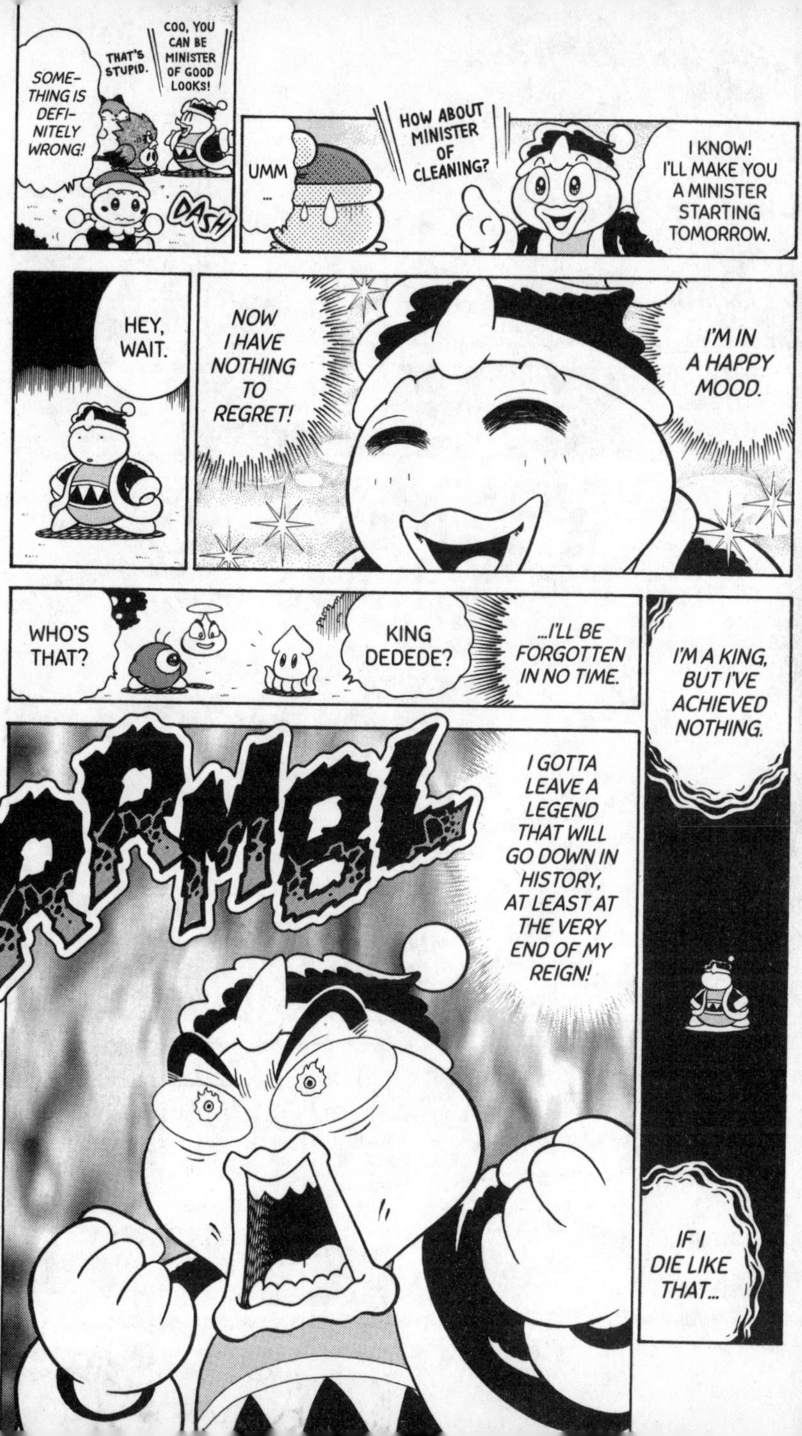
I KNOW! I'LL MAKE YOU A MINISTER STARTING TOMORROW.
HOW ABOUT MINISTER OF CLEANING?
UMM ...
COO, YOU CAN BE MINISTER OF GOOD LOOKS!
THAT'S STUPID.
SOME-THING IS DEFI-NITELY WRONG!
DASH
I'M IN A HAPPY MOOD.
NOW I HAVE NOTHING TO REGRET!
HEY, WAIT.
I'M A KING, BUT I'VE ACHIEVED NOTHING.
IF I DIE LIKE THAT...
...I'LL BE FORGOTTEN IN NO TIME.
KING DEDEDE?
WHO'S THAT?
I GOTTA LEAVE A LEGEND THAT WILL GO DOWN IN HISTORY, AT LEAST AT THE VERY END OF MY REIGN!
RRMBL

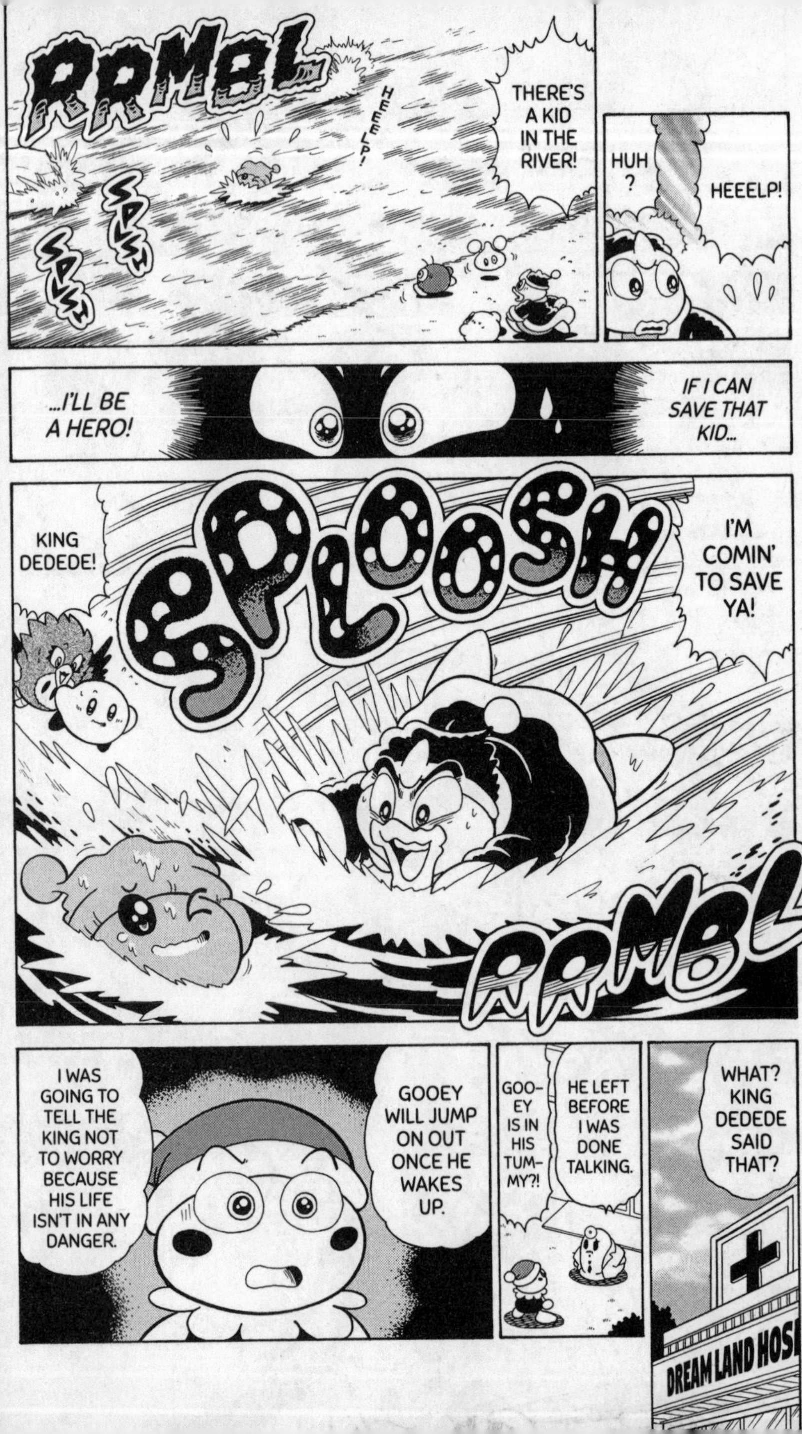
HEEELP!
HUH?
THERE'S A KID IN THE RIVER!
HEEELP!
RRMBL
SPLSH
SPLSH
IF I CAN SAVE THAT KID...
...I'LL BE A HERO!
I'M COMIN' TO SAVE YA!
SPLOOSH
KING DEDEDE!
RRMBL
WHAT? KING DEDEDE SAID THAT?
DREAM LAND HOS
HE LEFT BEFORE I WAS DONE TALKING.
GOO-EY IS IN HIS TUM-MY?!
GOOEY WILL JUMP ON OUT ONCE HE WAKES UP.
I WAS GOING TO TELL THE KING NOT TO WORRY BECAUSE HIS LIFE ISN'T IN ANY DANGER.

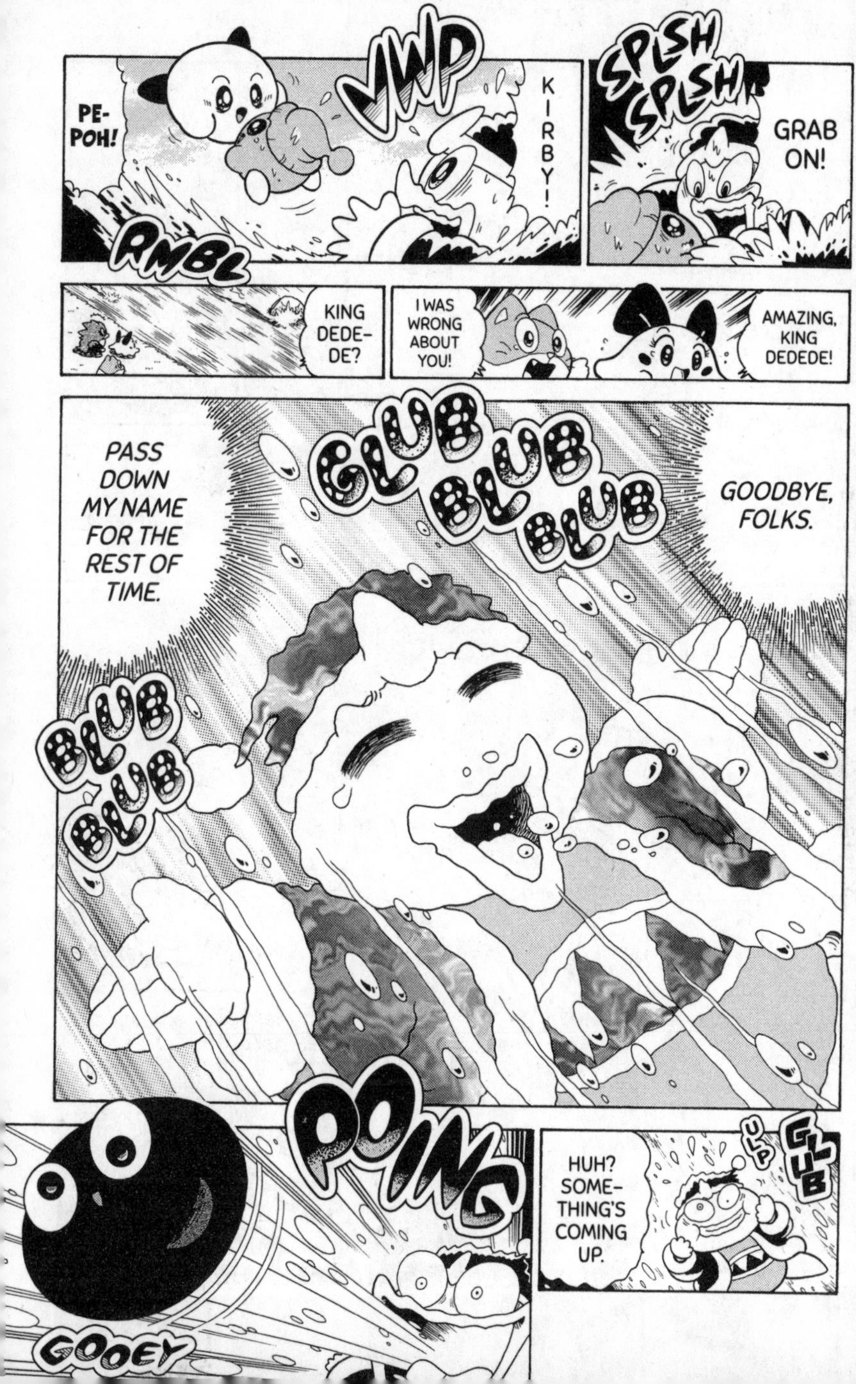
SPLSH SPLSH
GRAB ON!
VWP
KIRBY!
PE-POH!
RMBL
AMAZING, KING DEDEDE!
I WAS WRONG ABOUT YOU!
KING DEDE-DE?
GOODBYE, FOLKS.
GLUB BLUB BLUB
PASS DOWN MY NAME FOR THE REST OF TIME.
BLUB BLUB
GLUB
ULP
HUH? SOME-THING'S COMING UP.
POING
GOOEY

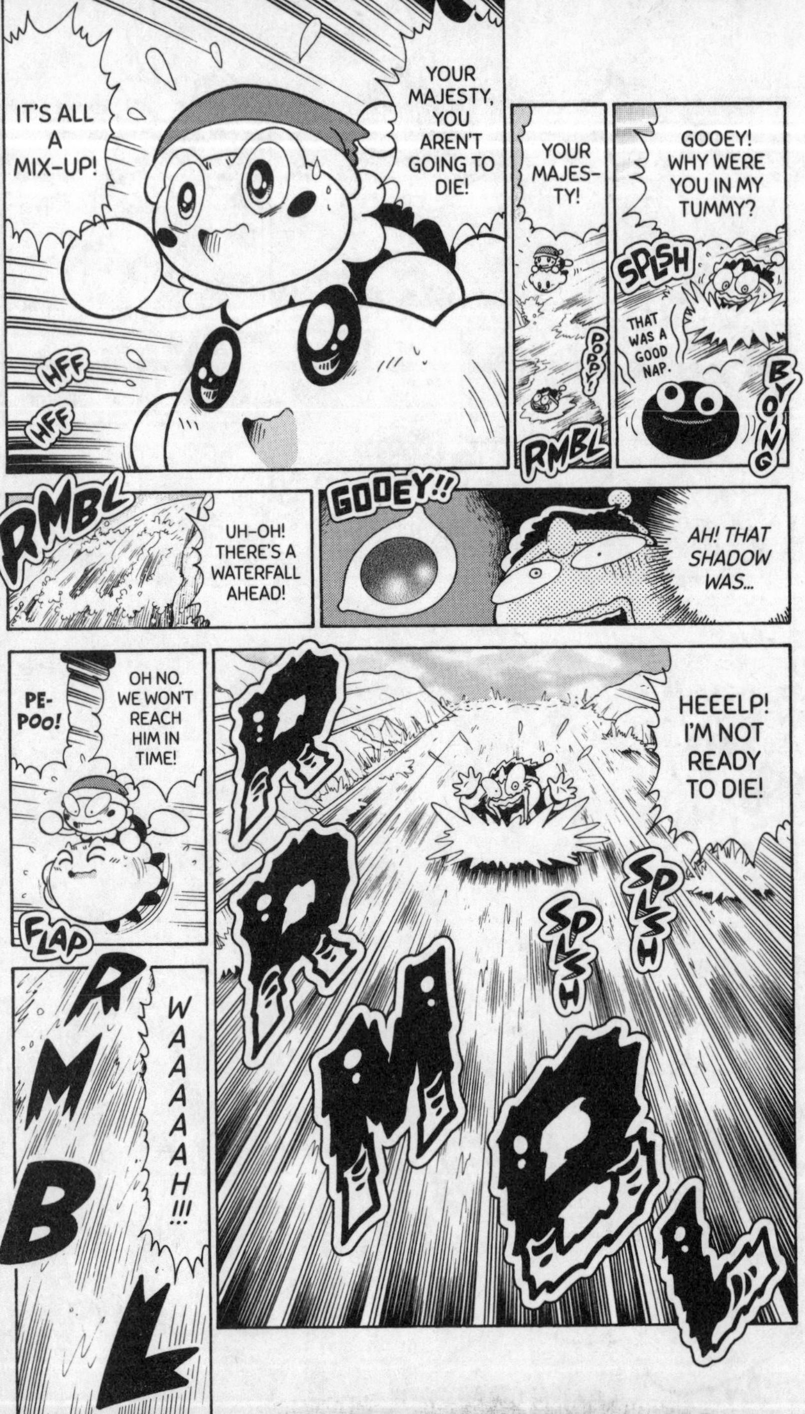
GOOEY! WHY WERE YOU IN MY TUMMY?
SPLSH
THAT WAS A GOOD NAP.
BYOING
YOUR MAJES-TY!
POPPY!
RMBL
YOUR MAJESTY, YOU AREN'T GOING TO DIE!
IT'S ALL A MIX-UP!
HFF
HFF
AH! THAT SHADOW WAS...
GOOEY!!
RMBL
UH-OH! THERE'S A WATERFALL AHEAD!
HEEELP! I'M NOT READY TO DIE!
SPLSH
SPLSH
RMBL
OH NO. WE WON'T REACH HIM IN TIME!
PE-POO!
FLAP
WAAAAAAH!!!
RMBL

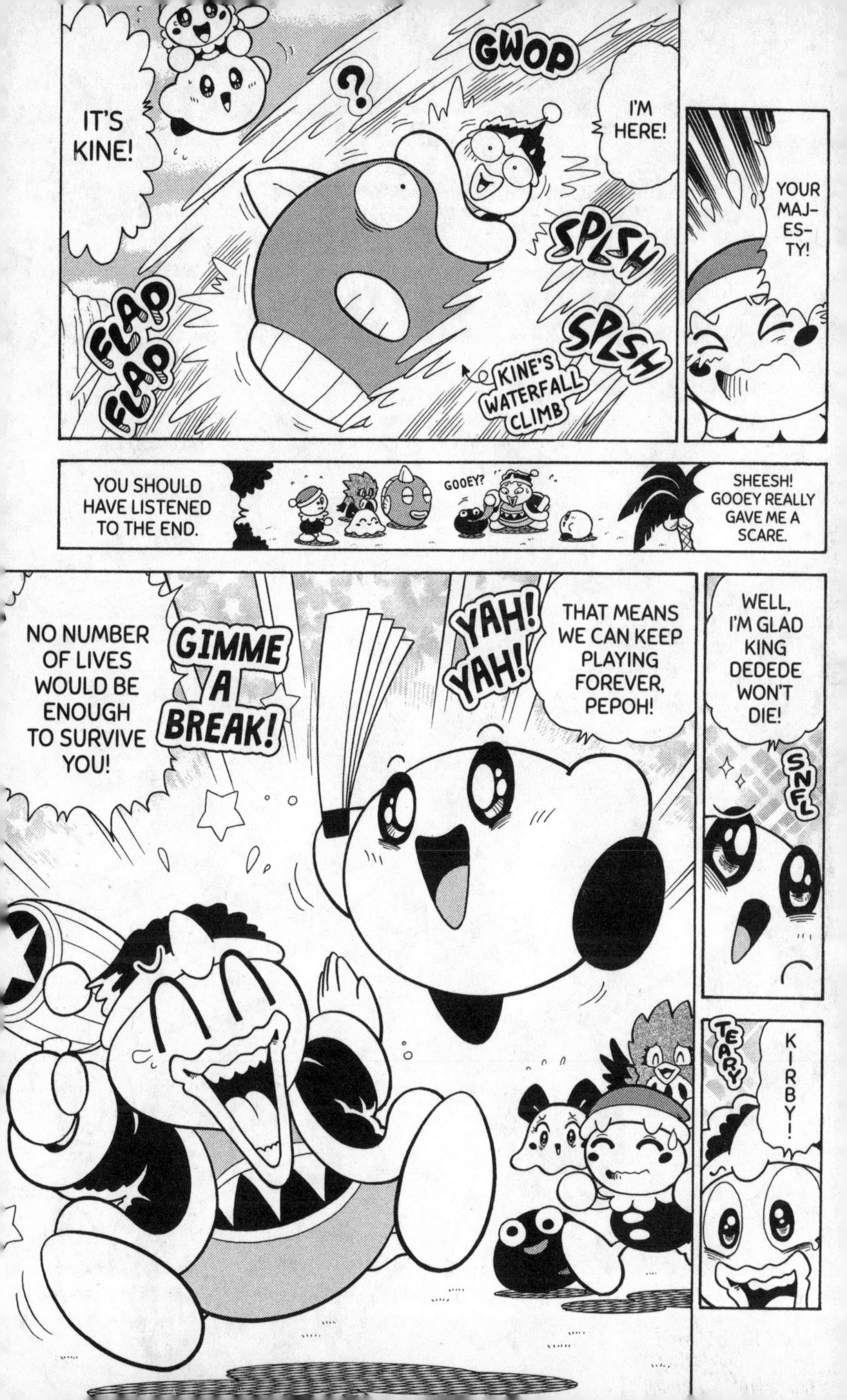
YOUR MAJESTY!
I'M HERE!
GWOP
?
IT'S KINE!
SPLSH
SPLSH
KINE'S WATERFALL CLIMB
FLAP FLAP
SHEESH! GOOEY REALLY GAVE ME A SCARE.
GOOEY?
YOU SHOULD HAVE LISTENED TO THE END.
WELL, I'M GLAD KING DEDEDE WON'T DIE!
SNFL
KIRBY!
TEARY
THAT MEANS WE CAN KEEP PLAYING FOREVER, PEPOH!
YAH! YAH!
GIMME A BREAK!
NO NUMBER OF LIVES WOULD BE ENOUGH TO SURVIVE YOU!

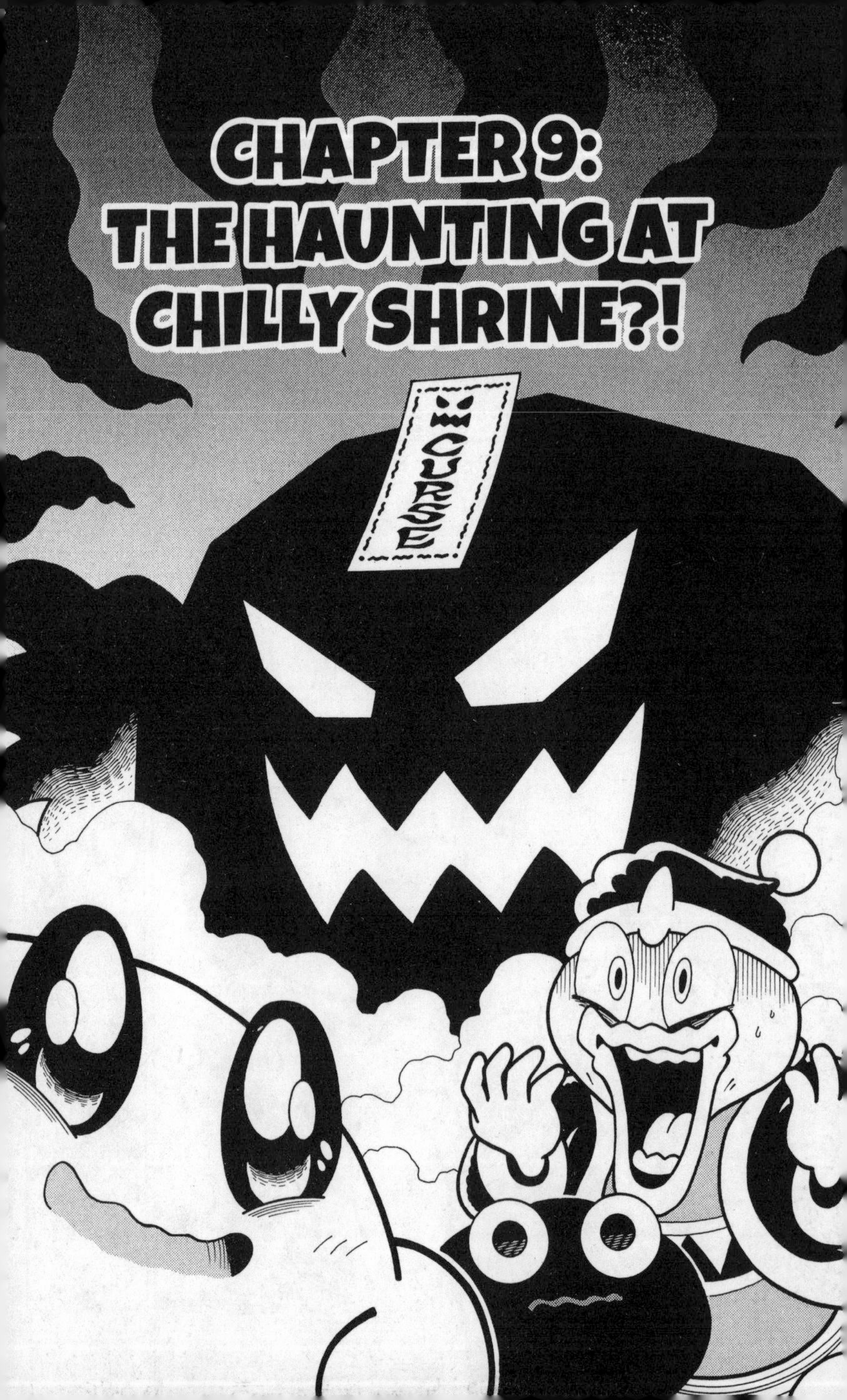
CHAPTER 9:
THE HAUNTING AT
CHILLY SHRINE?!
CURSE

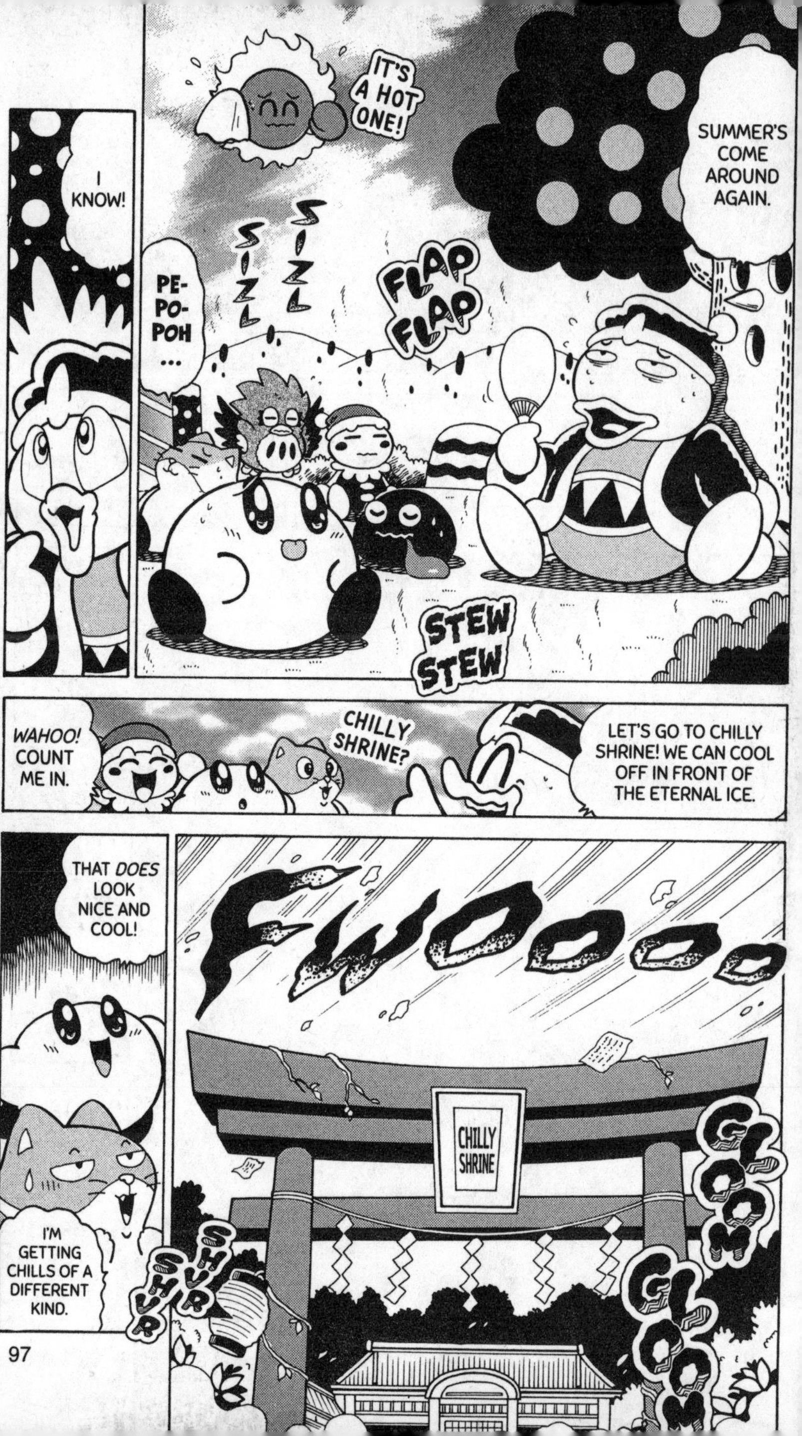
SUMMER'S COME AROUND AGAIN.
IT'S A HOT ONE!
FLAP FLAP
SIZZL SIZZL
PE-PO-POH...
STEW STEW
I KNOW!
LET'S GO TO CHILLY SHRINE! WE CAN COOL OFF IN FRONT OF THE ETERNAL ICE.
CHILLY SHRINE?
WAHOO! COUNT ME IN.
FWOOooo
CHILLY SHRINE
GLOOM GLOOM
SHURR SHURR
THAT *DOES* LOOK NICE AND COOL!
I'M GETTING CHILLS OF A DIFFERENT KIND.

AUTHOR'S COMMENT

THEY SAY THE DIFFERENCE BETWEEN HORROR AND COMEDY IS PAPER-THIN. IT'S ALL ABOUT RELIEVING THE TENSION. AT THE TIME I DREW THIS STORY, THOUGH, I WASN'T THINKING ABOUT ANY OF THAT. I NEED TO STUDY COMEDY SOME MORE.

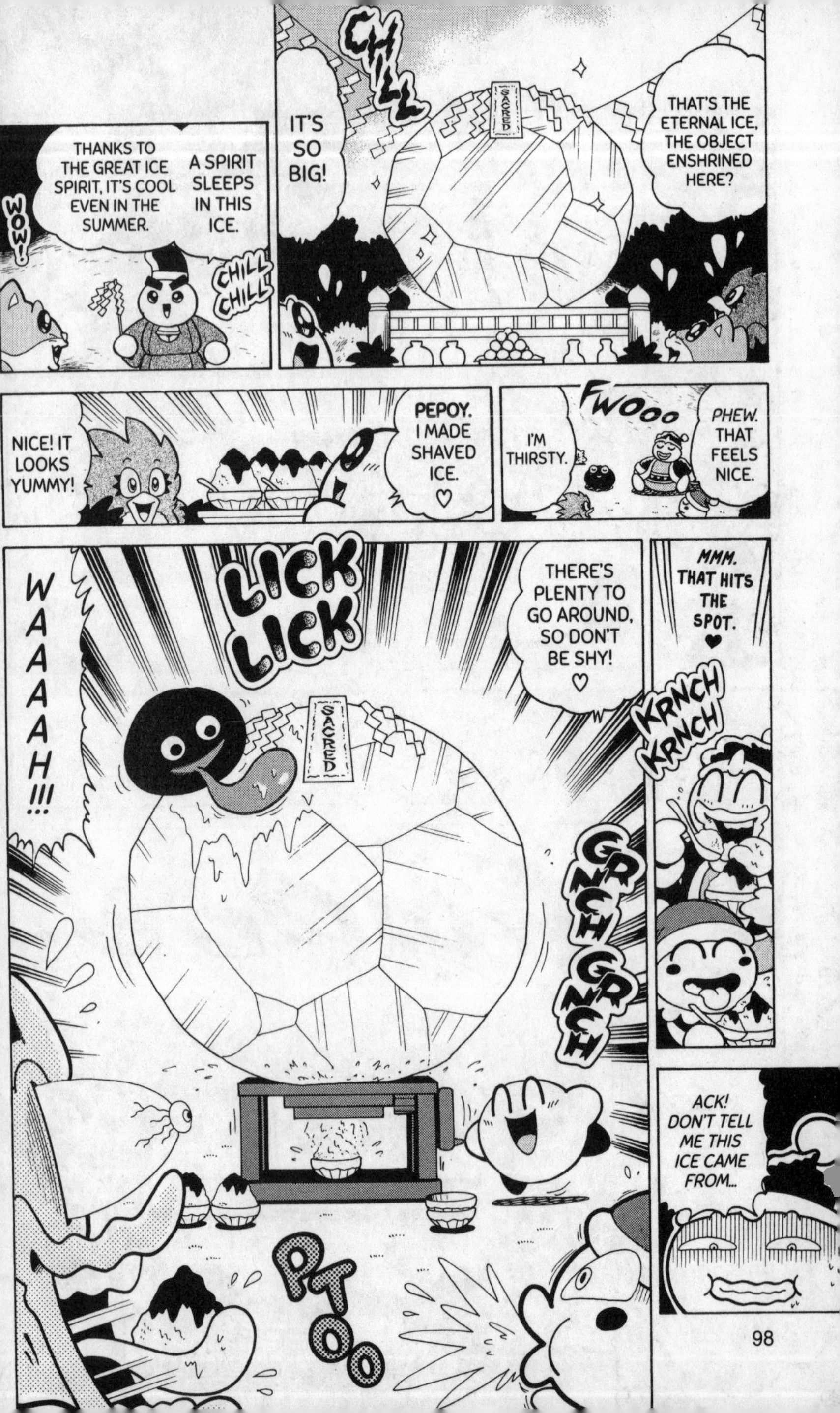
THAT'S THE ETERNAL ICE, THE OBJECT ENSHRINED HERE?
CHILL
SACRED
IT'S SO BIG!
A SPIRIT SLEEPS IN THIS ICE.
THANKS TO THE GREAT ICE SPIRIT, IT'S COOL EVEN IN THE SUMMER.
WOW!
CHILL CHILL
PHEW. THAT FEELS NICE.
FWOOO
I'M THIRSTY.
PEPOY. I MADE SHAVED ICE. ♡
NICE! IT LOOKS YUMMY!
MMM. THAT HITS THE SPOT. ♥
KRNCH KRNCH
ACK! DON'T TELL ME THIS ICE CAME FROM...
THERE'S PLENTY TO GO AROUND, SO DON'T BE SHY! ♡
GRNCH GRNCH
LICK LICK
SACRED
WAAAAAH!!!
PTOO

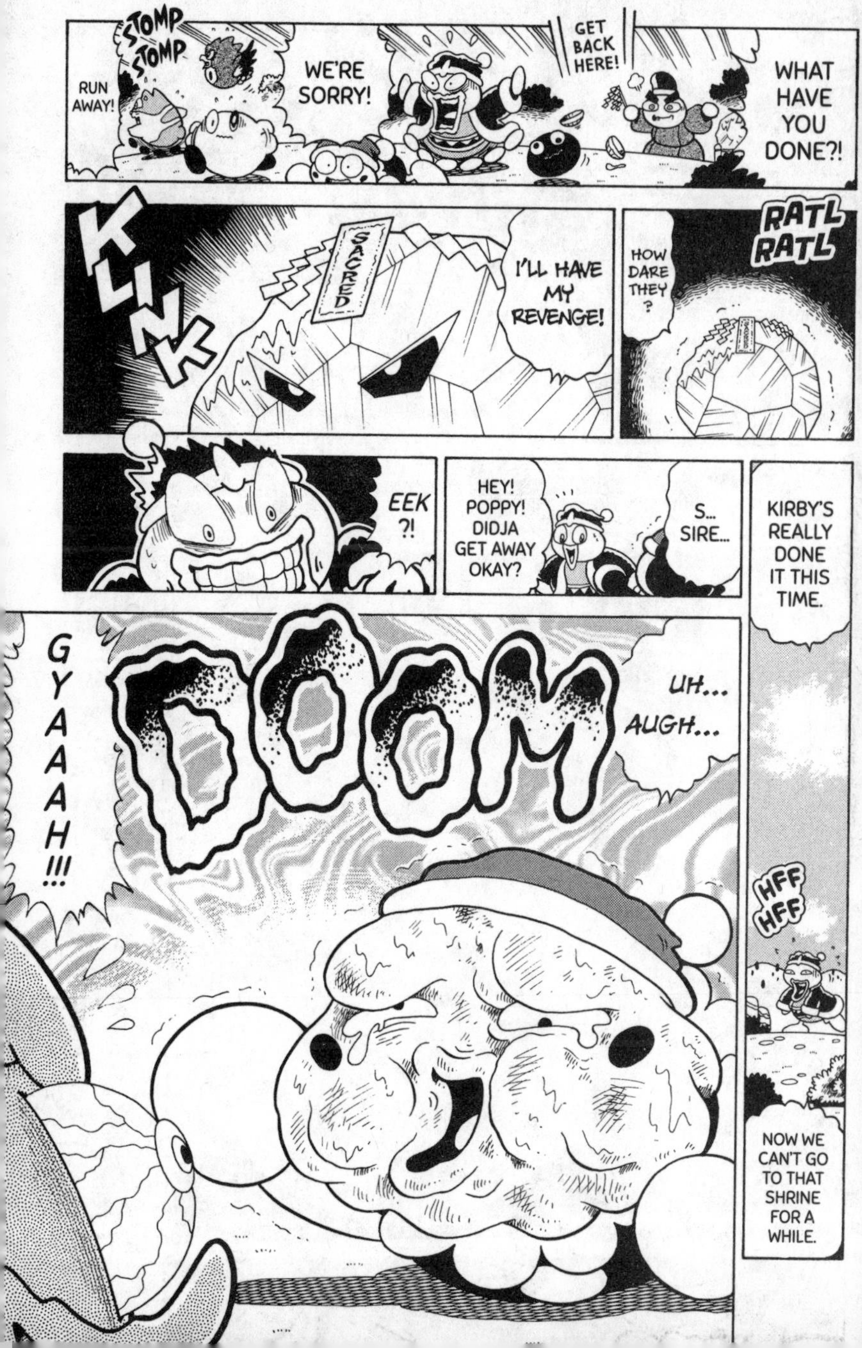
WHAT HAVE YOU DONE?!
GET BACK HERE!
WE'RE SORRY!
STOMP STOMP
RUN AWAY!
RATL RATL
HOW DARE THEY?
I'LL HAVE MY REVENGE!
SACRED
KLINK
KIRBY'S REALLY DONE IT THIS TIME.
HFF HFF
NOW WE CAN'T GO TO THAT SHRINE FOR A WHILE.
S... SIRE...
HEY! POPPY! DIDJA GET AWAY OKAY?
EEK?!
UH... AUGH...
DOOM
GYAAAAH!!!

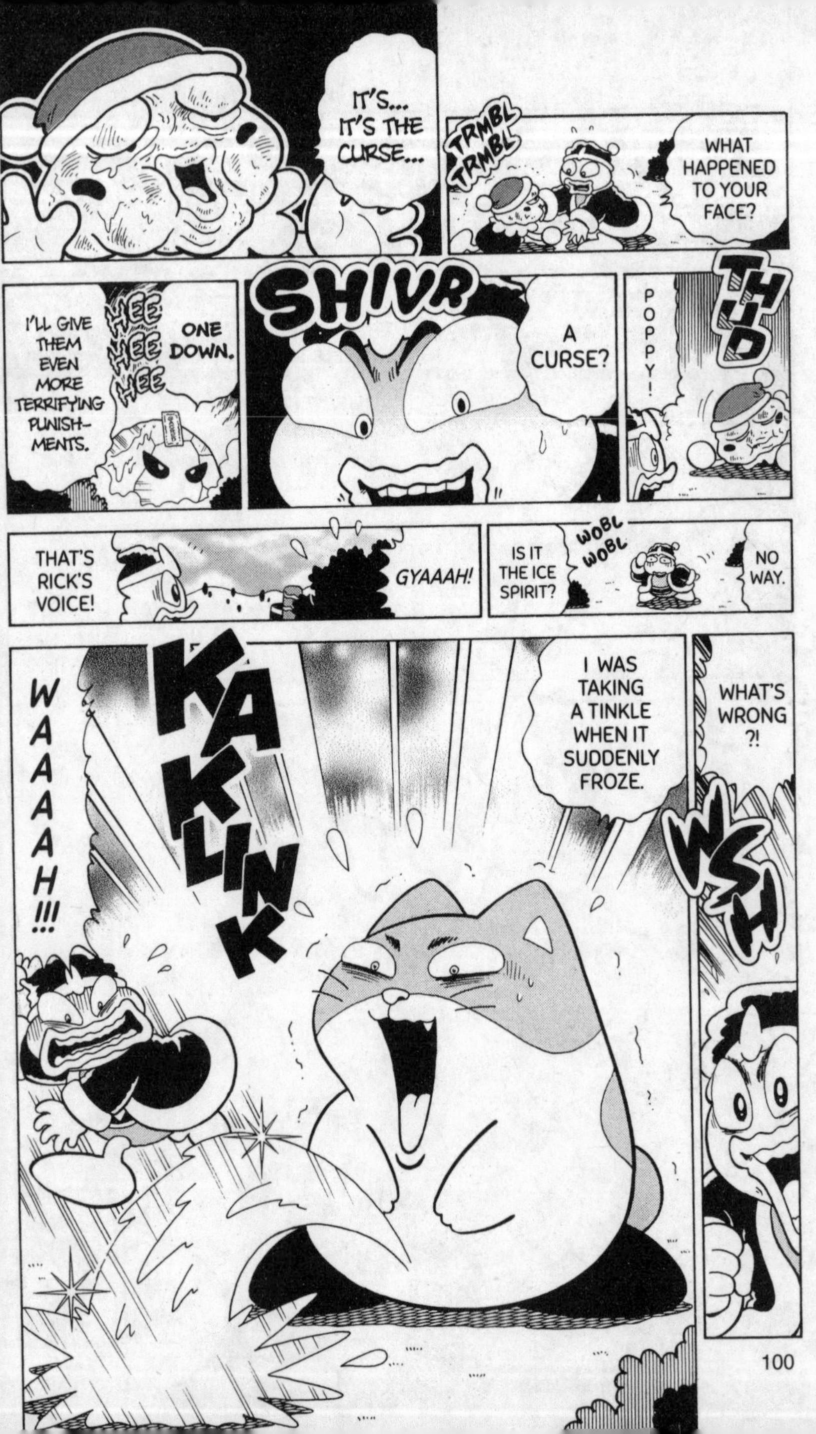
TRMBL TRMBL
WHAT HAPPENED TO YOUR FACE?
IT'S... IT'S THE CURSE...
THUD
POPPY!
SHIVR
A CURSE?
ONE DOWN.
HEE HEE HEE
I'LL GIVE THEM EVEN MORE TERRIFYING PUNISH-MENTS.
WOBL WOBL
NO WAY.
IS IT THE ICE SPIRIT?
GYAAAH!
THAT'S RICK'S VOICE!
WHAT'S WRONG?!
WSH
I WAS TAKING A TINKLE WHEN IT SUDDENLY FROZE.
KAKLINK
WAAAAAAH!!!

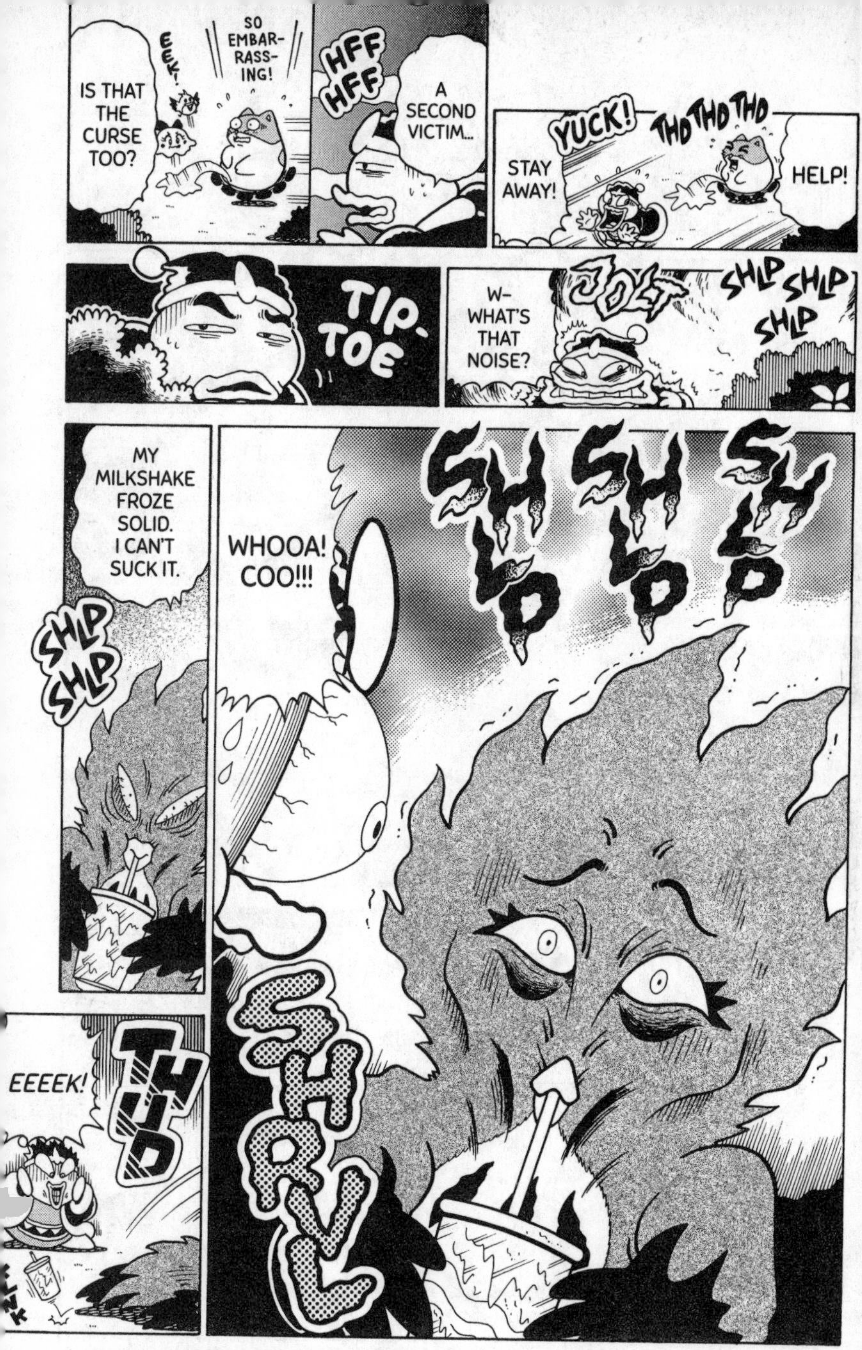
HELP!
THD THD THD
YUCK!
STAY AWAY!
HFF HFF
A SECOND VICTIM...
SO EMBARRASSING!
EEK!
IS THAT THE CURSE TOO?
SHLP SHLP SHLP
JOLT
W-WHAT'S THAT NOISE?
TIP-TOE
SHLOP SHLOP SHLP
WHOOA! COO!!!
SHRVL
MY MILKSHAKE FROZE SOLID. I CAN'T SUCK IT.
SHLP SHLP
THUD
EEEEK!

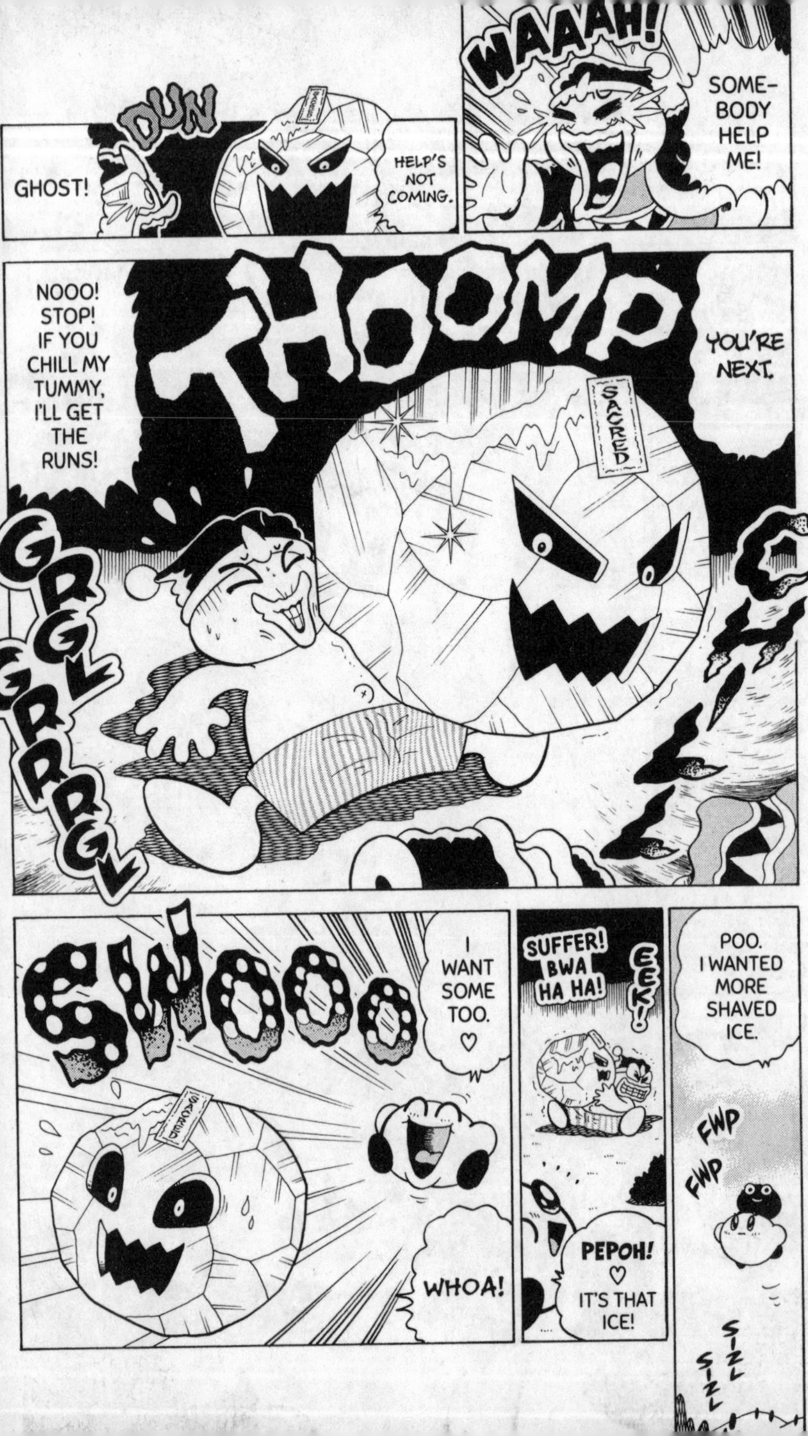
WAAAH!
SOME-BODY HELP ME!
DUN
HELP'S NOT COMING.
GHOST!
YOU'RE NEXT.
THOOMP
NOOO! STOP! IF YOU CHILL MY TUMMY, I'LL GET THE RUNS!
GRGL GRRRGL
POO. I WANTED MORE SHAVED ICE.
FWP
FWP
SIZL
SIZL
EEK!
SUFFER! BWA HA HA!
PEPOH! ♡ IT'S THAT ICE!
I WANT SOME TOO. ♡
SWOOOO
WHOA!

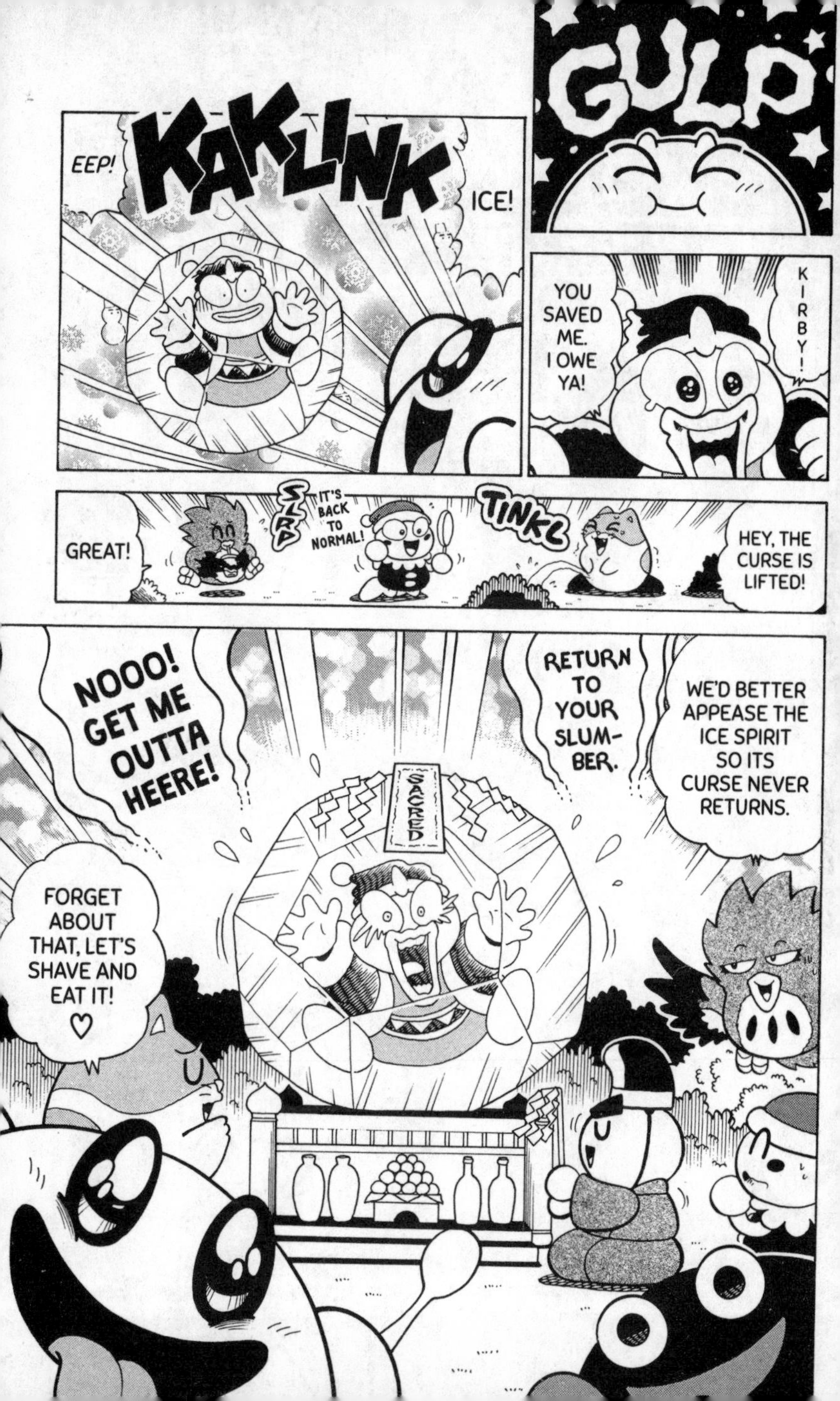
GULP
KIRBY!
YOU SAVED ME. I OWE YA!
KAKLINK
ICE!
EEP!
HEY, THE CURSE IS LIFTED!
TINKL
IT'S BACK TO NORMAL!
SLRP
GREAT!
WE'D BETTER APPEASE THE ICE SPIRIT SO ITS CURSE NEVER RETURNS.
RETURN TO YOUR SLUMBER.
NOOO! GET ME OUTTA HEERE!
SACRED
FORGET ABOUT THAT, LET'S SHAVE AND EAT IT! ♡

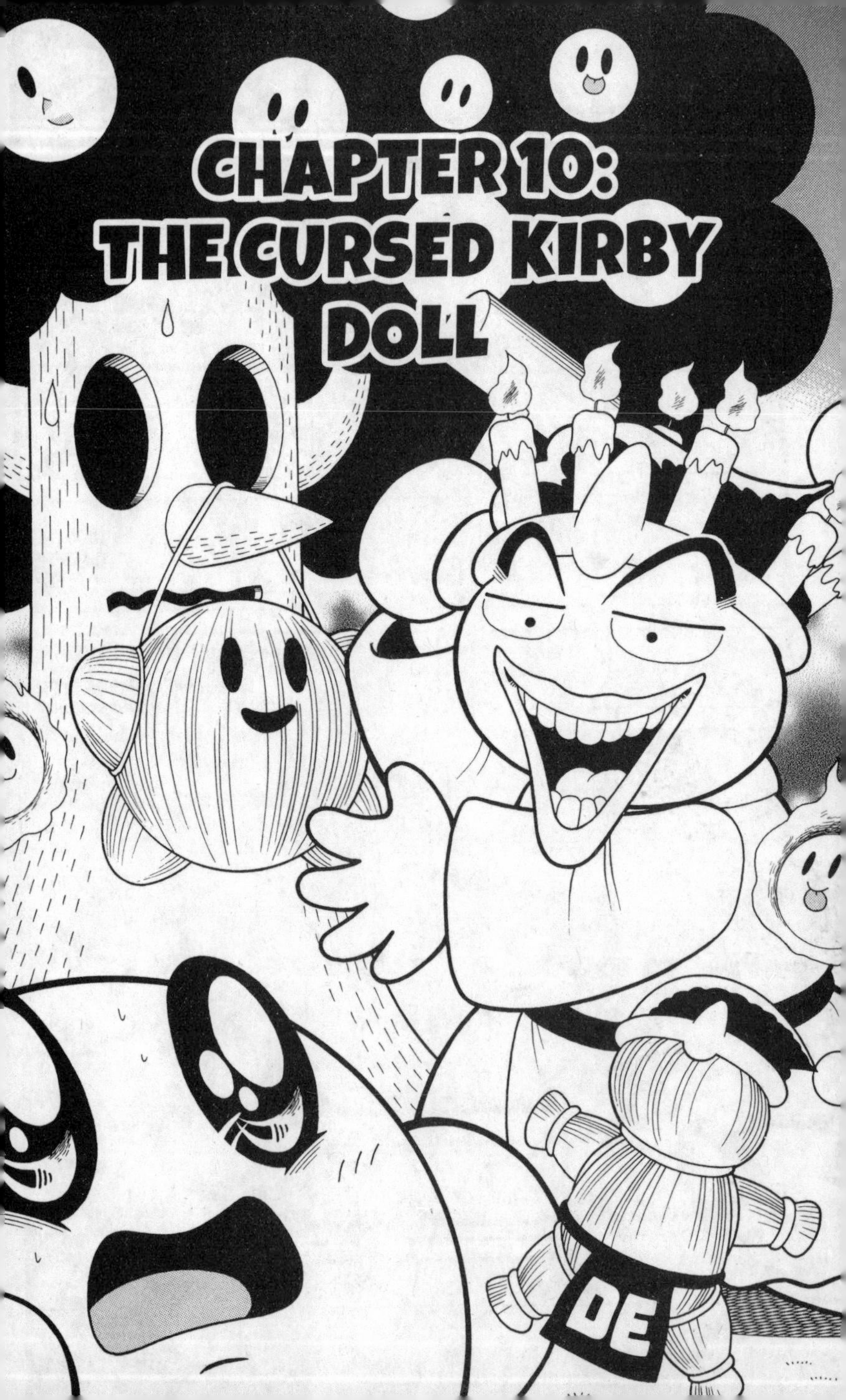
CHAPTER 10:
THE CURSED KIRBY DOLL
DE

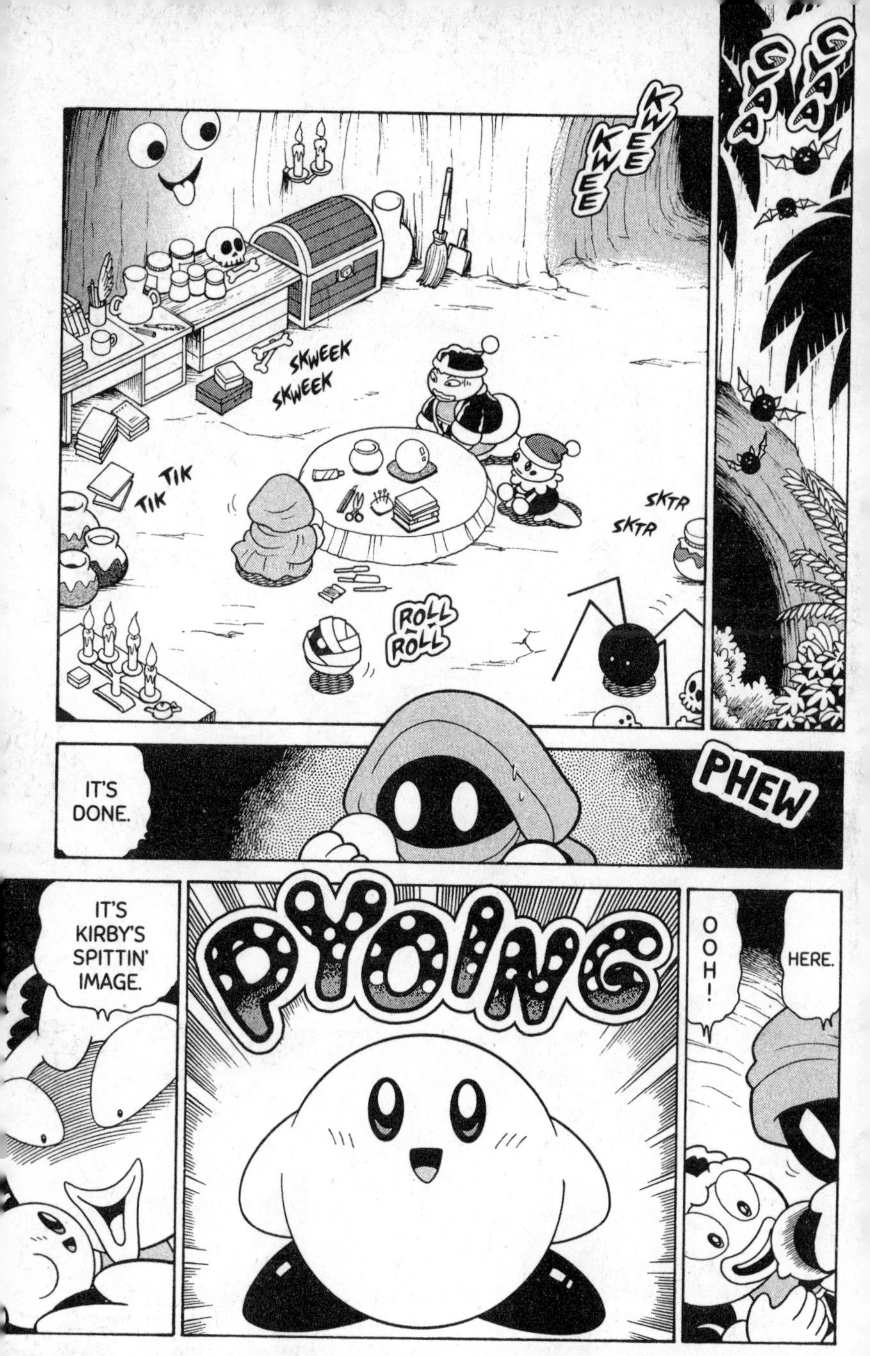
GYAA
GYAA
KWEE
KWEE
SKWEEK
SKWEEK
TIK
TIK
SKTR
SKTR
ROLL
ROLL
PHEW
IT'S DONE.
HERE.
OOH!
PYOING
IT'S KIRBY'S SPITTIN' IMAGE.

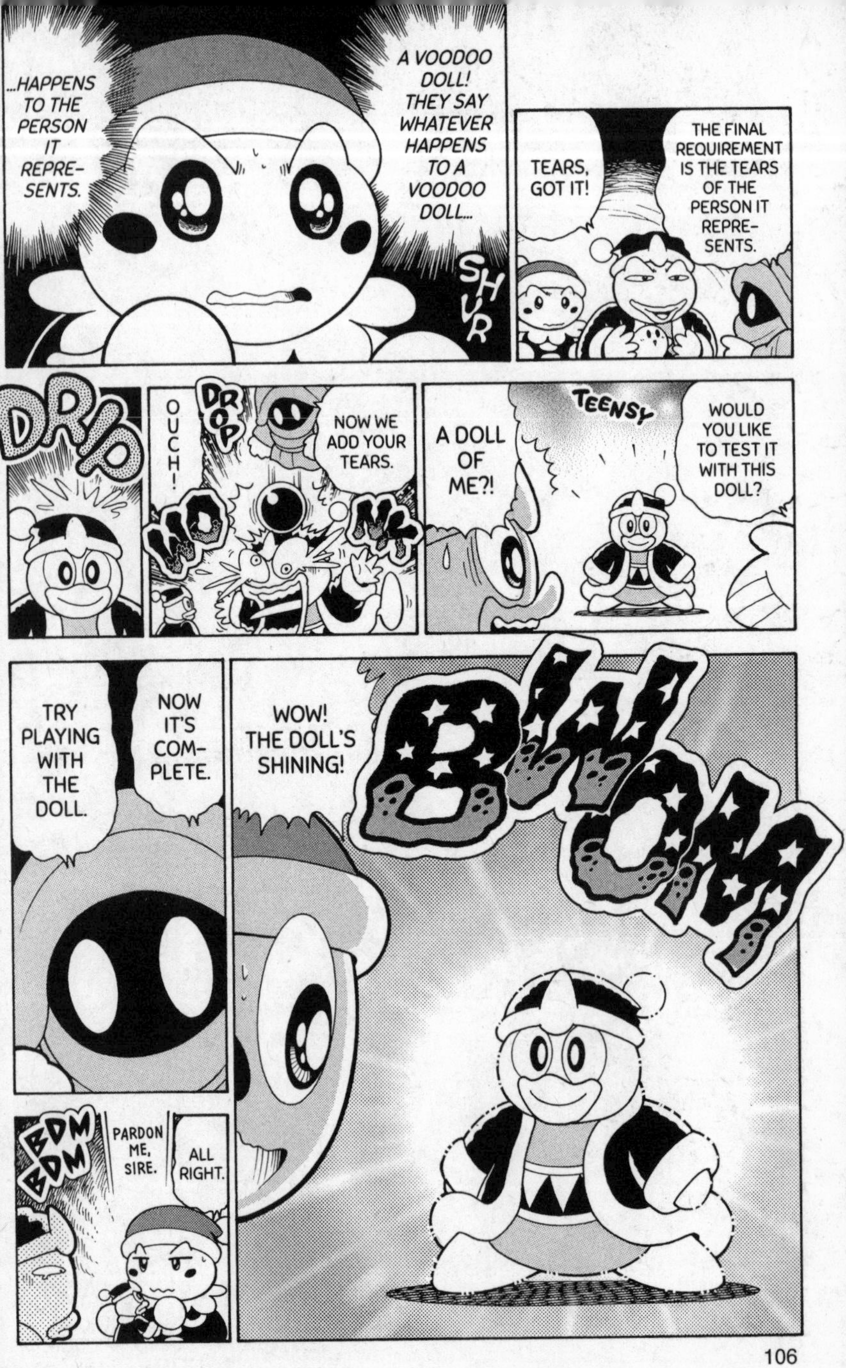
THE FINAL REQUIREMENT IS THE TEARS OF THE PERSON IT REPRESENTS.
TEARS, GOT IT!
A VOODOO DOLL! THEY SAY WHATEVER HAPPENS TO A VOODOO DOLL...
...HAPPENS TO THE PERSON IT REPRESENTS.
SHUR
WOULD YOU LIKE TO TEST IT WITH THIS DOLL?
TEENSY
A DOLL OF ME?!
NOW WE ADD YOUR TEARS.
DROP
OUCH!
DRIP
WOW! THE DOLL'S SHINING!
BWOM
NOW IT'S COMPLETE.
TRY PLAYING WITH THE DOLL.
ALL RIGHT.
PARDON ME, SIRE.
BDM BDM

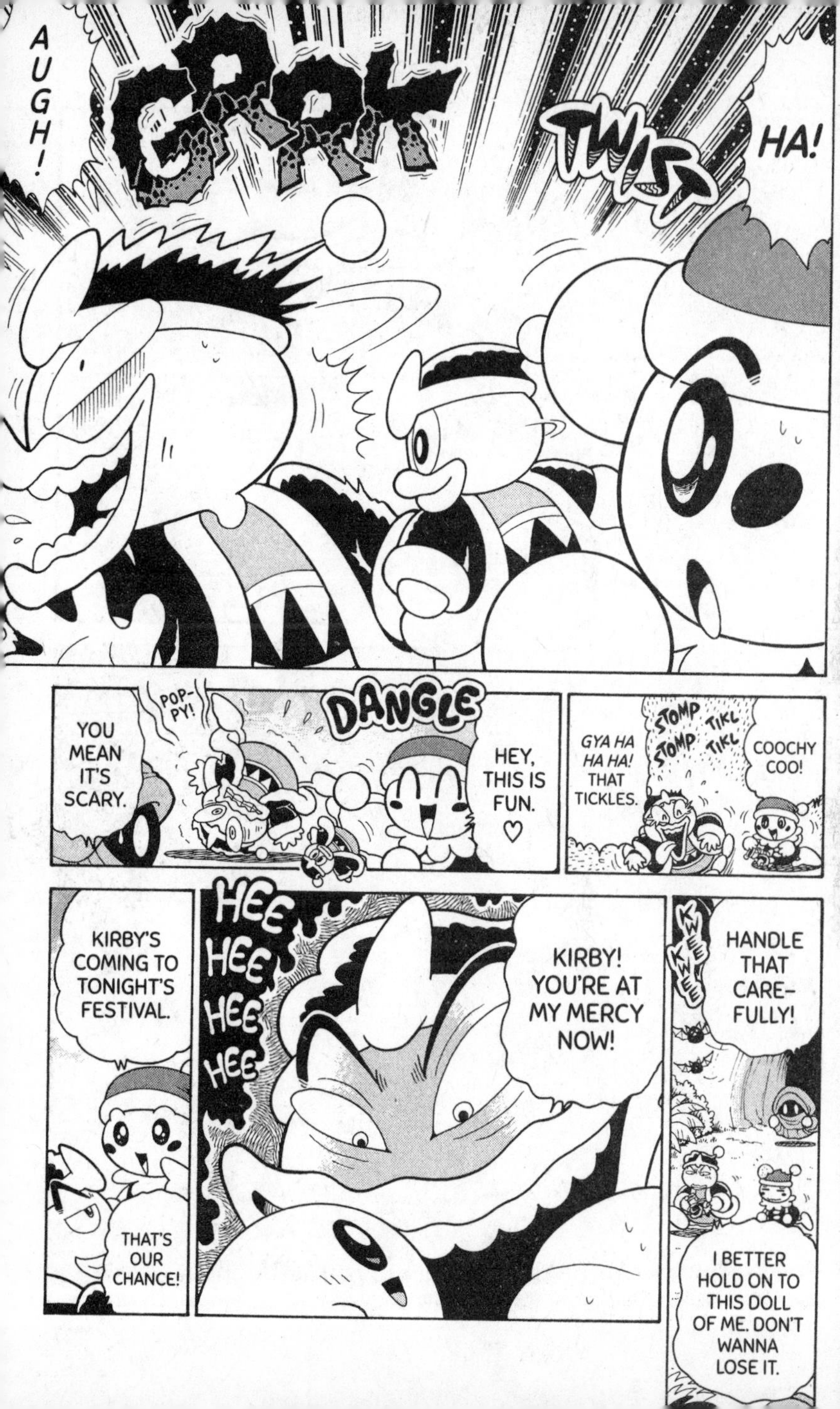
HA!
TWIST
CRRK
AUGH!
COOCHY COO!
TIKL TIKL
STOMP STOMP
GYA HA HA HA! THAT TICKLES.
HEY, THIS IS FUN. ♡
DANGLE
POP-PY!
YOU MEAN IT'S SCARY.
KWEE KWEE
HANDLE THAT CARE-FULLY!
I BETTER HOLD ON TO THIS DOLL OF ME. DON'T WANNA LOSE IT.
KIRBY! YOU'RE AT MY MERCY NOW!
HEE HEE HEE HEE
KIRBY'S COMING TO TONIGHT'S FESTIVAL.
THAT'S OUR CHANCE!

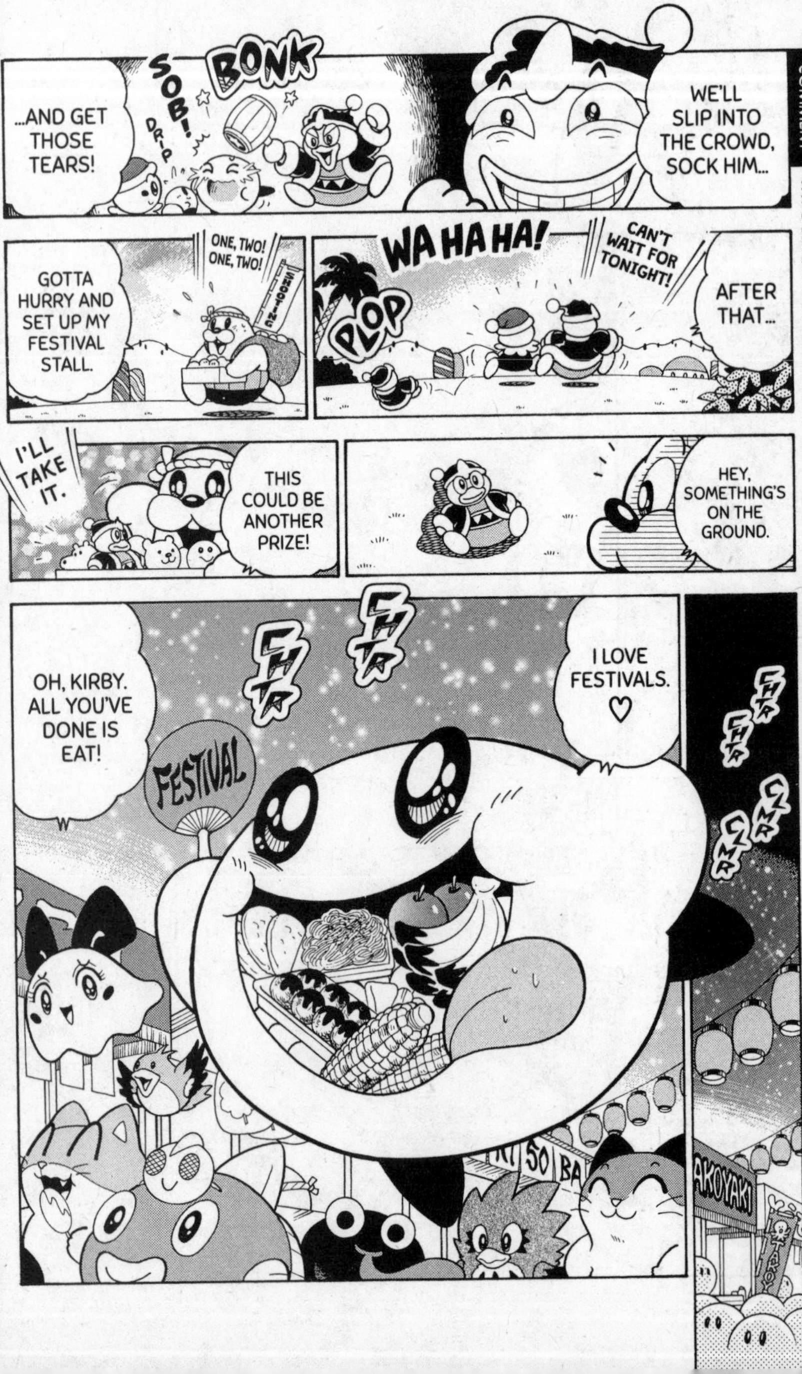
WE'LL SLIP INTO THE CROWD, SOCK HIM...
BONK
SOB!
DRIP
...AND GET THOSE TEARS!
CAN'T WAIT FOR TONIGHT!
AFTER THAT...
WA HA HA!
PLOP
ONE, TWO! ONE, TWO!
SHOOTING
GOTTA HURRY AND SET UP MY FESTIVAL STALL.
HEY, SOMETHING'S ON THE GROUND.
THIS COULD BE ANOTHER PRIZE!
I'LL TAKE IT.
I LOVE FESTIVALS. ♥
OH, KIRBY. ALL YOU'VE DONE IS EAT!
FESTIVAL
KI SO BA
AKOYAKI

AUTHOR'S COMMENT

FOR GAG MANGA, THE VOODOO DOLL CHAPTER IS A WORN-OUT CLICHÉ. STILL, I WANTED TO TRY DOING IT WITH KIRBY AND KING DEDEDE. I'M GRATEFUL FOR KING DEDEDE'S GREAT REACTIONS.

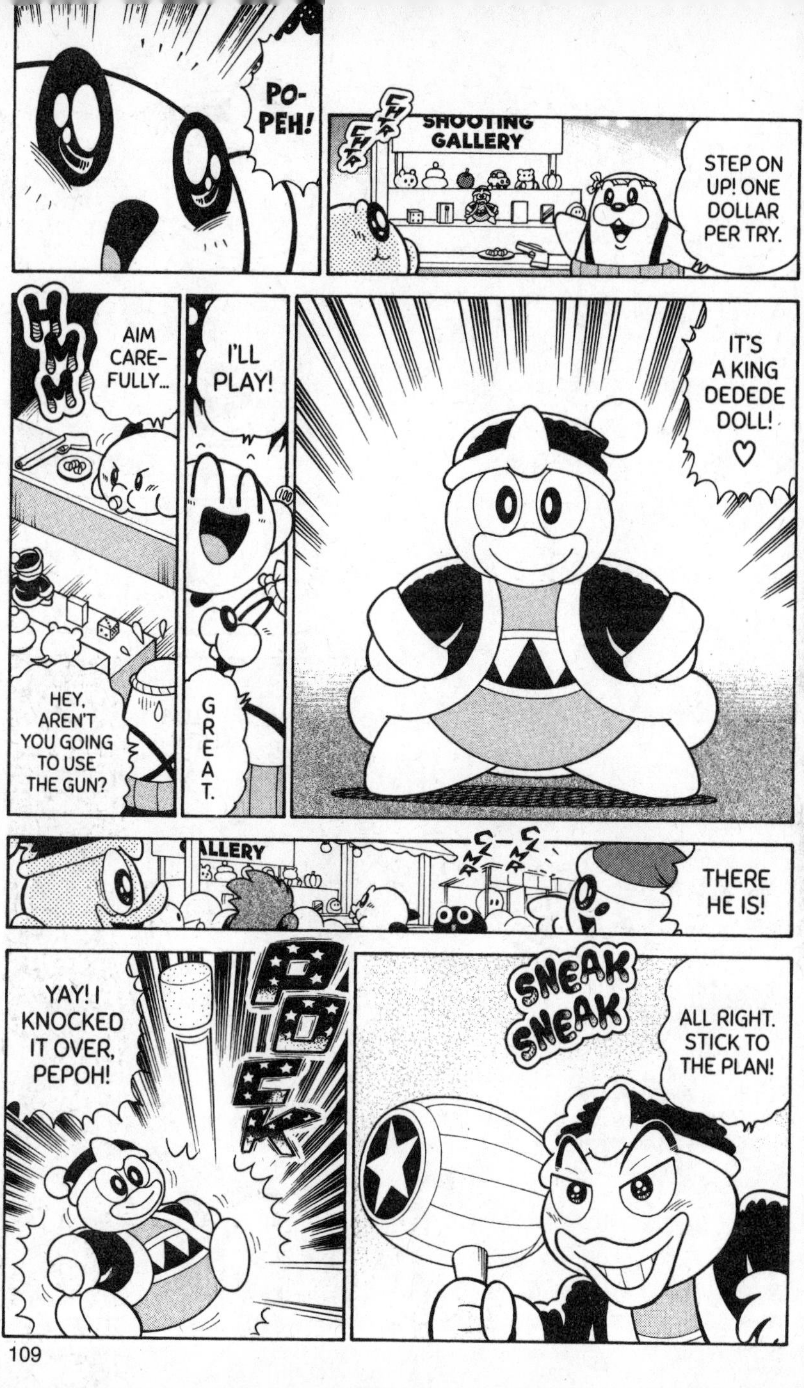
CHTR CHTR
SHOOTING GALLERY
STEP ON UP! ONE DOLLAR PER TRY.
PO-PEH!
IT'S A KING DEDEDE DOLL! ♡
I'LL PLAY!
GREAT.
HMMM
AIM CAREFULLY...
HEY, AREN'T YOU GOING TO USE THE GUN?
CLMR CLMR
GALLERY
THERE HE IS!
SNEAK SNEAK
ALL RIGHT. STICK TO THE PLAN!
POCK
YAY! I KNOCKED IT OVER, PEPOH!

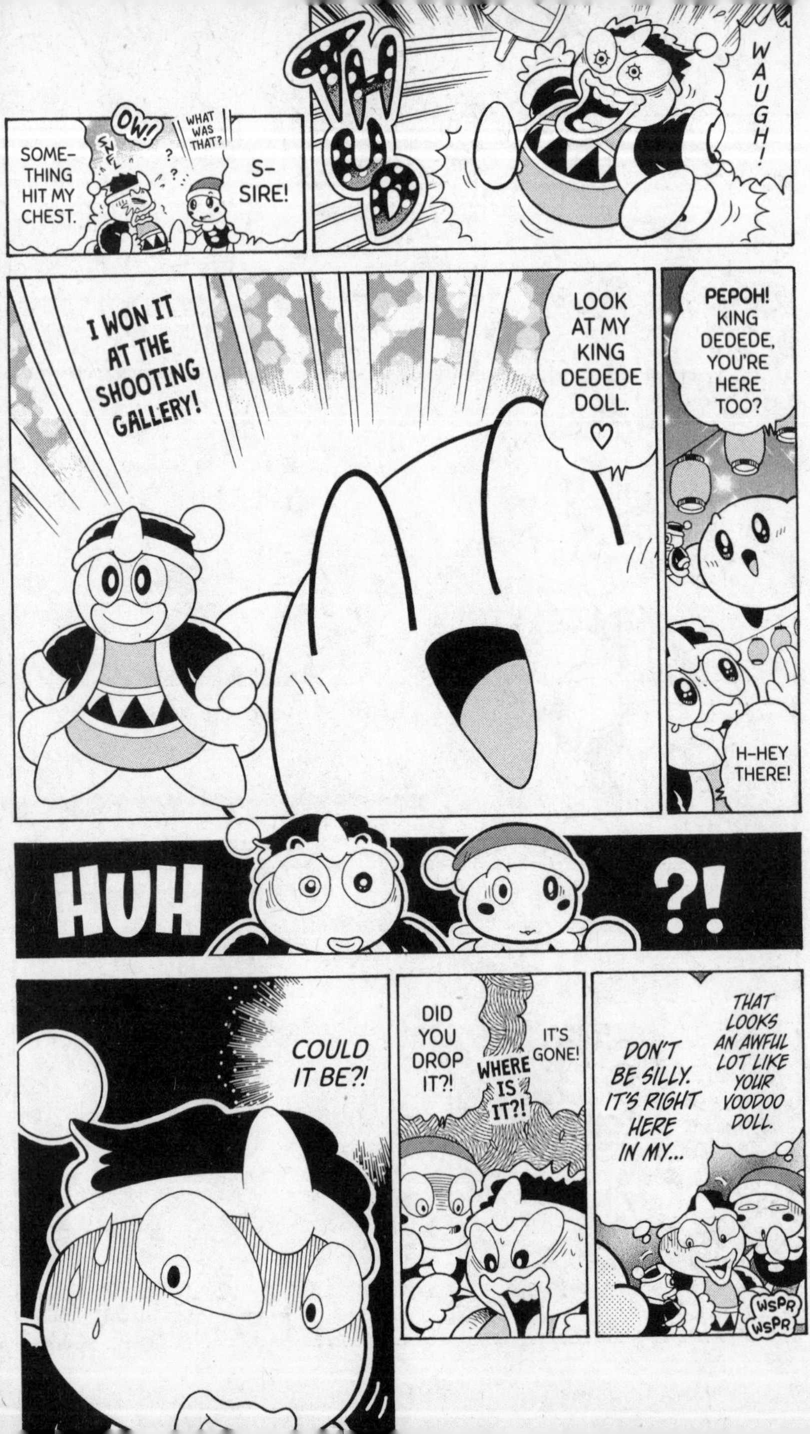
WAUGH!
THUD
WHAT WAS THAT?
S-SIRE!
OW!
SNFL
SOME-THING HIT MY CHEST.
PEPOH! KING DEDEDE, YOU'RE HERE TOO?
H-HEY THERE!
LOOK AT MY KING DEDEDE DOLL. ♥
I WON IT AT THE SHOOTING GALLERY!
HUH ?!
THAT LOOKS AN AWFUL LOT LIKE YOUR VOODOO DOLL.
DON'T BE SILLY. IT'S RIGHT HERE IN MY...
WSPR WSPR
IT'S GONE!
WHERE IS IT?!
DID YOU DROP IT?!
COULD IT BE?!

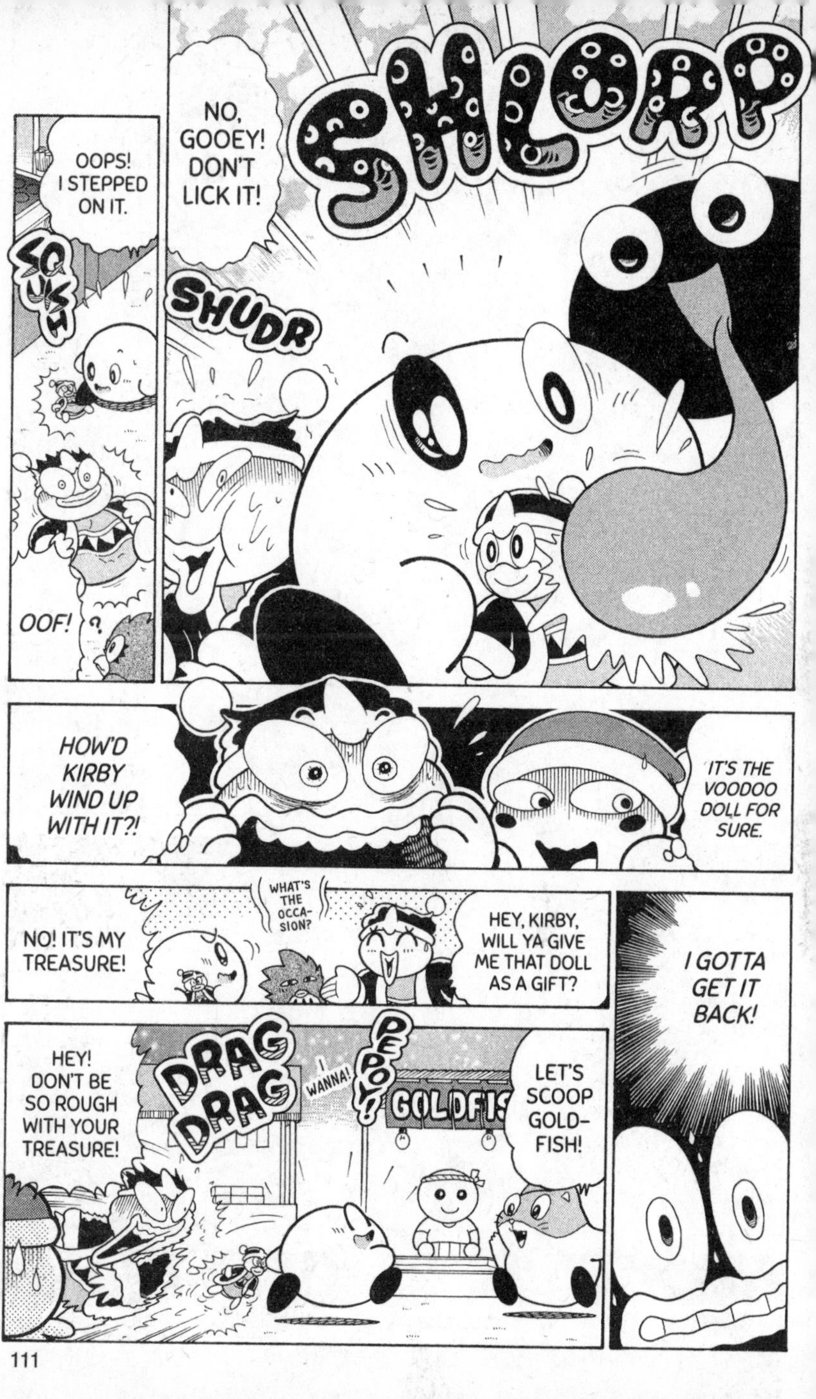
SHLORP
NO, GOOEY! DON'T LICK IT!
SHUDR
OOPS! I STEPPED ON IT.
SQUISH
OOF!
?
IT'S THE VOODOO DOLL FOR SURE.
HOW'D KIRBY WIND UP WITH IT?!
I GOTTA GET IT BACK!
HEY, KIRBY, WILL YA GIVE ME THAT DOLL AS A GIFT?
WHAT'S THE OCCASION?
NO! IT'S MY TREASURE!
LET'S SCOOP GOLD-FISH!
PEPOY!
GOLDFIS
I WANNA!
DRAG DRAG
HEY! DON'T BE SO ROUGH WITH YOUR TREASURE!

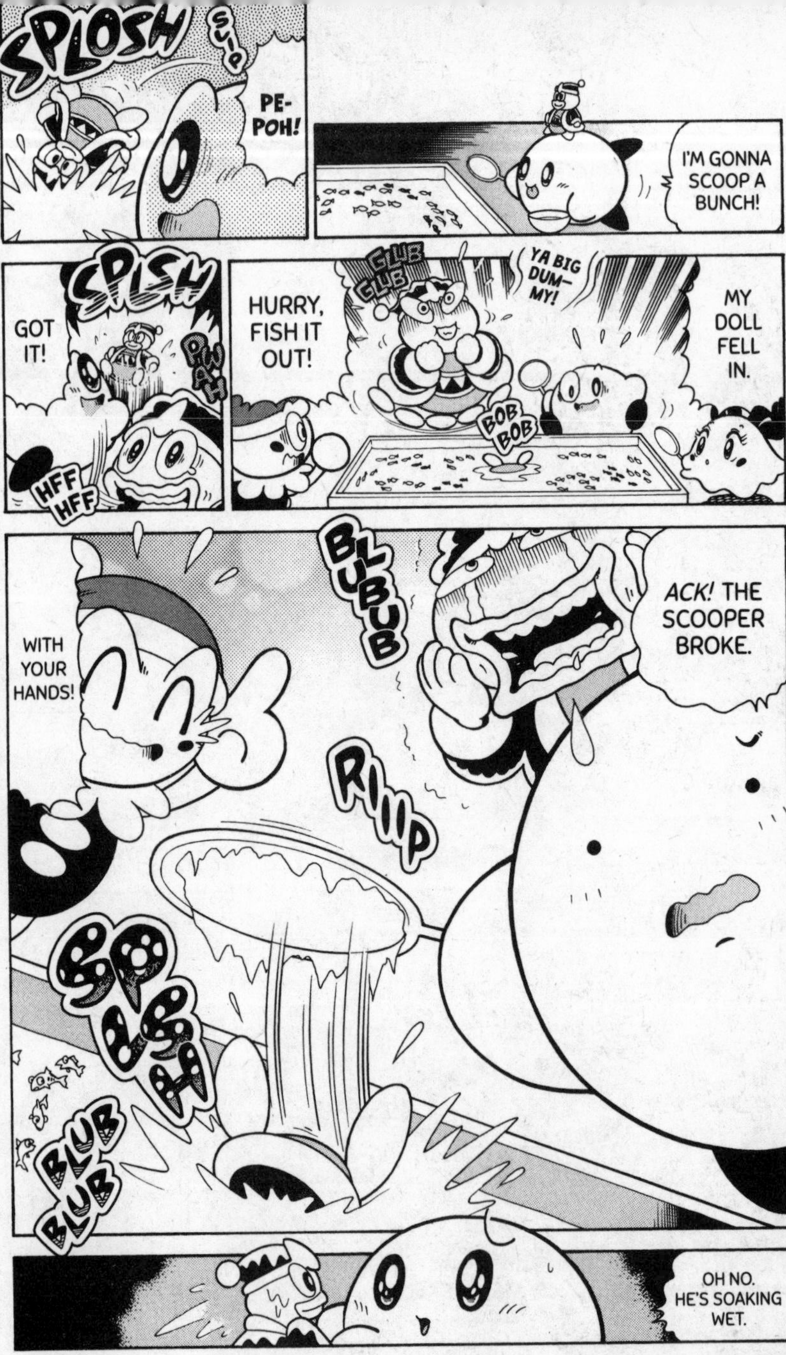
I'M GONNA SCOOP A BUNCH!
SPLOSH
SLIP
PE-POH!
MY DOLL FELL IN.
YA BIG DUMMY!
GLUB GLUB
BOB BOB
HURRY, FISH IT OUT!
SPLISH
GOT IT!
PWAH
HFF HFF
ACK! THE SCOOPER BROKE.
BLUBUB
RIIIP
WITH YOUR HANDS!
SPLOSH
BLUB BLUB
OH NO. HE'S SOAKING WET.

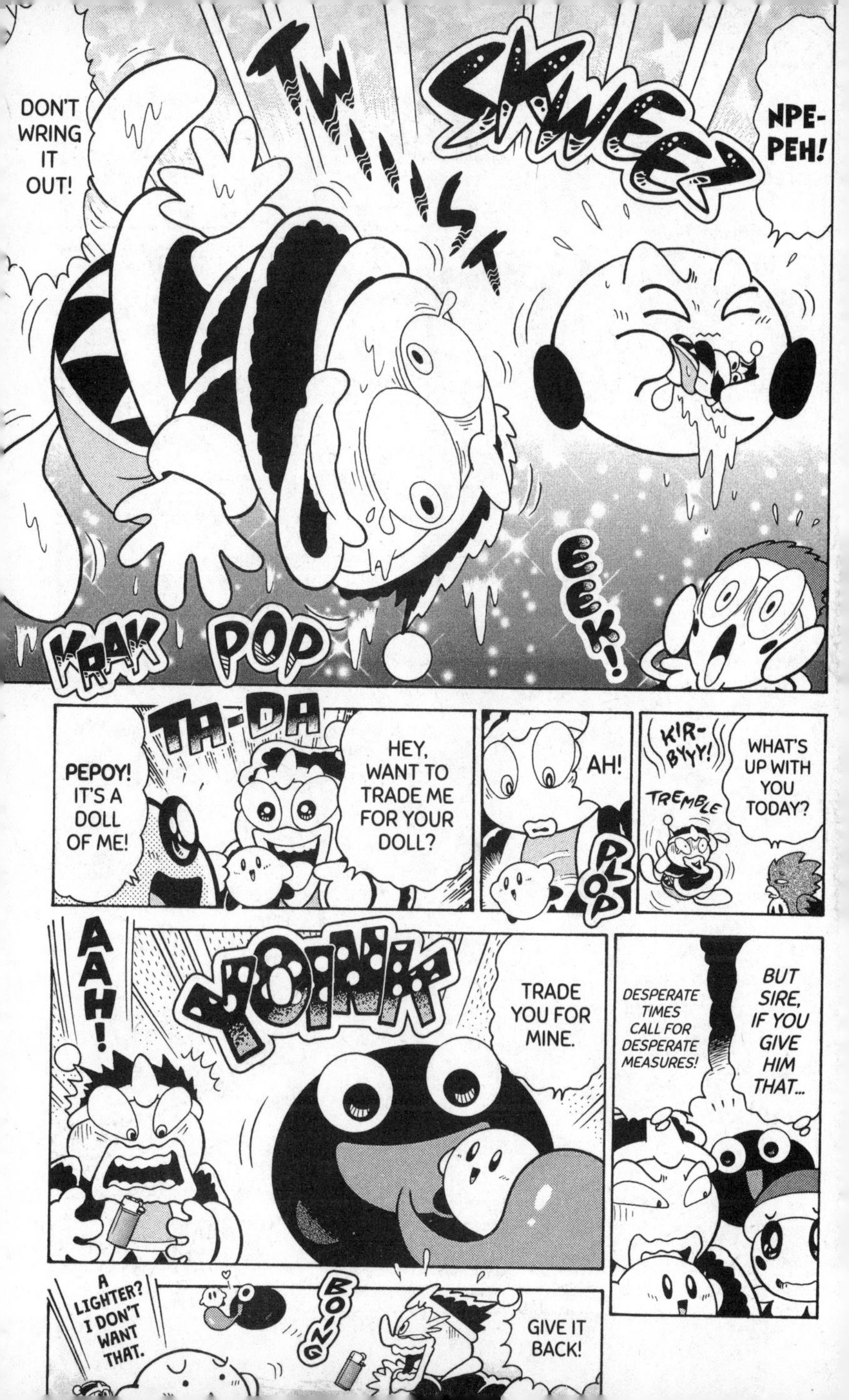
NPE-PEH!
SKWEEZ
TWIST
DON'T WRING IT OUT!
EEK!
POP
KRAK
WHAT'S UP WITH YOU TODAY?
KIR-BYYY!
TREMBLE
AH!
PLOP
HEY, WANT TO TRADE ME FOR YOUR DOLL?
TA-DA
PEPOY! IT'S A DOLL OF ME!
BUT SIRE, IF YOU GIVE HIM THAT...
DESPERATE TIMES CALL FOR DESPERATE MEASURES!
TRADE YOU FOR MINE.
YOINK
AAH!
GIVE IT BACK!
BOING
A LIGHTER? I DON'T WANT THAT.

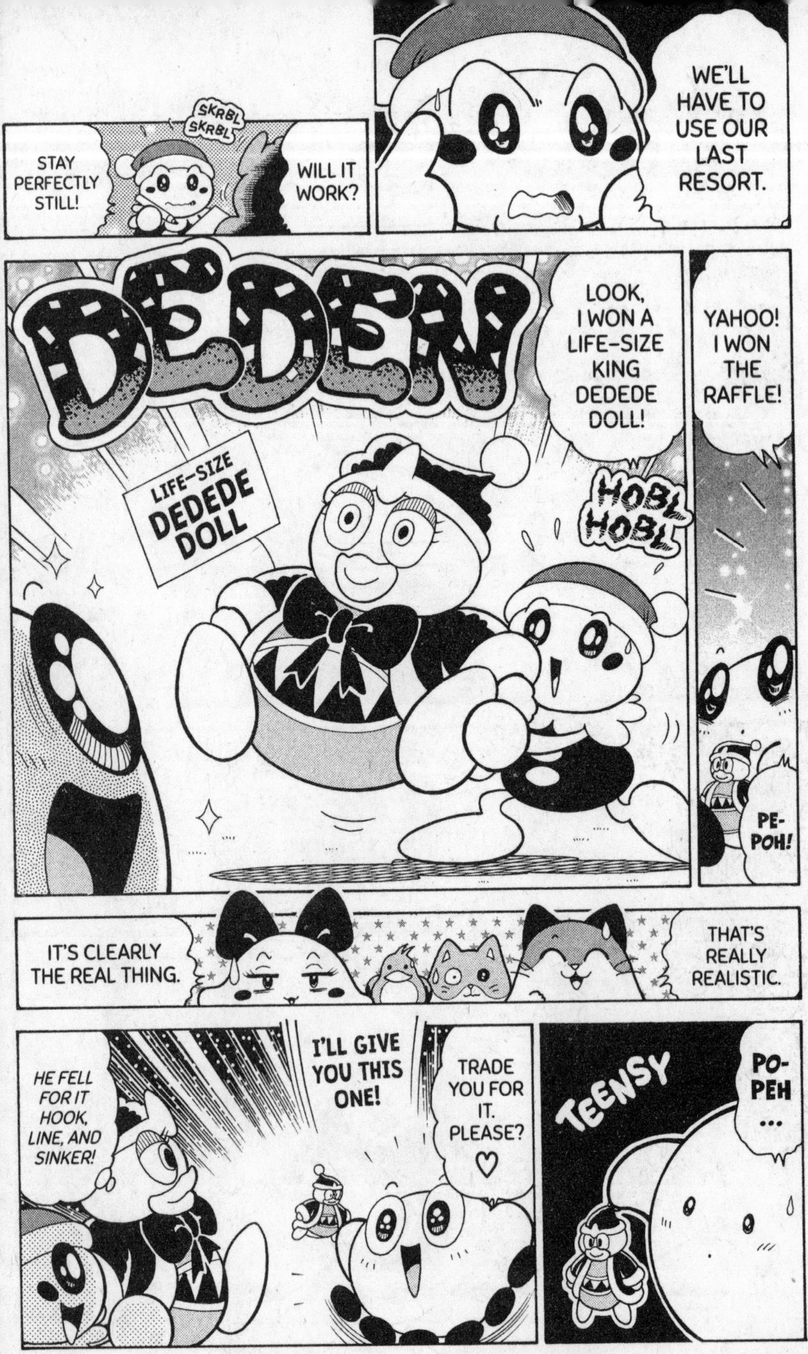
WE'LL HAVE TO USE OUR LAST RESORT.
WILL IT WORK?
SKRBL SKRBL
STAY PERFECTLY STILL!
YAHOO! I WON THE RAFFLE!
PE-POH!
LOOK, I WON A LIFE-SIZE KING DEDEDE DOLL!
DEDEN
HOBL HOBL
LIFE-SIZE DEDEDE DOLL
THAT'S REALLY REALISTIC.
IT'S CLEARLY THE REAL THING.
PO-PEH ...
TEENSY
TRADE YOU FOR IT. PLEASE? ♡
I'LL GIVE YOU THIS ONE!
HE FELL FOR IT HOOK, LINE, AND SINKER!

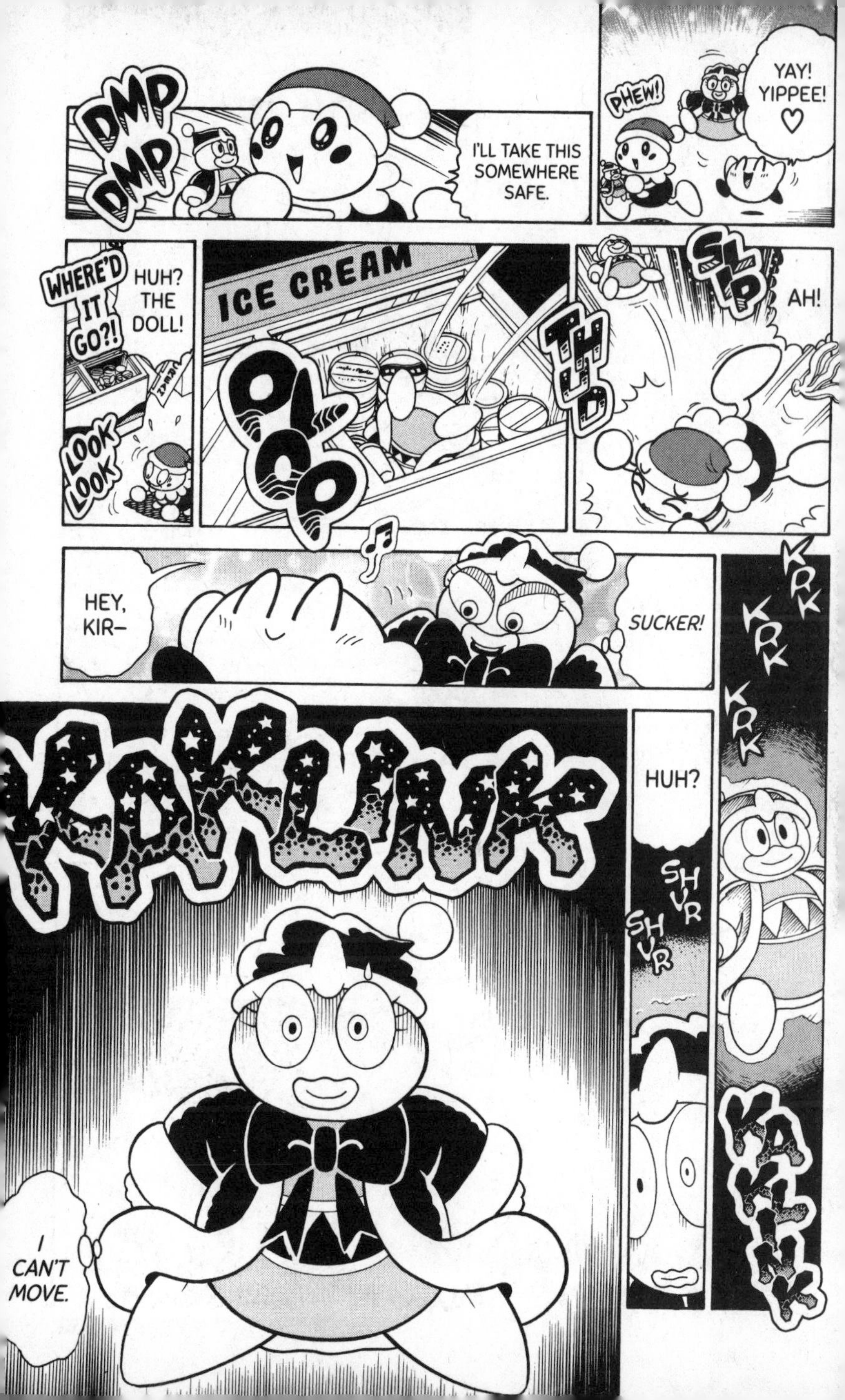
PHEW!
YAY! YIPPEE! ♥
DMP DMP
I'LL TAKE THIS SOMEWHERE SAFE.
SLIP
AH!
THUD
ICE CREAM
PLOP
HUH? THE DOLL!
WHERE'D IT GO?!
LOOK LOOK
KRK KRK KRK KRK
KAKLINK
HEY, KIR–
SUCKER!
HUH?
SHUR SHUR
KAKLINK
I CAN'T MOVE.

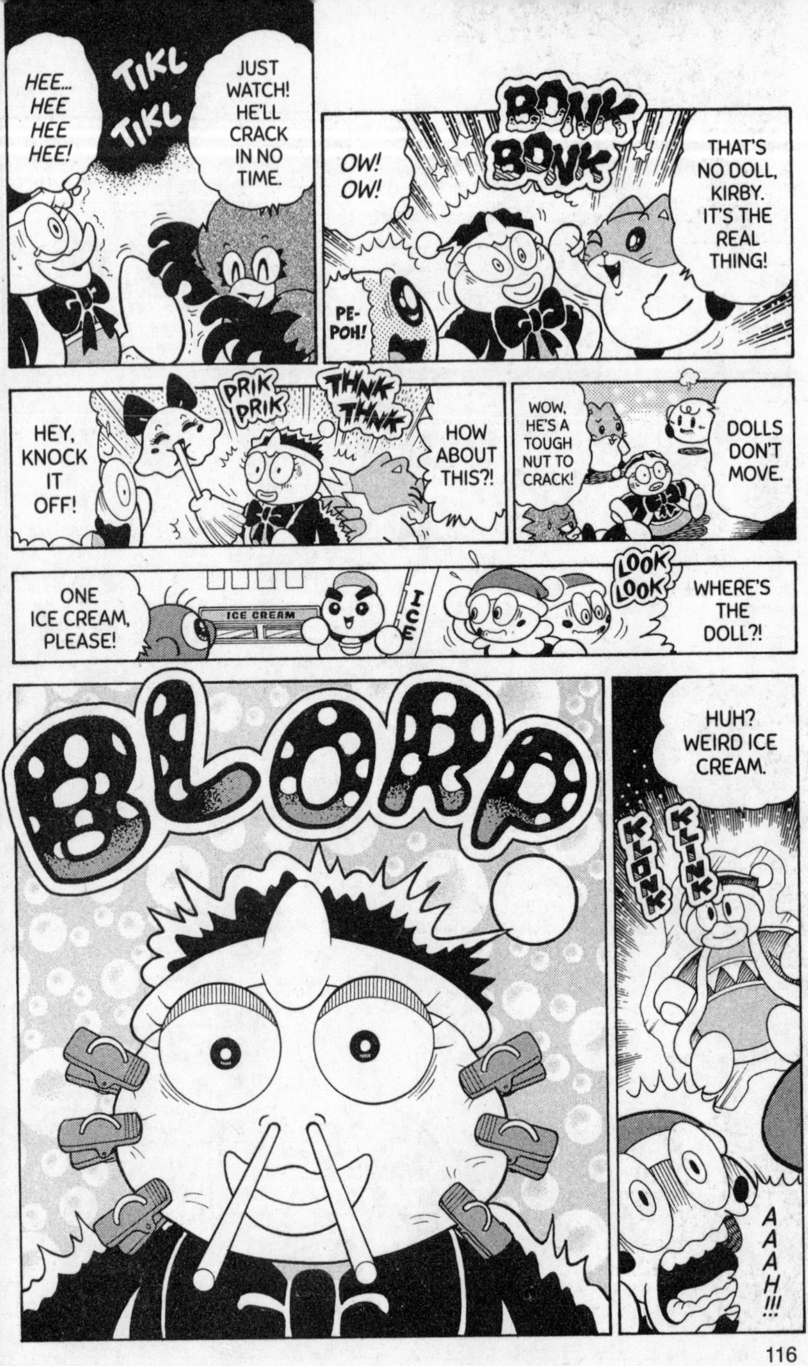
BONK BONK
THAT'S NO DOLL, KIRBY. IT'S THE REAL THING!
OW! OW!
PE-POH!
JUST WATCH! HE'LL CRACK IN NO TIME.
TIKL TIKL
HEE... HEE HEE HEE!
DOLLS DON'T MOVE.
WOW, HE'S A TOUGH NUT TO CRACK!
HOW ABOUT THIS?!
THNK THNK
PRIK PRIK
HEY, KNOCK IT OFF!
WHERE'S THE DOLL?!
LOOK LOOK
ICE
ICE CREAM
ONE ICE CREAM, PLEASE!
HUH? WEIRD ICE CREAM.
KLINK
KLONK
AAAAH!!!
BLORP

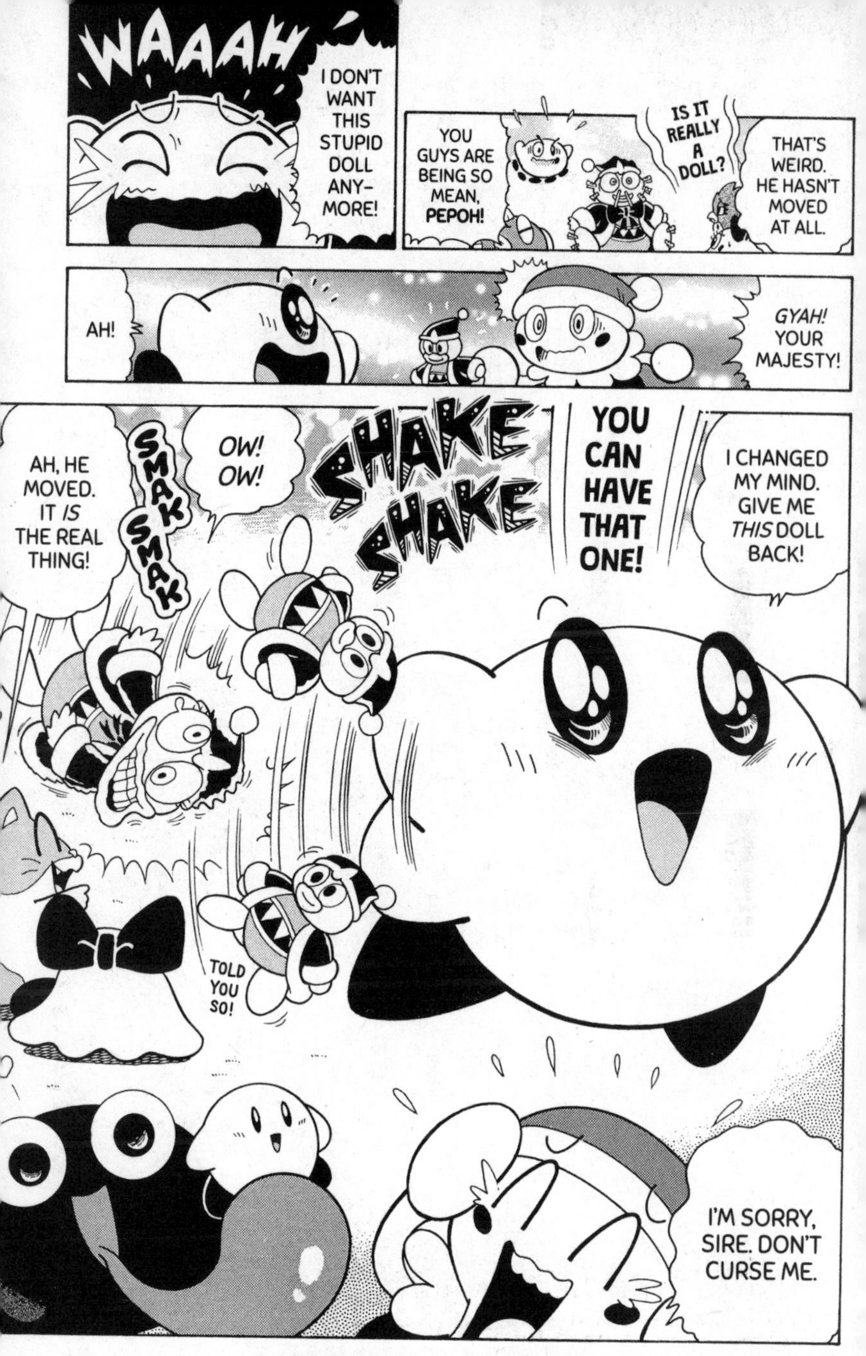
THAT'S WEIRD. HE HASN'T MOVED AT ALL.
IS IT REALLY A DOLL?
YOU GUYS ARE BEING SO MEAN, PEPOH!
WAAAH
I DON'T WANT THIS STUPID DOLL ANY-MORE!
GYAH! YOUR MAJESTY!
AH!
I CHANGED MY MIND. GIVE ME THIS DOLL BACK!
YOU CAN HAVE THAT ONE!
SHAKE SHAKE
OW! OW!
SMAK SMAK
AH, HE MOVED. IT IS THE REAL THING!
TOLD YOU SO!
I'M SORRY, SIRE. DON'T CURSE ME.

CHAPTER 11: TRAINING IN SECRET SWEEPSTAKES TECHNIQUES!

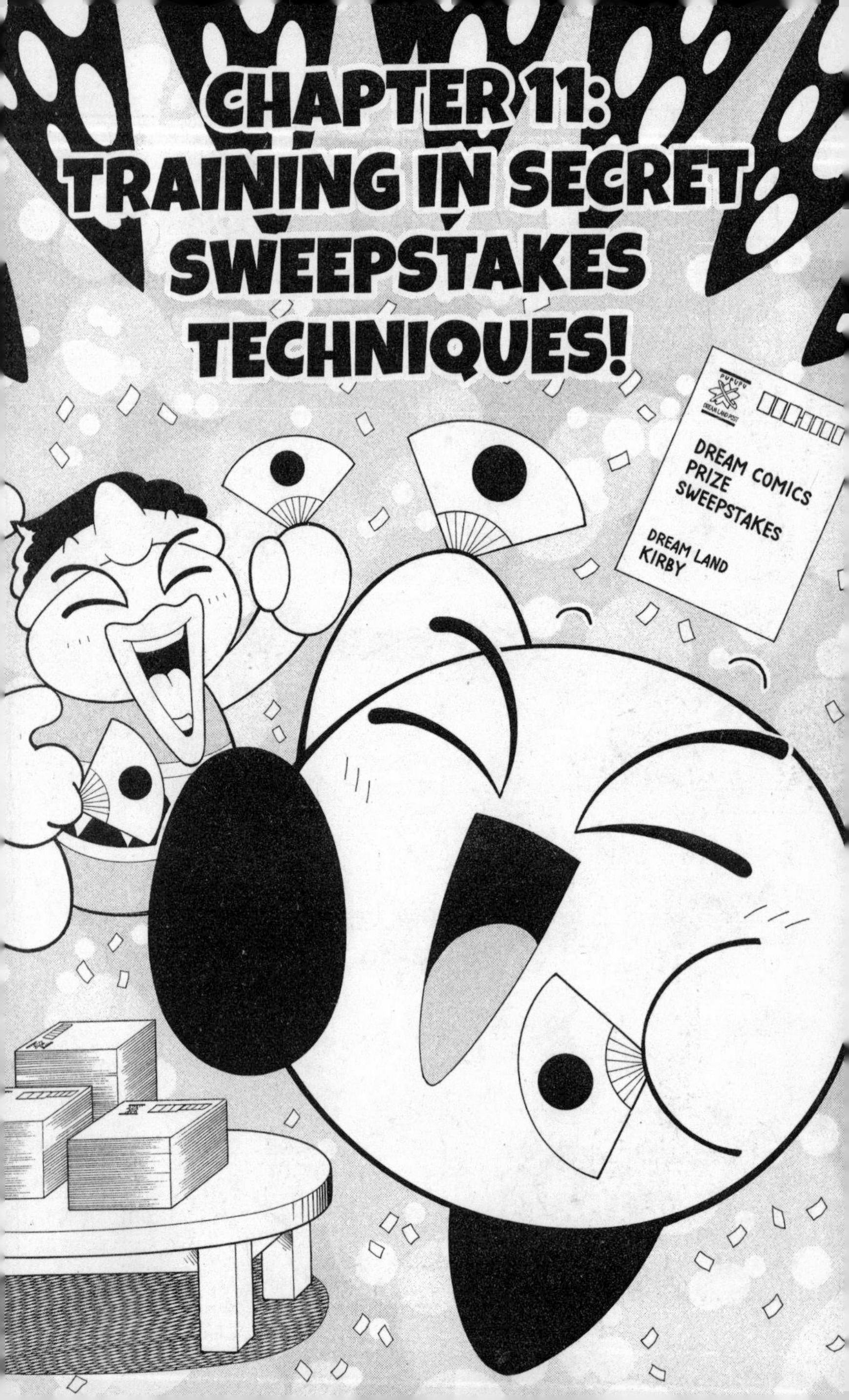
DREAM COMICS
PRIZE
SWEEPSTAKES
DREAM LAND
KIRBY

AUTHOR'S COMMENT

SWEEPSTAKES! I'VE NEVER WON ONE BEFORE. I'M ENVIOUS OF PEOPLE WHO HAVE LUCK WITH SWEEPSTAKES OR GAMBLING! WAIT A SEC. I GET TO DRAW *KIRBY*! I'M LUCKY AFTER ALL!

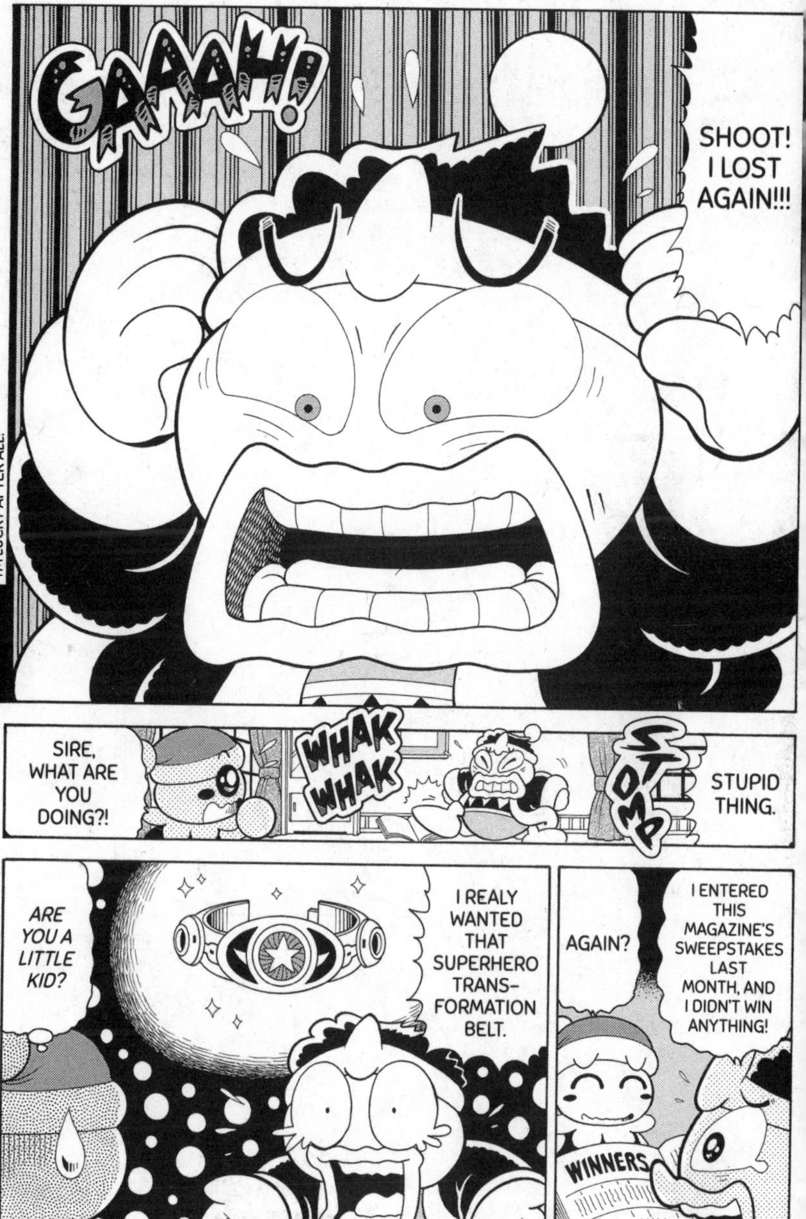
GAAAH!
SHOOT! I LOST AGAIN!!!
STUPID THING.
STOMP
WHAK WHAK
SIRE, WHAT ARE YOU DOING?!
I ENTERED THIS MAGAZINE'S SWEEPSTAKES LAST MONTH, AND I DIDN'T WIN ANYTHING!
AGAIN?
WINNERS
I REALY WANTED THAT SUPERHERO TRANS-FORMATION BELT.
ARE YOU A LITTLE KID?

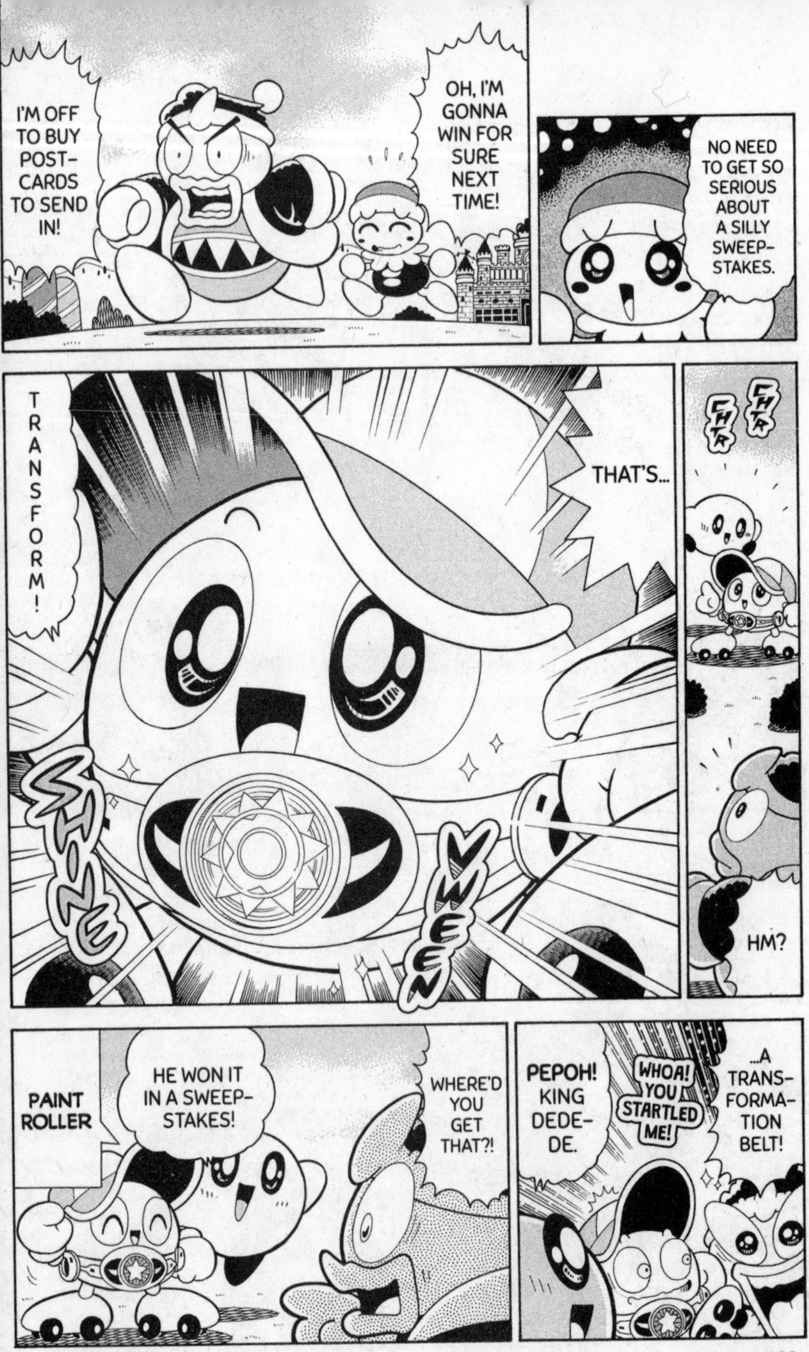
NO NEED TO GET SO SERIOUS ABOUT A SILLY SWEEP-STAKES.
OH, I'M GONNA WIN FOR SURE NEXT TIME!
I'M OFF TO BUY POST-CARDS TO SEND IN!
CHTR CHTR
HM?
THAT'S...
TRANSFORM!
VWEEN
SHINE
...A TRANS-FORMA-TION BELT!
WHOA! YOU STARTLED ME!
PEPOH! KING DEDE-DE.
WHERE'D YOU GET THAT?!
HE WON IT IN A SWEEP-STAKES!
PAINT ROLLER

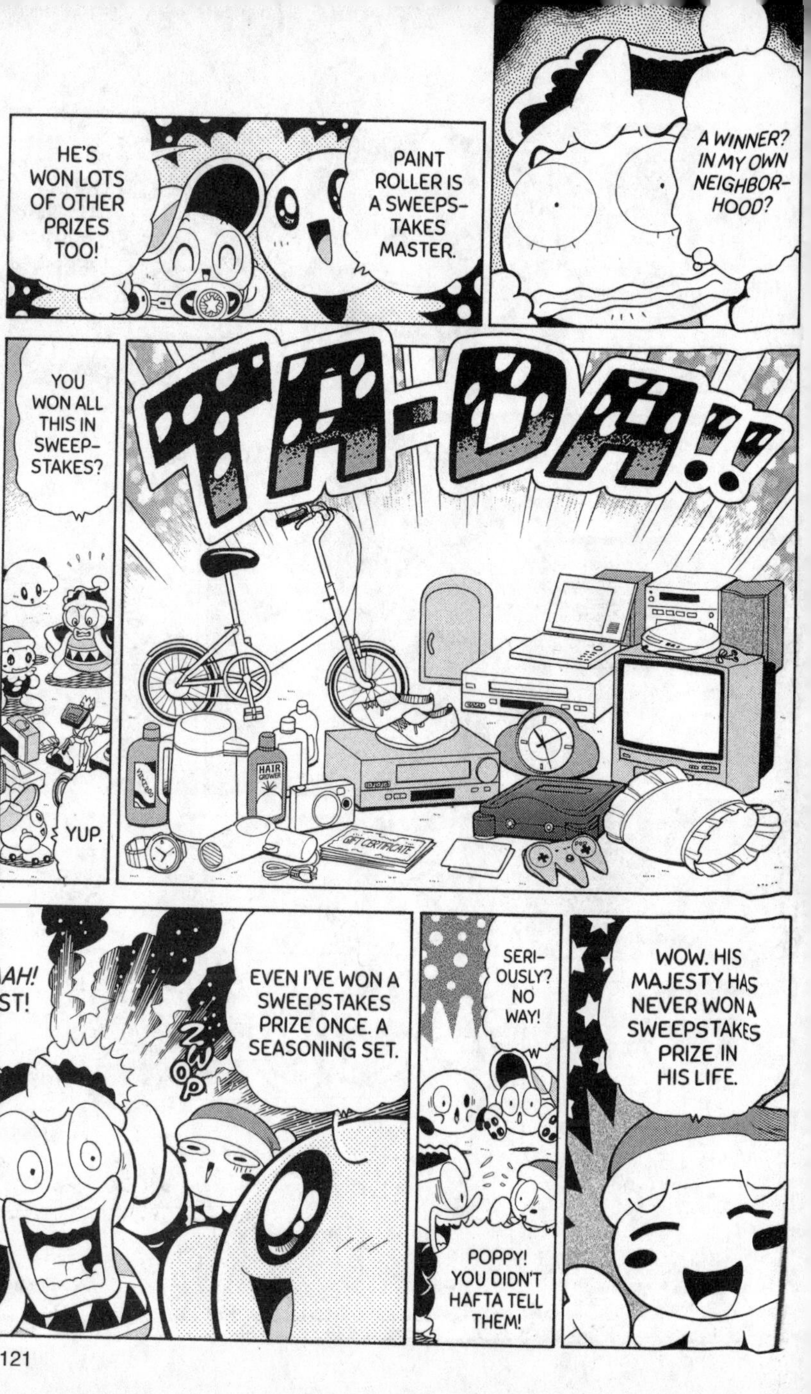
A WINNER? IN MY OWN NEIGHBOR-HOOD?
PAINT ROLLER IS A SWEEPS-TAKES MASTER.
HE'S WON LOTS OF OTHER PRIZES TOO!
TA-DA!!
HAIR GROWER
GIFT CERTIFICATE
YOU WON ALL THIS IN SWEEP-STAKES?
YUP.
WOW. HIS MAJESTY HAS NEVER WON A SWEEPSTAKES PRIZE IN HIS LIFE.
SERI-OUSLY? NO WAY!
POPPY! YOU DIDN'T HAFTA TELL THEM!
EVEN I'VE WON A SWEEPSTAKES PRIZE ONCE. A SEASONING SET.
ZWOOP
GAAAH! I LOST!

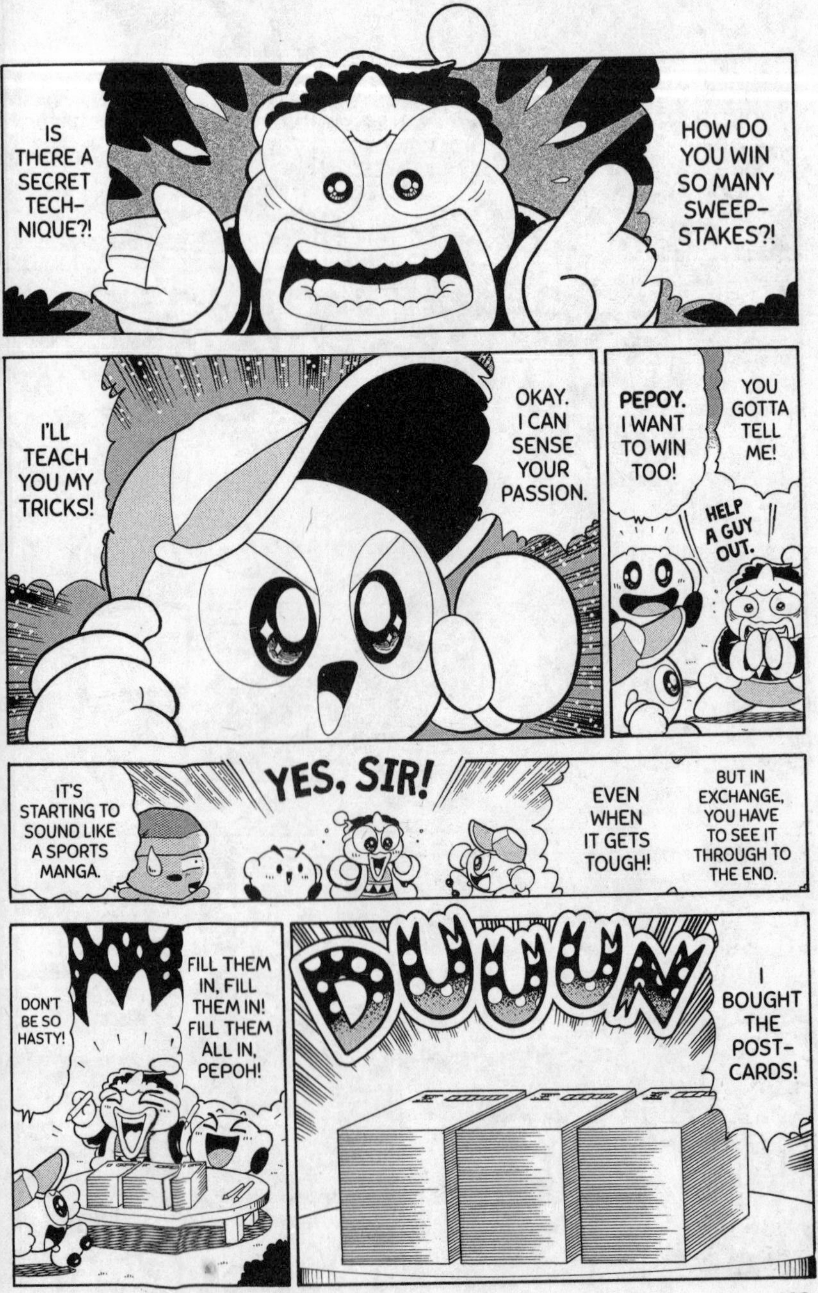
HOW DO YOU WIN SO MANY SWEEPSTAKES?!
IS THERE A SECRET TECHNIQUE?!
YOU GOTTA TELL ME!
PEPOY. I WANT TO WIN TOO!
HELP A GUY OUT.
OKAY. I CAN SENSE YOUR PASSION.
I'LL TEACH YOU MY TRICKS!
BUT IN EXCHANGE, YOU HAVE TO SEE IT THROUGH TO THE END.
EVEN WHEN IT GETS TOUGH!
YES, SIR!
IT'S STARTING TO SOUND LIKE A SPORTS MANGA.
DUUUN
I BOUGHT THE POSTCARDS!
FILL THEM IN, FILL THEM IN! FILL THEM ALL IN, PEPOH!
DON'T BE SO HASTY!

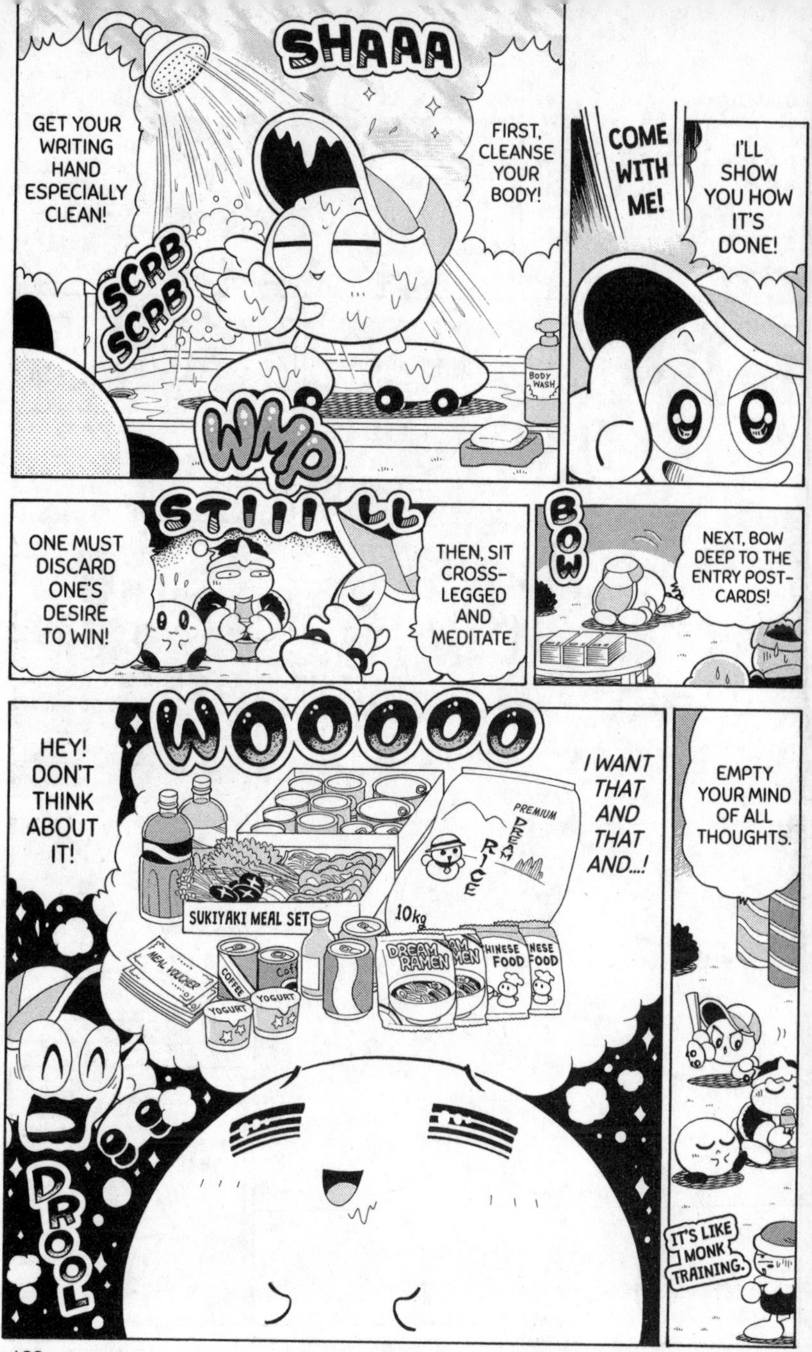
COME WITH ME!
I'LL SHOW YOU HOW IT'S DONE!
SHAAA
FIRST, CLEANSE YOUR BODY!
GET YOUR WRITING HAND ESPECIALLY CLEAN!
SCRB SCRB
BODY WASH
WMP
BOW
NEXT, BOW DEEP TO THE ENTRY POST-CARDS!
STIIILL
THEN, SIT CROSS-LEGGED AND MEDITATE.
ONE MUST DISCARD ONE'S DESIRE TO WIN!
EMPTY YOUR MIND OF ALL THOUGHTS.
IT'S LIKE MONK TRAINING.
WOOOOO
I WANT THAT AND THAT AND...!
HEY! DON'T THINK ABOUT IT!
PREMIUM DREAM RICE
10kg
SUKIYAKI MEAL SET
MEAL VOUCHER
COFFEE
YOGURT
YOGURT
DREAM RAMEN
DROOL

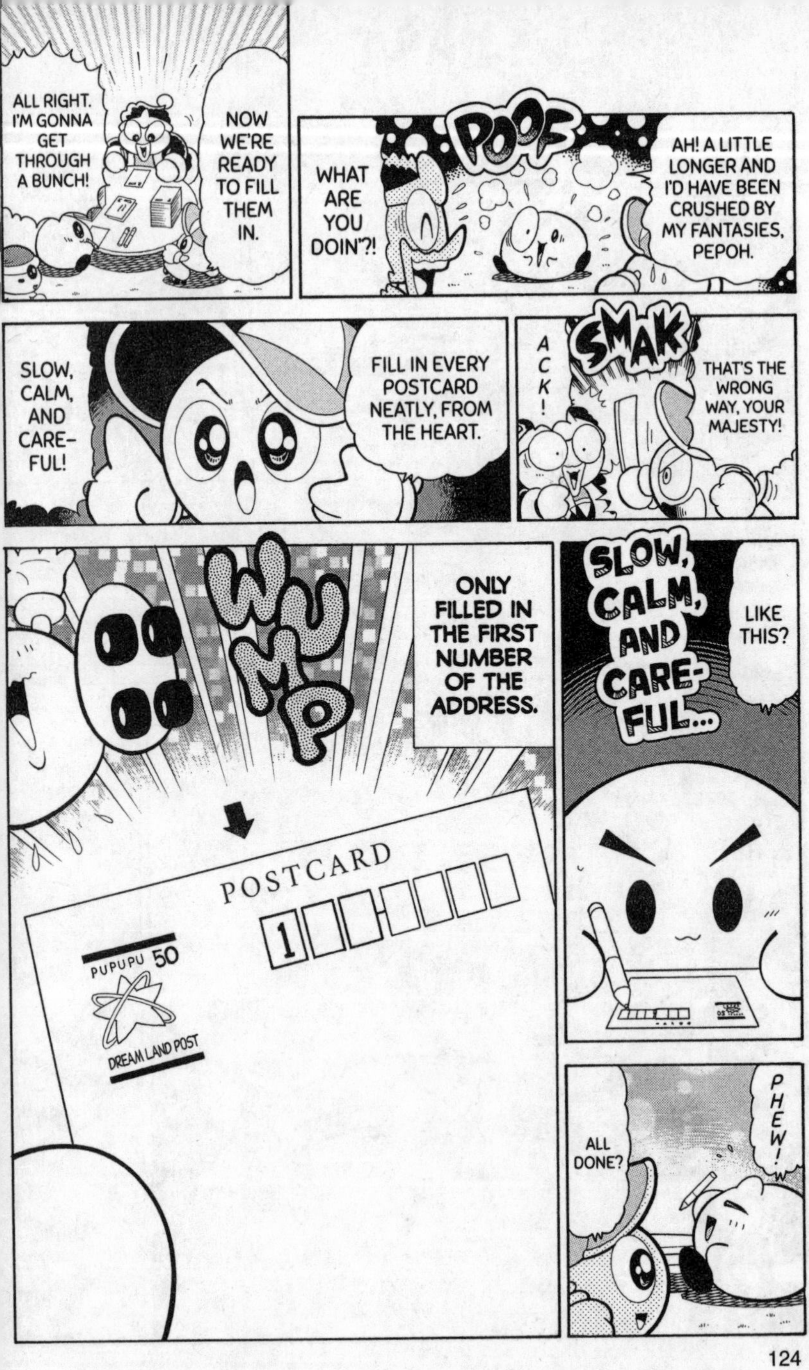

POOF
AH! A LITTLE LONGER AND I'D HAVE BEEN CRUSHED BY MY FANTASIES, PEPOH.
WHAT ARE YOU DOIN'?!
NOW WE'RE READY TO FILL THEM IN.
ALL RIGHT. I'M GONNA GET THROUGH A BUNCH!
THAT'S THE WRONG WAY, YOUR MAJESTY!
SMAK
ACK!
FILL IN EVERY POSTCARD NEATLY, FROM THE HEART.
SLOW, CALM, AND CARE-FUL!
LIKE THIS?
SLOW, CALM, AND CARE-FUL...
PHEW!
ALL DONE?
ONLY FILLED IN THE FIRST NUMBER OF THE ADDRESS.
WUMP
POSTCARD
1
PUPUPU 50
DREAM LAND POST

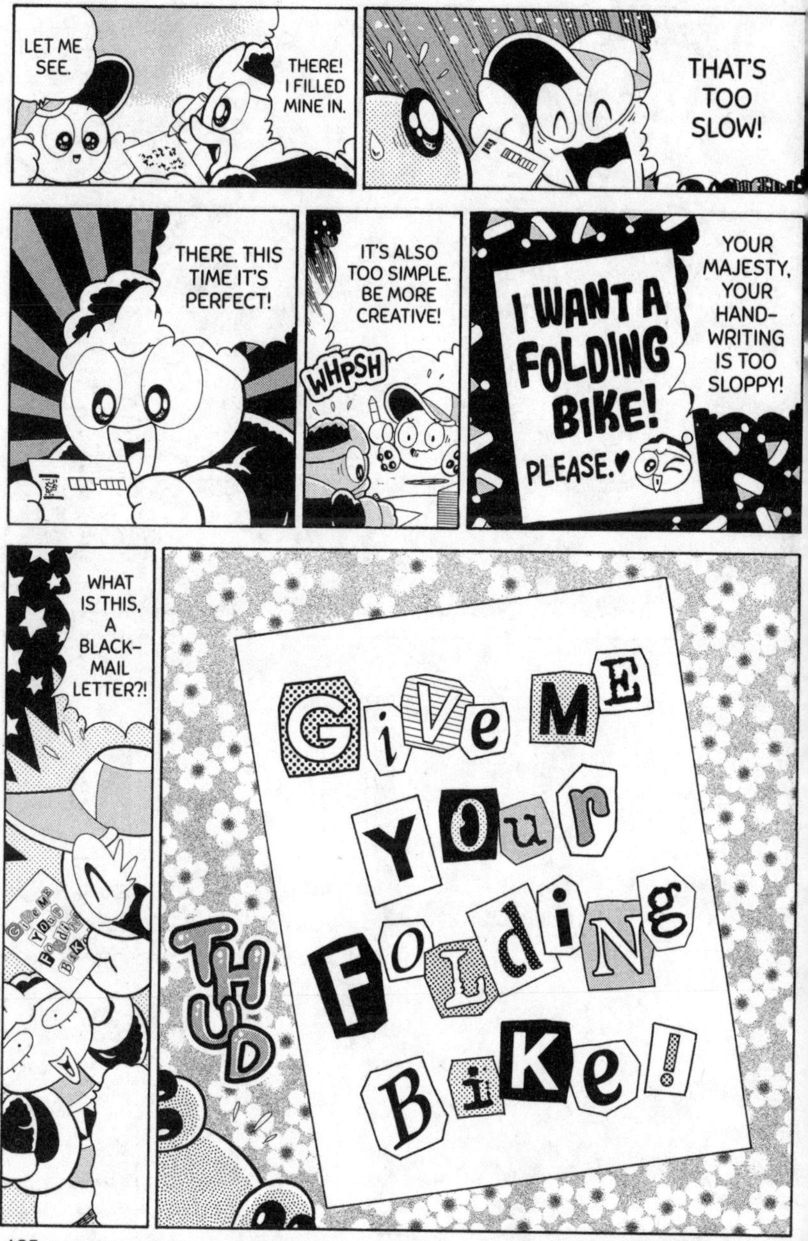
THAT'S TOO SLOW!
THERE! I FILLED MINE IN.
LET ME SEE.
YOUR MAJESTY, YOUR HAND-WRITING IS TOO SLOPPY!
I WANT A FOLDING BIKE! PLEASE.♥
IT'S ALSO TOO SIMPLE. BE MORE CREATIVE!
WHPSH
THERE. THIS TIME IT'S PERFECT!
GiVe ME YOUr FOLdiNg BiKe!
THUD
WHAT IS THIS, A BLACK-MAIL LETTER?!

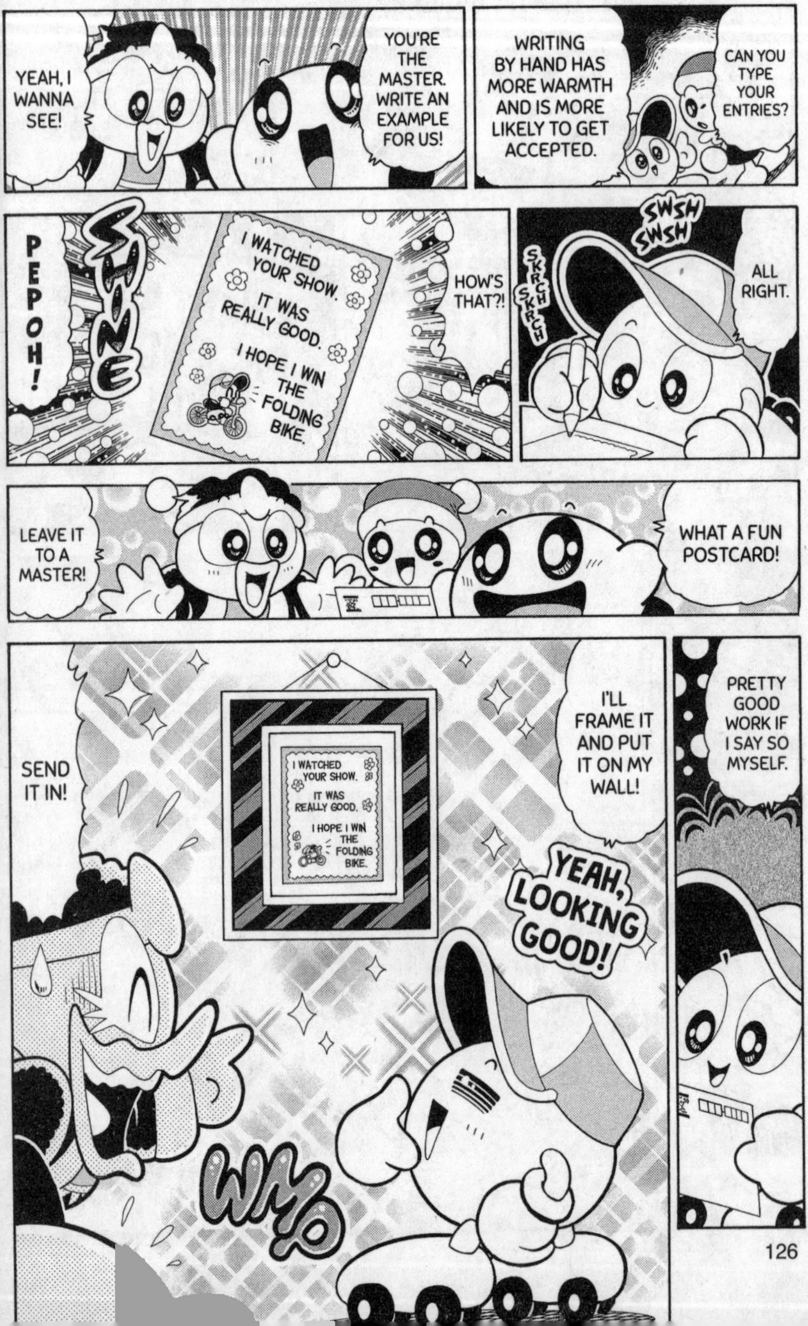
CAN YOU TYPE YOUR ENTRIES?
WRITING BY HAND HAS MORE WARMTH AND IS MORE LIKELY TO GET ACCEPTED.
YOU'RE THE MASTER. WRITE AN EXAMPLE FOR US!
YEAH, I WANNA SEE!
SWSH SWSH
SKRCH SKRCH
ALL RIGHT.
HOW'S THAT?!
I WATCHED YOUR SHOW. IT WAS REALLY GOOD. I HOPE I WIN THE FOLDING BIKE.
SHINE
PEPOH!
WHAT A FUN POSTCARD!
LEAVE IT TO A MASTER!
PRETTY GOOD WORK IF I SAY SO MYSELF.
I'LL FRAME IT AND PUT IT ON MY WALL!
YEAH, LOOKING GOOD!
I WATCHED YOUR SHOW. IT WAS REALLY GOOD. I HOPE I WIN THE FOLDING BIKE.
SEND IT IN!
WMP

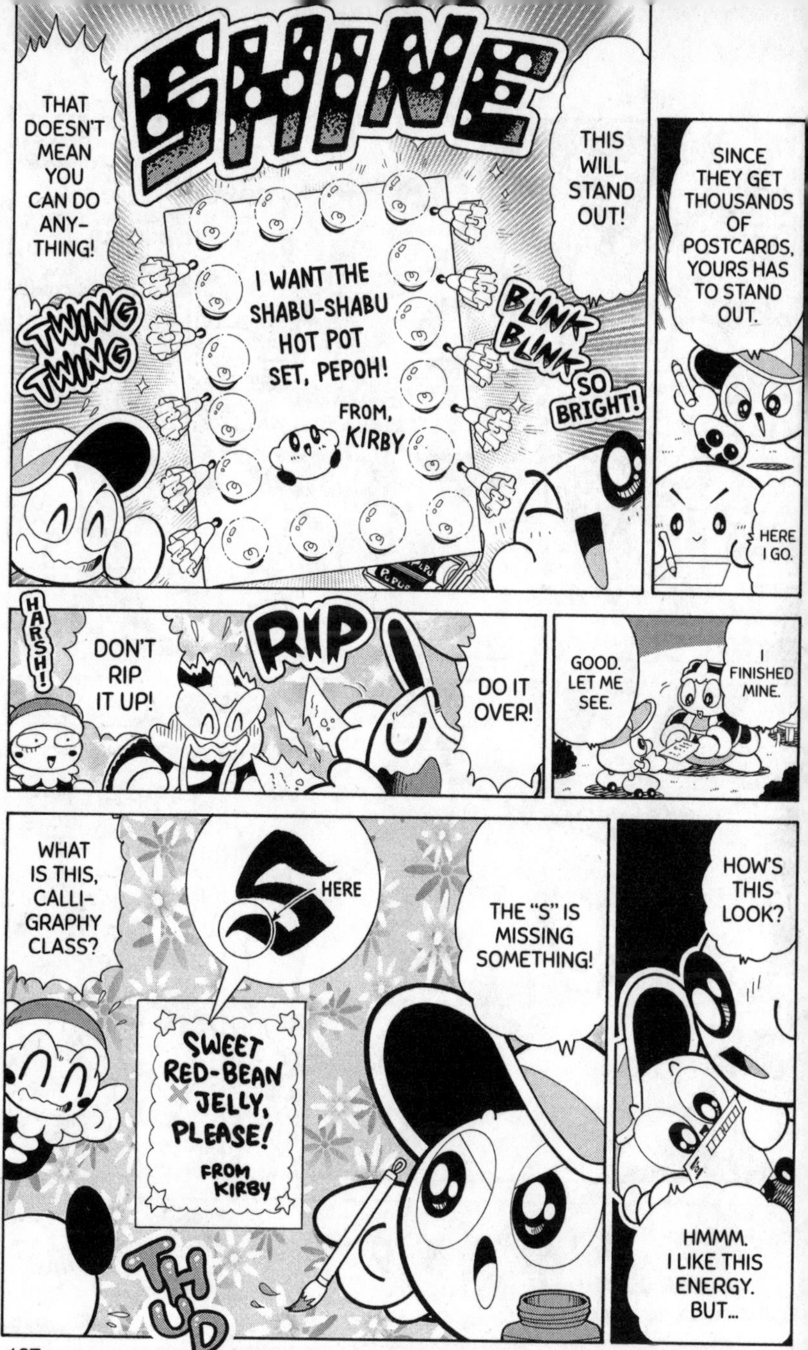
SINCE THEY GET THOUSANDS OF POSTCARDS, YOURS HAS TO STAND OUT.
HERE I GO.
THIS WILL STAND OUT!
SHINE
THAT DOESN'T MEAN YOU CAN DO ANY-THING!
BLINK BLINK
SO BRIGHT!
I WANT THE SHABU-SHABU HOT POT SET, PEPOH!
FROM, KIRBY
TWING TWING
I FINISHED MINE.
GOOD. LET ME SEE.
DO IT OVER!
RIP
DON'T RIP IT UP!
HARSH!
HOW'S THIS LOOK?
HMMM. I LIKE THIS ENERGY. BUT...
THE "S" IS MISSING SOMETHING!
HERE
WHAT IS THIS, CALLI-GRAPHY CLASS?
SWEET RED-BEAN JELLY, PLEASE!
FROM KIRBY
THUD

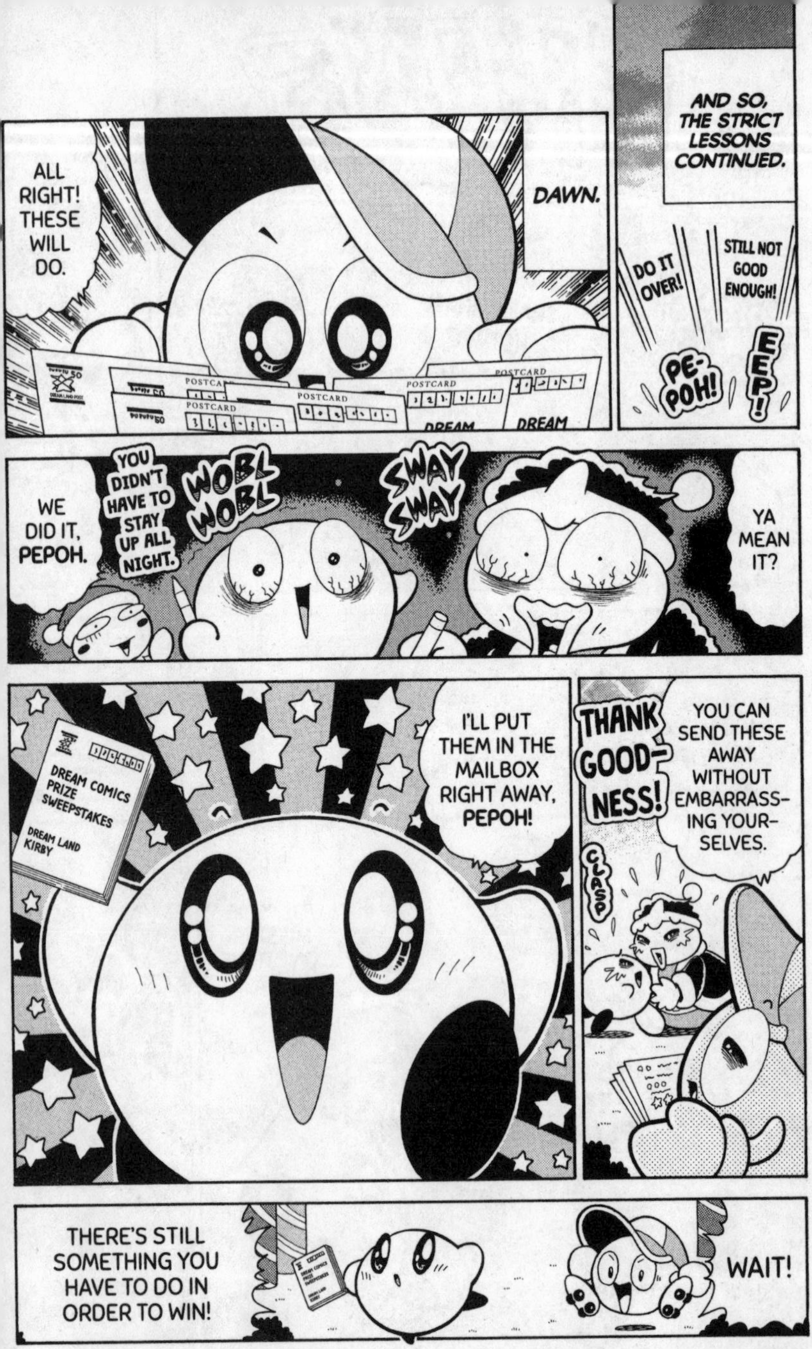
AND SO, THE STRICT LESSONS CONTINUED.
STILL NOT GOOD ENOUGH!
DO IT OVER!
EEP!
PE-POH!
DAWN.
ALL RIGHT! THESE WILL DO.
POSTCARD
DREAM
YA MEAN IT?
SWAY SWAY
WOBL WOBL
YOU DIDN'T HAVE TO STAY UP ALL NIGHT.
WE DID IT, PEPOH.
YOU CAN SEND THESE AWAY WITHOUT EMBARRASS-ING YOUR-SELVES.
THANK GOOD-NESS!
CLASP
I'LL PUT THEM IN THE MAILBOX RIGHT AWAY, PEPOH!
DREAM COMICS PRIZE SWEEPSTAKES
DREAM LAND KIRBY
WAIT!
THERE'S STILL SOMETHING YOU HAVE TO DO IN ORDER TO WIN!

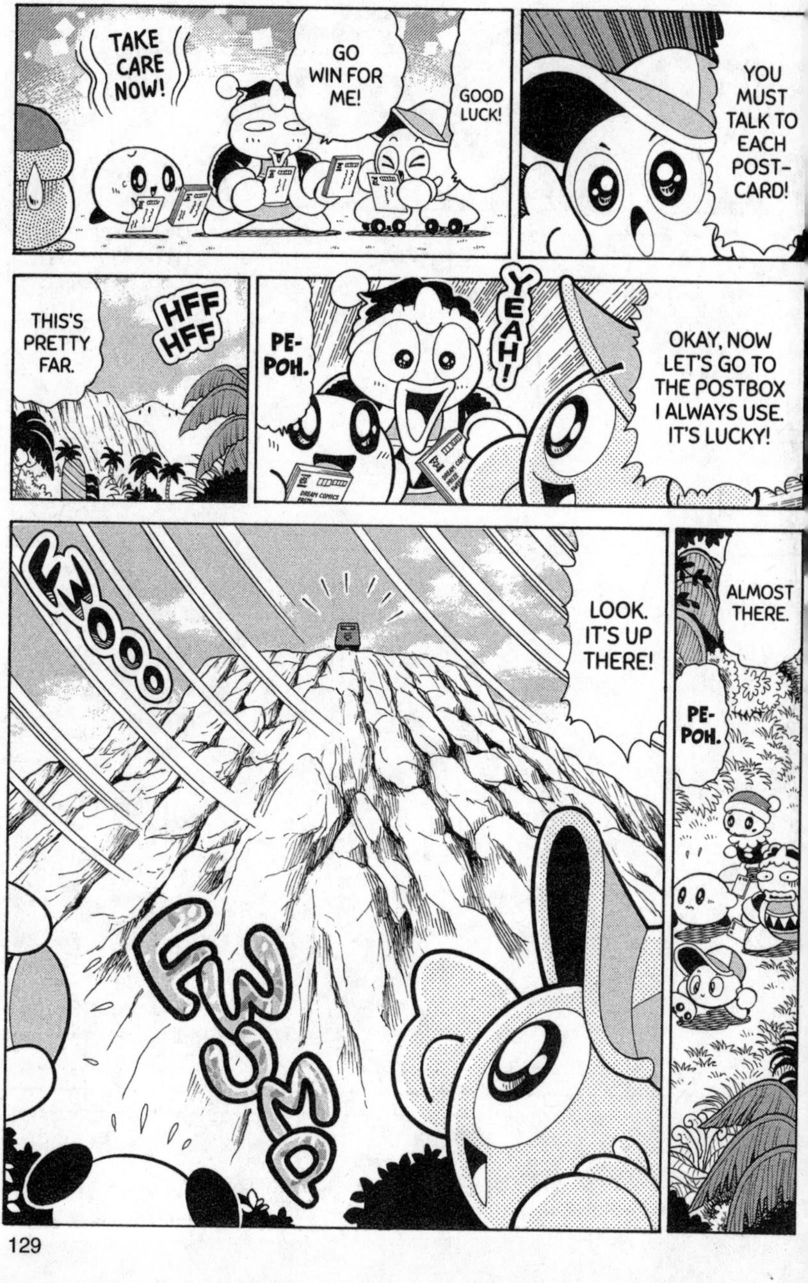
YOU MUST TALK TO EACH POST-CARD!
GOOD LUCK!
GO WIN FOR ME!
TAKE CARE NOW!
OKAY, NOW LET'S GO TO THE POSTBOX I ALWAYS USE. IT'S LUCKY!
YEAH!
PE-POH.
HFF HFF
THIS'S PRETTY FAR.
ALMOST THERE.
PE-POH.
LOOK. IT'S UP THERE!
FWOOO
FWUMP

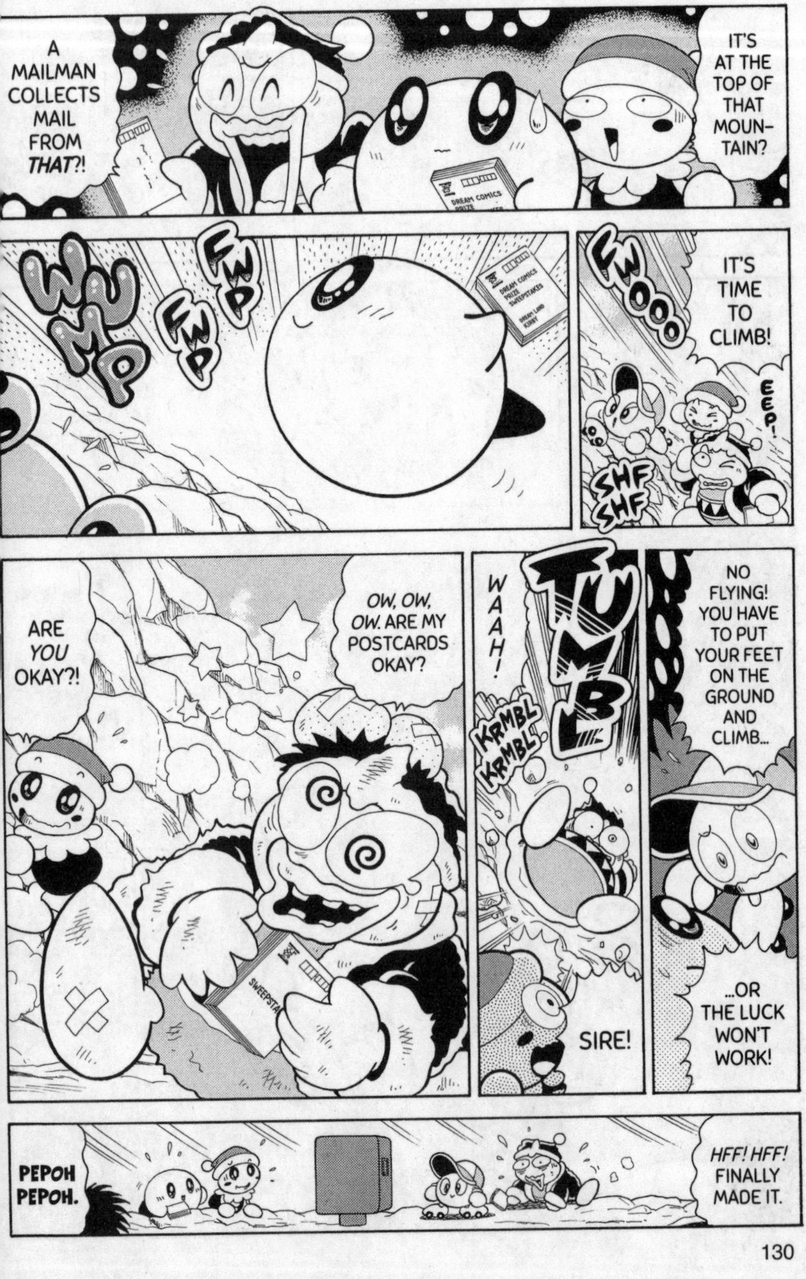
IT'S AT THE TOP OF THAT MOUNTAIN?
A MAILMAN COLLECTS MAIL FROM *THAT*?!
FWOOO
IT'S TIME TO CLIMB!
EEP!
SHF SHF
DREAM COMICS PRIZE SWEEPSTAKES DREAM LAND KIRBY
FWP FWP
FWP
WUMP
NO FLYING! YOU HAVE TO PUT YOUR FEET ON THE GROUND AND CLIMB...
...OR THE LUCK WON'T WORK!
TUMBLE
WAAH!
KRMBL KRMBL
SIRE!
OW, OW, OW. ARE MY POSTCARDS OKAY?
ARE *YOU* OKAY?!
HFF! HFF! FINALLY MADE IT.
PEPOH PEPOH.

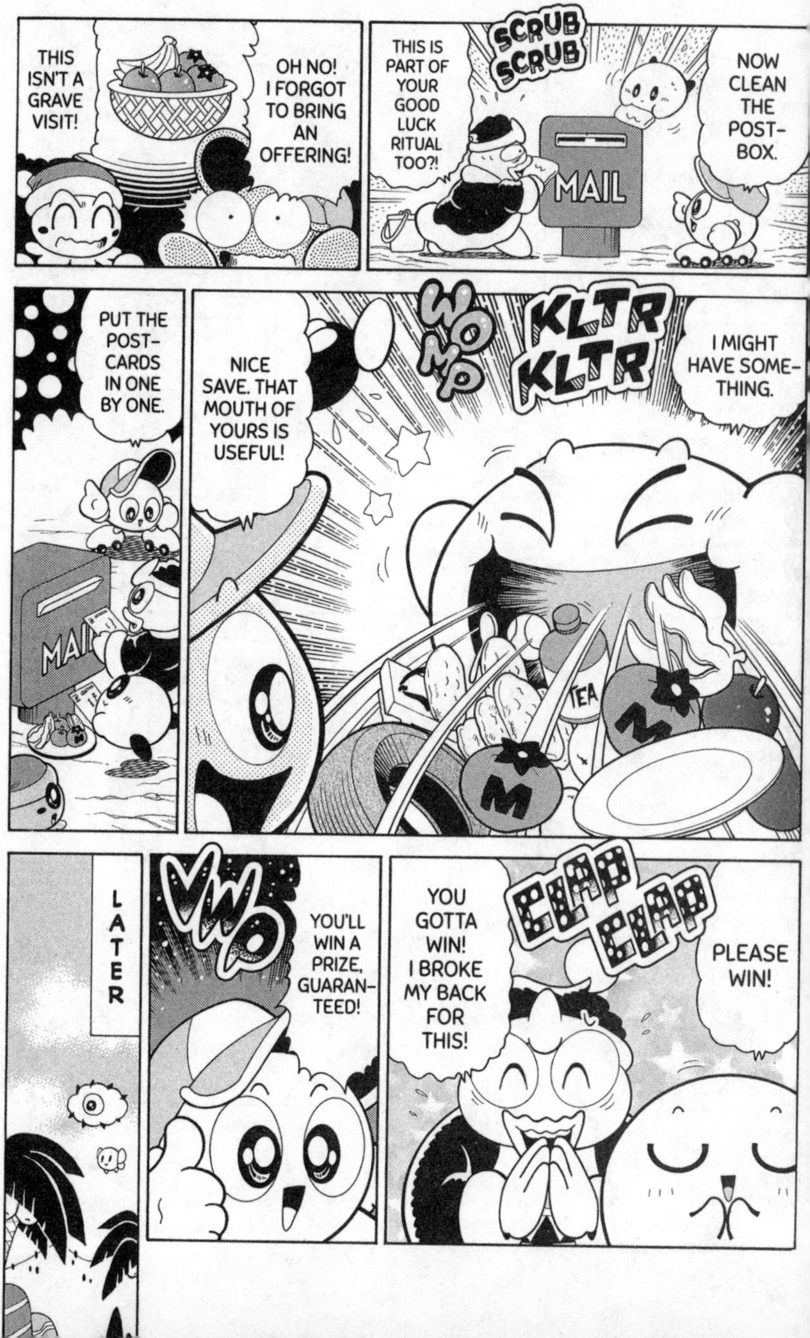
SCRUB SCRUB
NOW CLEAN THE POST-BOX.
THIS IS PART OF YOUR GOOD LUCK RITUAL TOO?!
OH NO! I FORGOT TO BRING AN OFFERING!
THIS ISN'T A GRAVE VISIT!
I MIGHT HAVE SOME-THING.
KLTR KLTR
WOMP
NICE SAVE. THAT MOUTH OF YOURS IS USEFUL!
PUT THE POST-CARDS IN ONE BY ONE.
TEA
MAIL
PLEASE WIN!
CLAP CLAP
YOU GOTTA WIN! I BROKE MY BACK FOR THIS!
YOU'LL WIN A PRIZE, GUARAN-TEED!
LATER

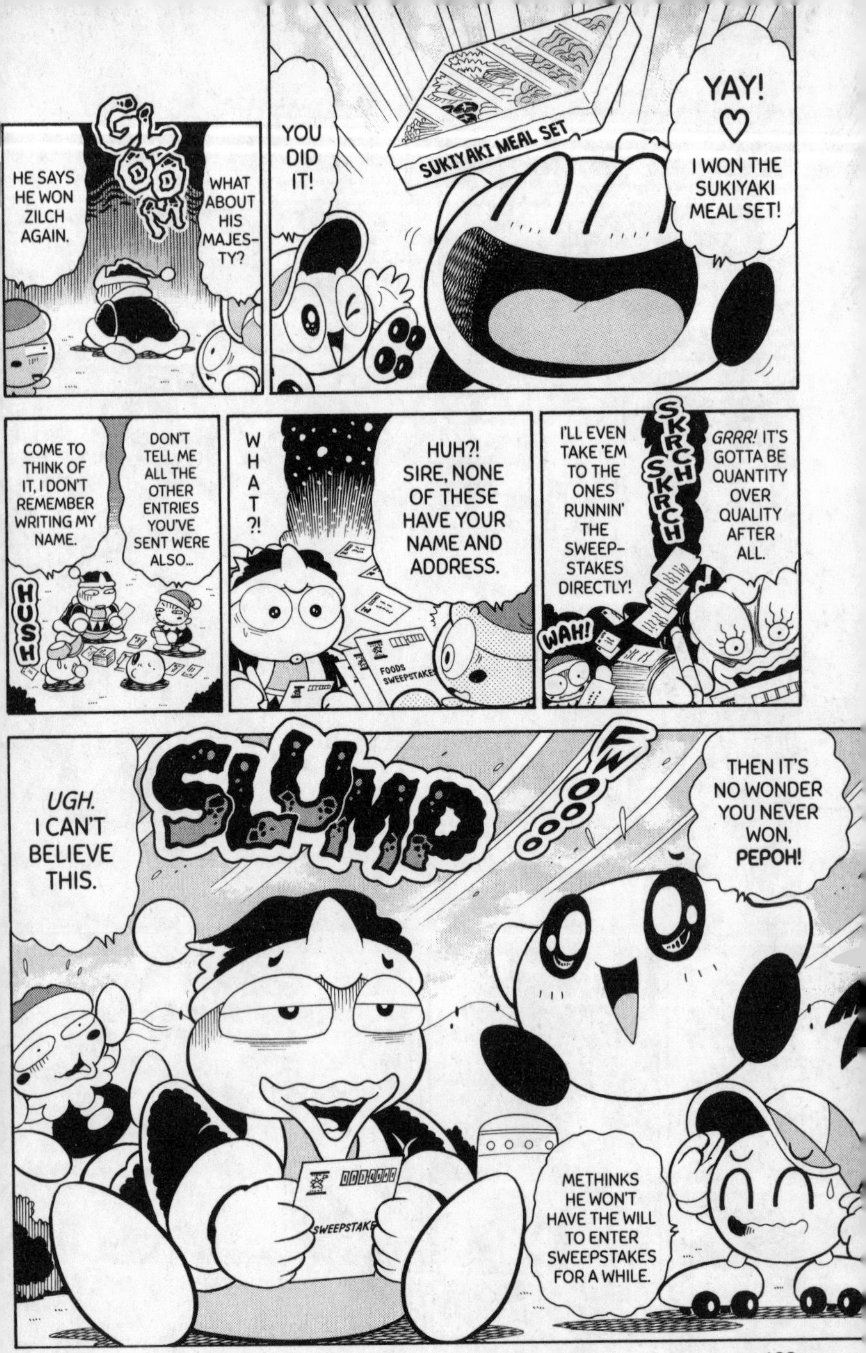
YAY! ♡ I WON THE SUKIYAKI MEAL SET!
SUKIYAKI MEAL SET
YOU DID IT!
WHAT ABOUT HIS MAJESTY?
GLOOM
HE SAYS HE WON ZILCH AGAIN.
GRRR! IT'S GOTTA BE QUANTITY OVER QUALITY AFTER ALL.
SKRCH SKRCH
I'LL EVEN TAKE 'EM TO THE ONES RUNNIN' THE SWEEPSTAKES DIRECTLY!
WAH!
HUH?! SIRE, NONE OF THESE HAVE YOUR NAME AND ADDRESS.
FOODS SWEEPSTAKES
WHAT?!
DON'T TELL ME ALL THE OTHER ENTRIES YOU'VE SENT WERE ALSO...
COME TO THINK OF IT, I DON'T REMEMBER WRITING MY NAME.
HUSH
THEN IT'S NO WONDER YOU NEVER WON, **PEPOH!**
FWOOOO
SLUMP
UGH. I CAN'T BELIEVE THIS.
METHINKS HE WON'T HAVE THE WILL TO ENTER SWEEPSTAKES FOR A WHILE.
SWEEPSTAKE

CHAPTER 12: LEGENDARY TEACHER KIRBY!

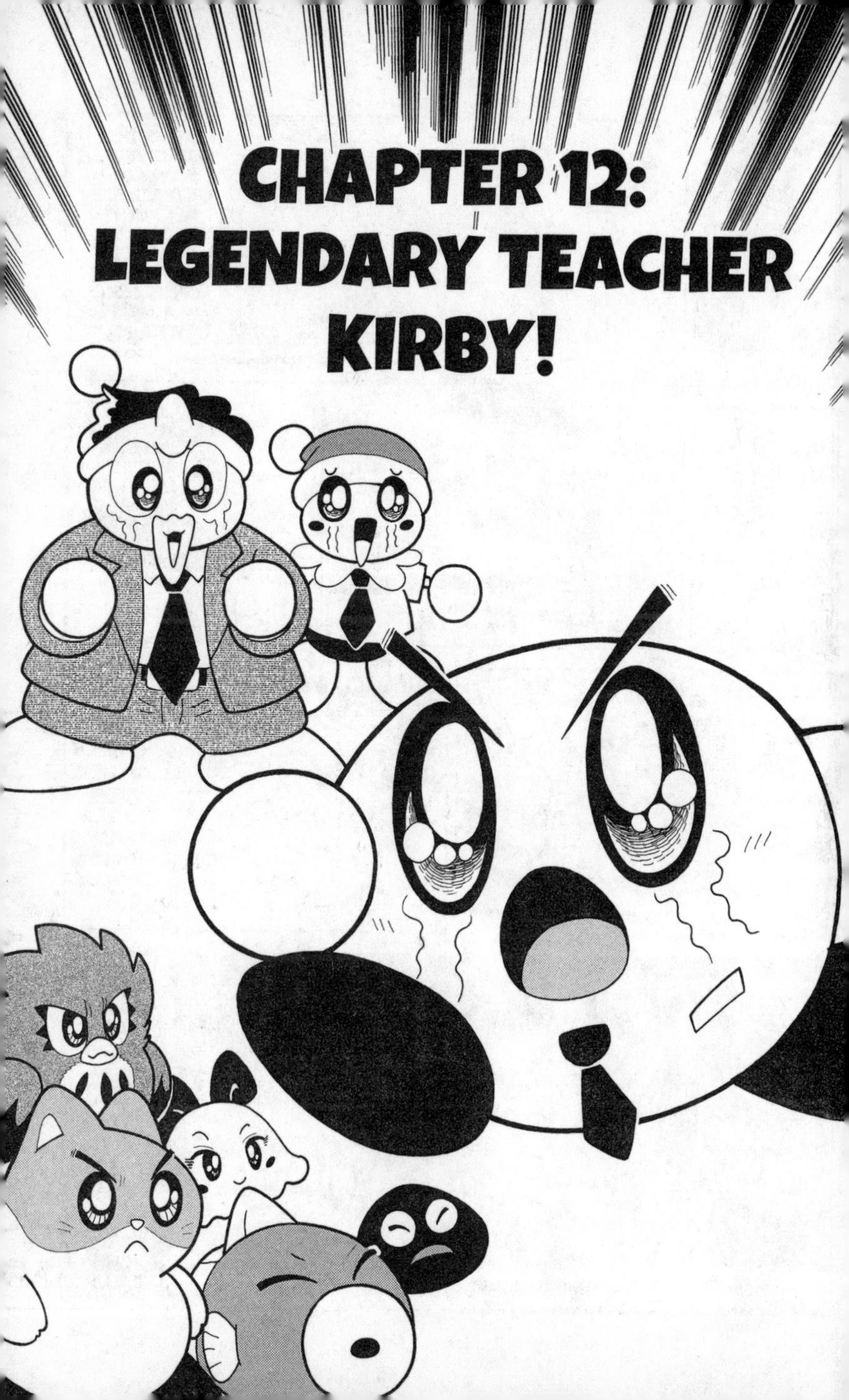

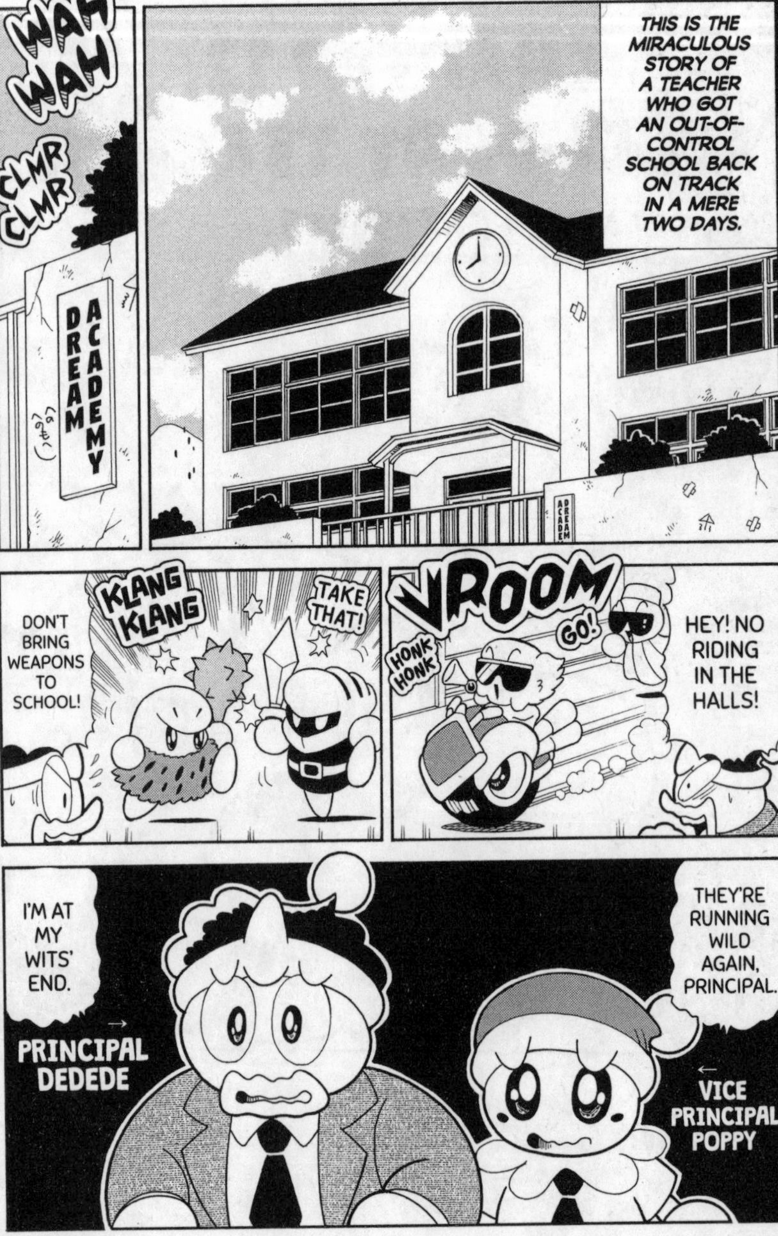
THIS IS THE MIRACULOUS STORY OF A TEACHER WHO GOT AN OUT-OF-CONTROL SCHOOL BACK ON TRACK IN A MERE TWO DAYS.
WAH WAH
CLMR CLMR
DREAM ACADEMY
VROOM
GO!
HONK HONK
HEY! NO RIDING IN THE HALLS!
TAKE THAT!
KLANG KLANG
DON'T BRING WEAPONS TO SCHOOL!
THEY'RE RUNNING WILD AGAIN, PRINCIPAL.
VICE PRINCIPAL POPPY
I'M AT MY WITS' END.
PRINCIPAL DEDEDE

AUTHOR'S COMMENT

THE STANDARD "TEACHERS" CHAPTER IS ALWAYS A SURE BET. KIRBY MIGHT BE A BETTER ACTOR THAN I THOUGHT. MAYBE I COULD HAVE DONE MORE "WHAT IF KIRBY WAS A..." CHAPTERS.

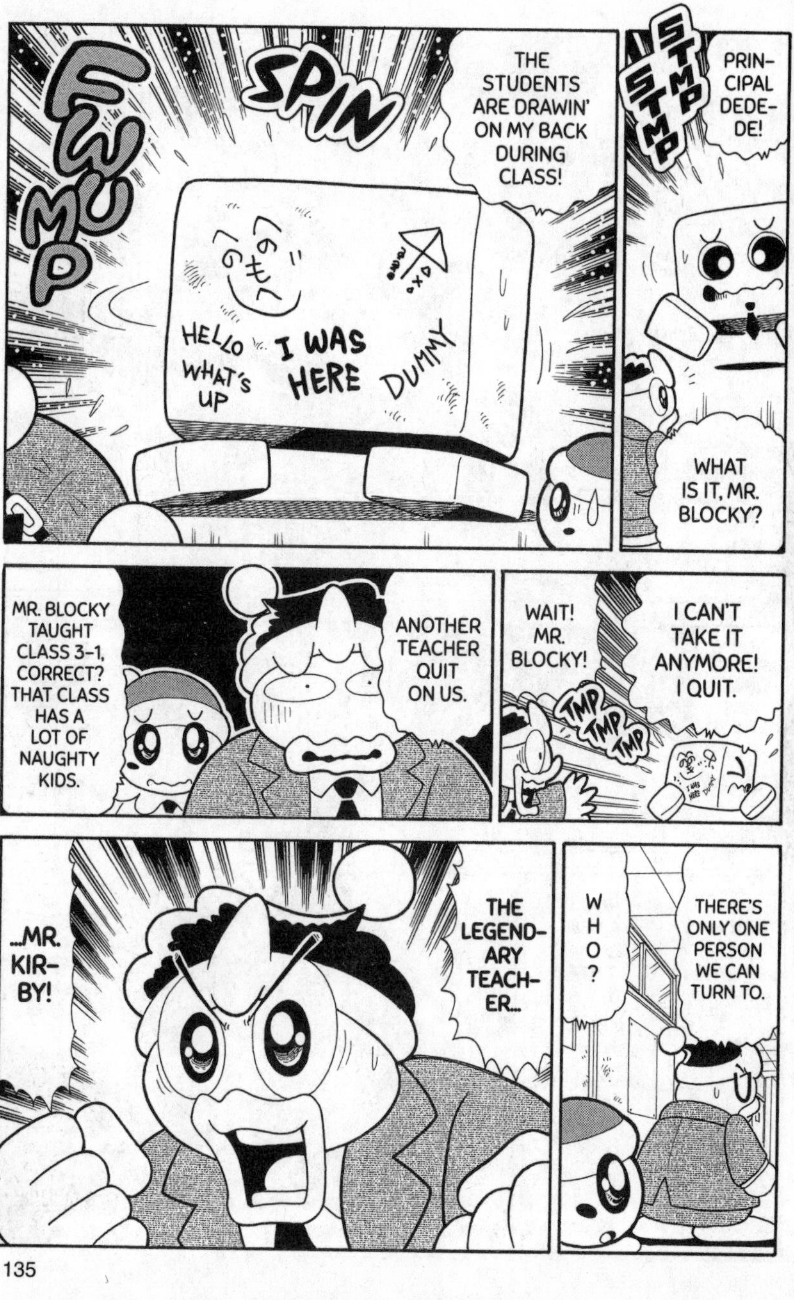
PRIN-CIPAL DEDE-DE!
STMP STMP
WHAT IS IT, MR. BLOCKY?
THE STUDENTS ARE DRAWIN' ON MY BACK DURING CLASS!
SPIN
FWUMP
DUMMY
I WAS HERE
HELLO WHAT'S UP
I CAN'T TAKE IT ANYMORE! I QUIT.
WAIT! MR. BLOCKY!
TMP TMP TMP
ANOTHER TEACHER QUIT ON US.
MR. BLOCKY TAUGHT CLASS 3-1, CORRECT? THAT CLASS HAS A LOT OF NAUGHTY KIDS.
THERE'S ONLY ONE PERSON WE CAN TURN TO.
WHO?
THE LEGEND-ARY TEACH-ER...
...MR. KIR-BY!

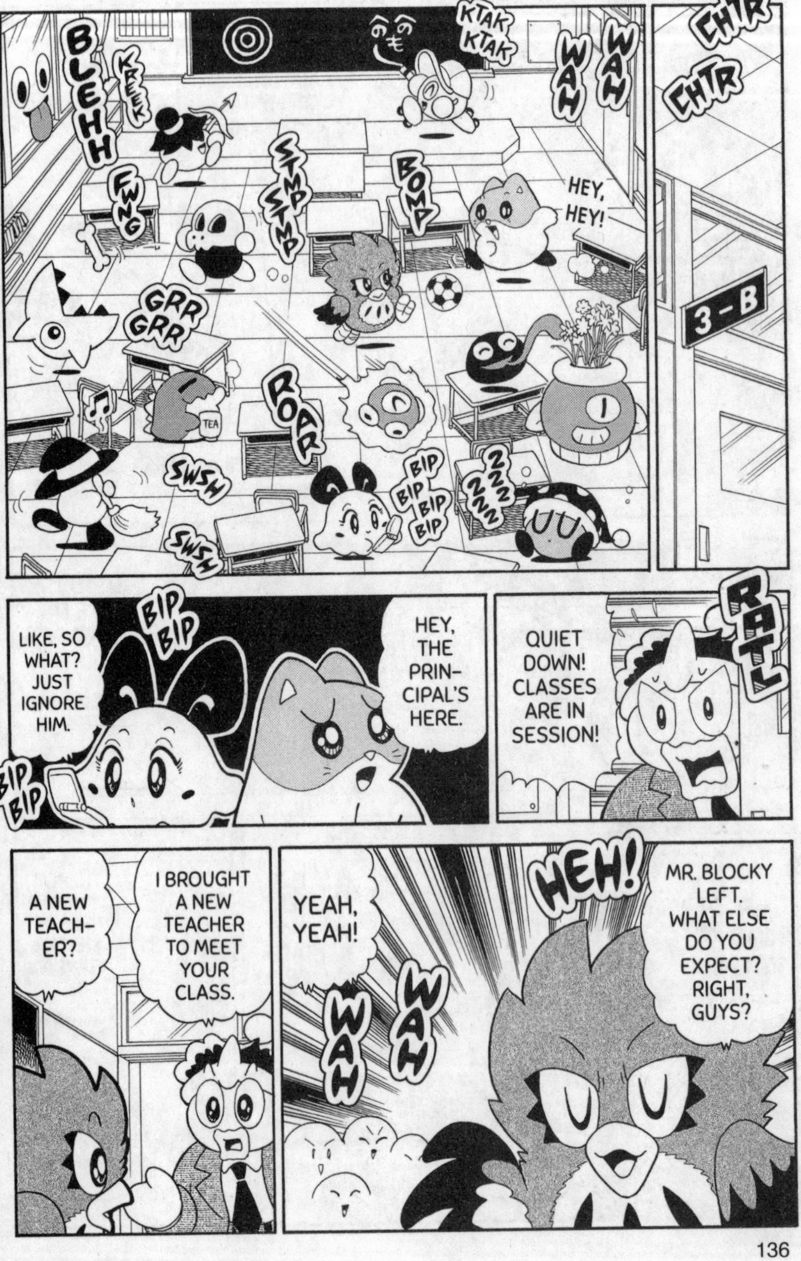
CHTR
CHTR
3-B
KTAK KTAK
WAH WAH
BLEHH
KREEK
STMP STMP
BOMP
HEY, HEY!
FWNG
GRR GRR
TEA
ROAR
SWSH
SWSH
BIP BIP BIP BIP
ZZZ ZZZ
RATL
QUIET DOWN! CLASSES ARE IN SESSION!
HEY, THE PRIN-CIPAL'S HERE.
BIP BIP
LIKE, SO WHAT? JUST IGNORE HIM.
BIP BIP
HEH!
MR. BLOCKY LEFT. WHAT ELSE DO YOU EXPECT? RIGHT, GUYS?
YEAH, YEAH!
WAH WAH
I BROUGHT A NEW TEACHER TO MEET YOUR CLASS.
A NEW TEACH-ER?

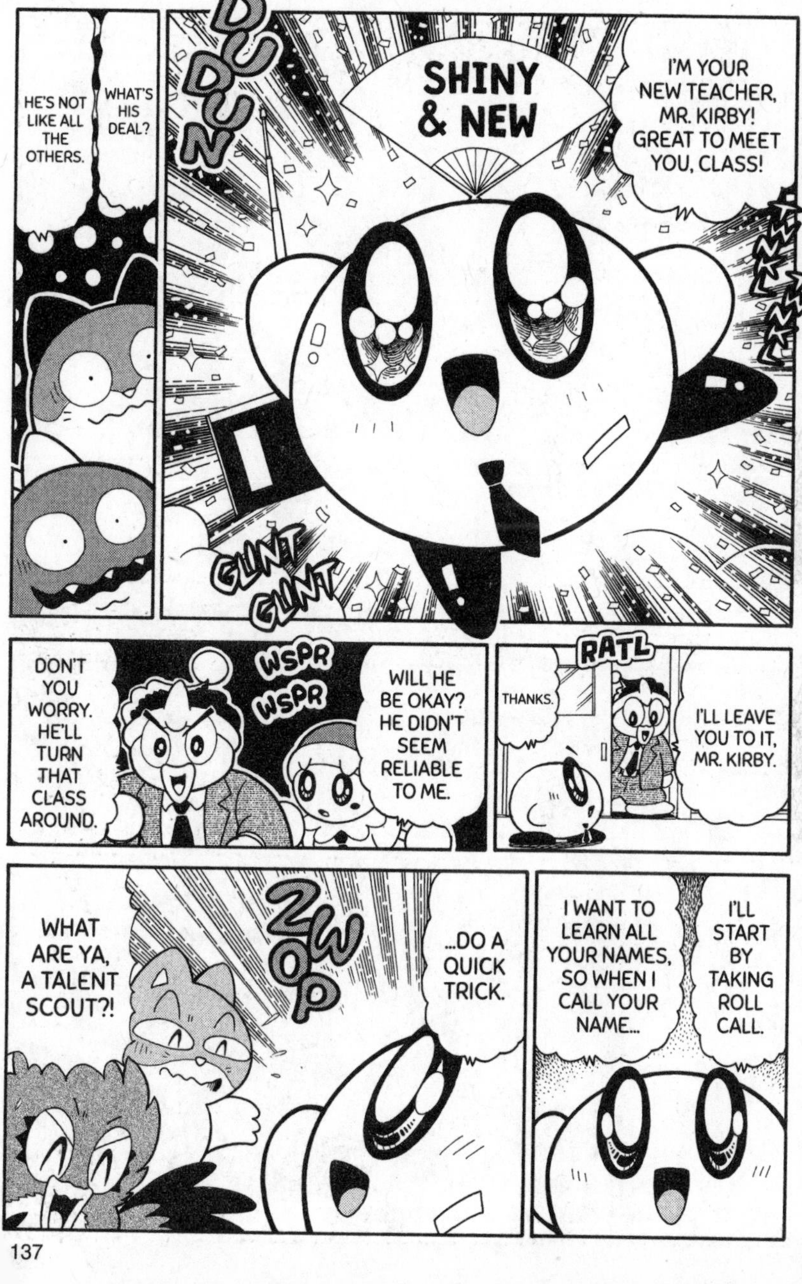
I'M YOUR NEW TEACHER, MR. KIRBY! GREAT TO MEET YOU, CLASS!
TINKL TINKL
SHINY & NEW
DUDUN
GLINT GLINT
WHAT'S HIS DEAL?
HE'S NOT LIKE ALL THE OTHERS.
RATL
I'LL LEAVE YOU TO IT, MR. KIRBY.
THANKS.
WILL HE BE OKAY? HE DIDN'T SEEM RELIABLE TO ME.
WSPR WSPR
DON'T YOU WORRY. HE'LL TURN THAT CLASS AROUND.
I'LL START BY TAKING ROLL CALL.
I WANT TO LEARN ALL YOUR NAMES, SO WHEN I CALL YOUR NAME...
...DO A QUICK TRICK.
ZWOP
WHAT ARE YA, A TALENT SCOUT?!

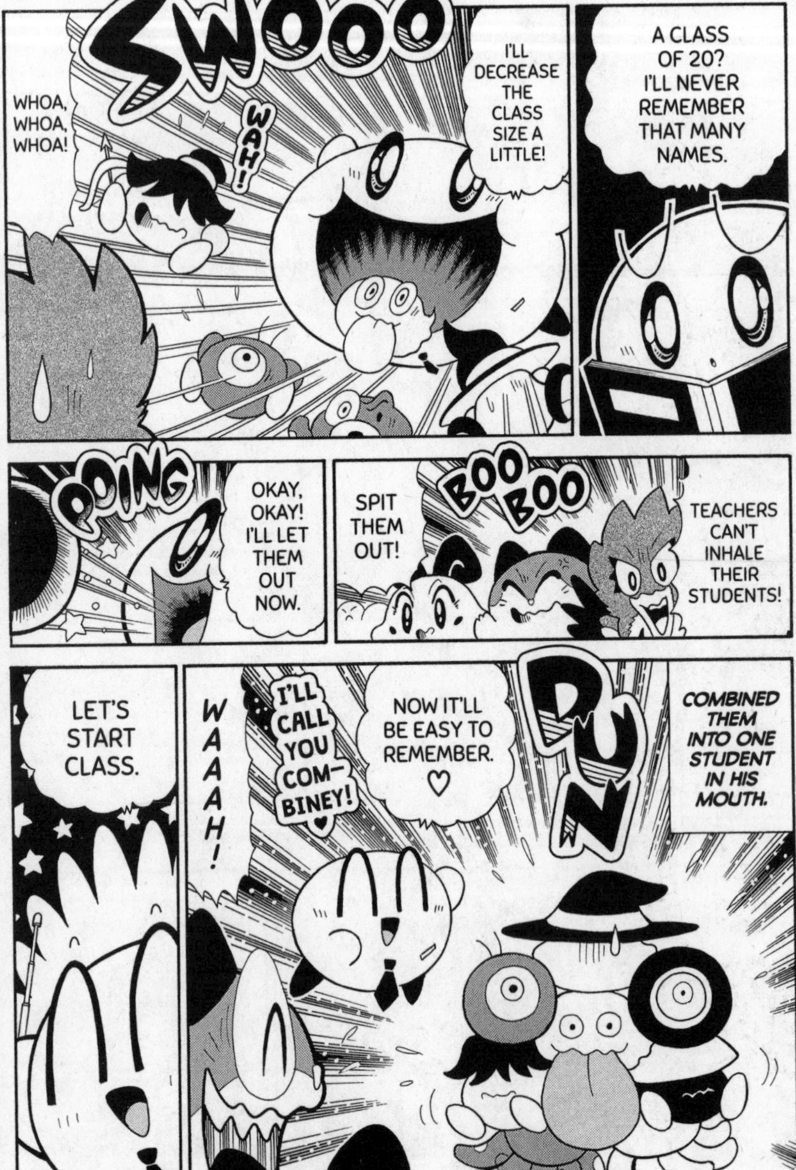
A CLASS OF 20? I'LL NEVER REMEMBER THAT MANY NAMES.
I'LL DECREASE THE CLASS SIZE A LITTLE!
SWOOO
WAH!
WHOA, WHOA, WHOA!
TEACHERS CAN'T INHALE THEIR STUDENTS!
BOO BOO
SPIT THEM OUT!
OKAY, OKAY! I'LL LET THEM OUT NOW.
POING
COMBINED THEM INTO ONE STUDENT IN HIS MOUTH.
DUN
NOW IT'LL BE EASY TO REMEMBER. ♡
I'LL CALL YOU COM-BINEY! ♥
WAAAAH!
LET'S START CLASS.

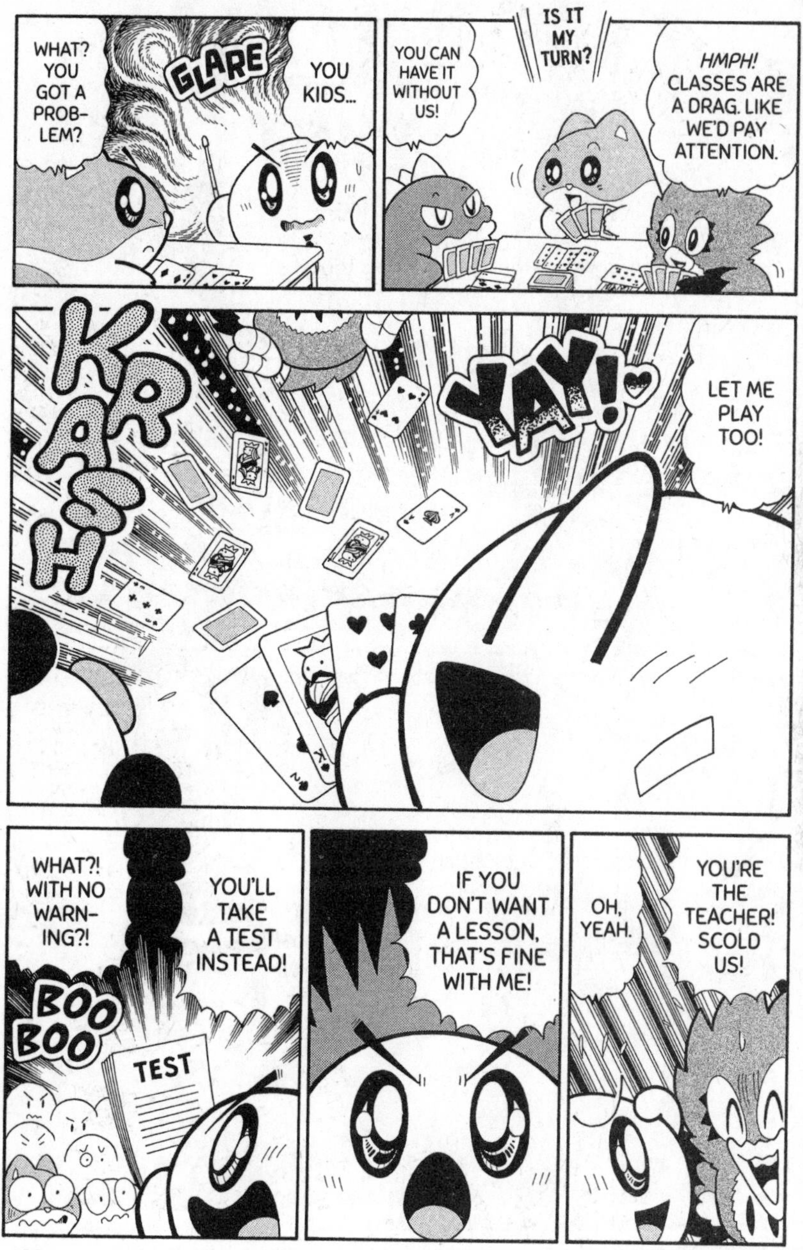
HMPH! CLASSES ARE A DRAG. LIKE WE'D PAY ATTENTION.
IS IT MY TURN?
YOU CAN HAVE IT WITHOUT US!
YOU KIDS...
GLARE
WHAT? YOU GOT A PROB-LEM?
LET ME PLAY TOO!
YAY!
KRASH
YOU'RE THE TEACHER! SCOLD US!
OH, YEAH.
IF YOU DON'T WANT A LESSON, THAT'S FINE WITH ME!
YOU'LL TAKE A TEST INSTEAD!
WHAT?! WITH NO WARNING?!
BOO BOO
TEST

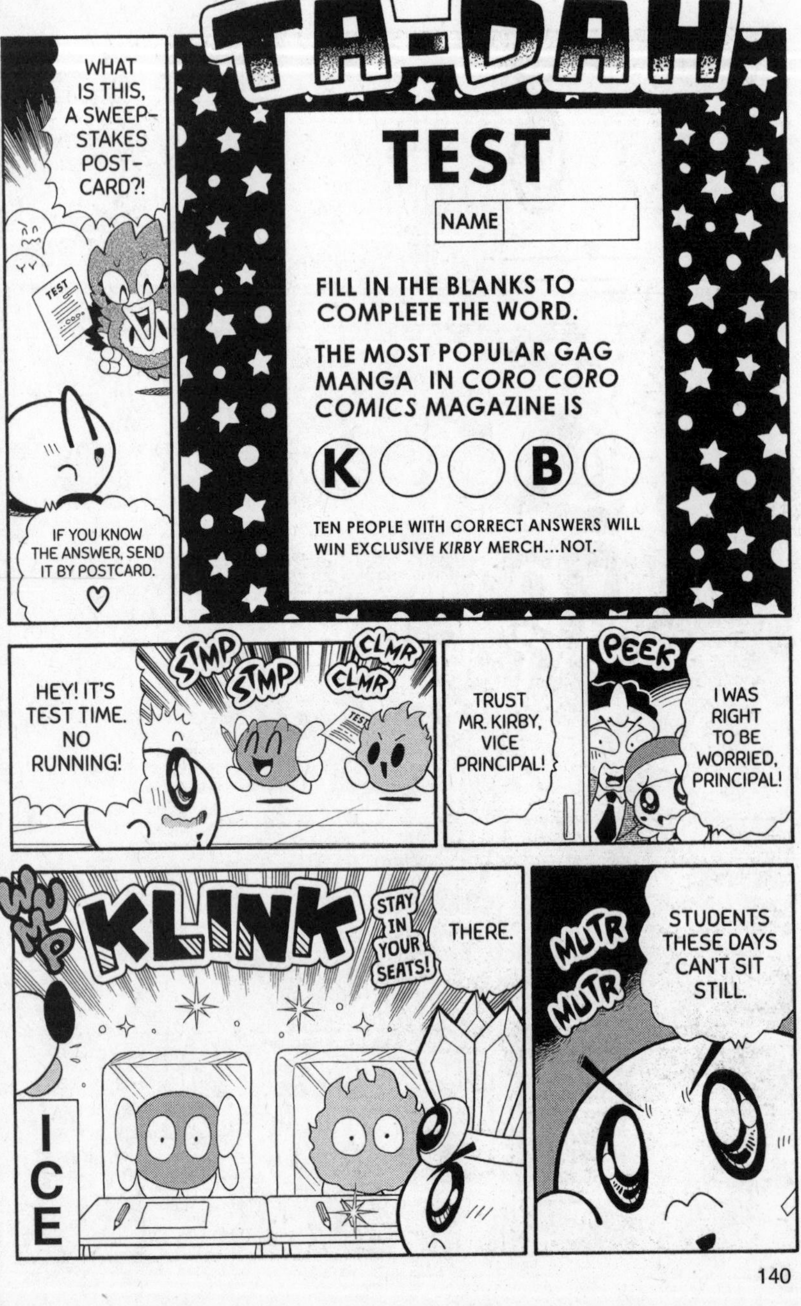
TA-DAH
TEST
NAME
FILL IN THE BLANKS TO COMPLETE THE WORD.
THE MOST POPULAR GAG MANGA IN *CORO CORO COMICS* MAGAZINE IS
K ○ ○ B ○
TEN PEOPLE WITH CORRECT ANSWERS WILL WIN EXCLUSIVE *KIRBY* MERCH...NOT.
WHAT IS THIS, A SWEEPSTAKES POSTCARD?!
IF YOU KNOW THE ANSWER, SEND IT BY POSTCARD. ♡
PEEK
I WAS RIGHT TO BE WORRIED, PRINCIPAL!
TRUST MR. KIRBY, VICE PRINCIPAL!
CLMR CLMR
STMP STMP
HEY! IT'S TEST TIME. NO RUNNING!
STUDENTS THESE DAYS CAN'T SIT STILL.
MUTR MUTR
THERE.
STAY IN YOUR SEATS!
KLINK
WMP
ICE

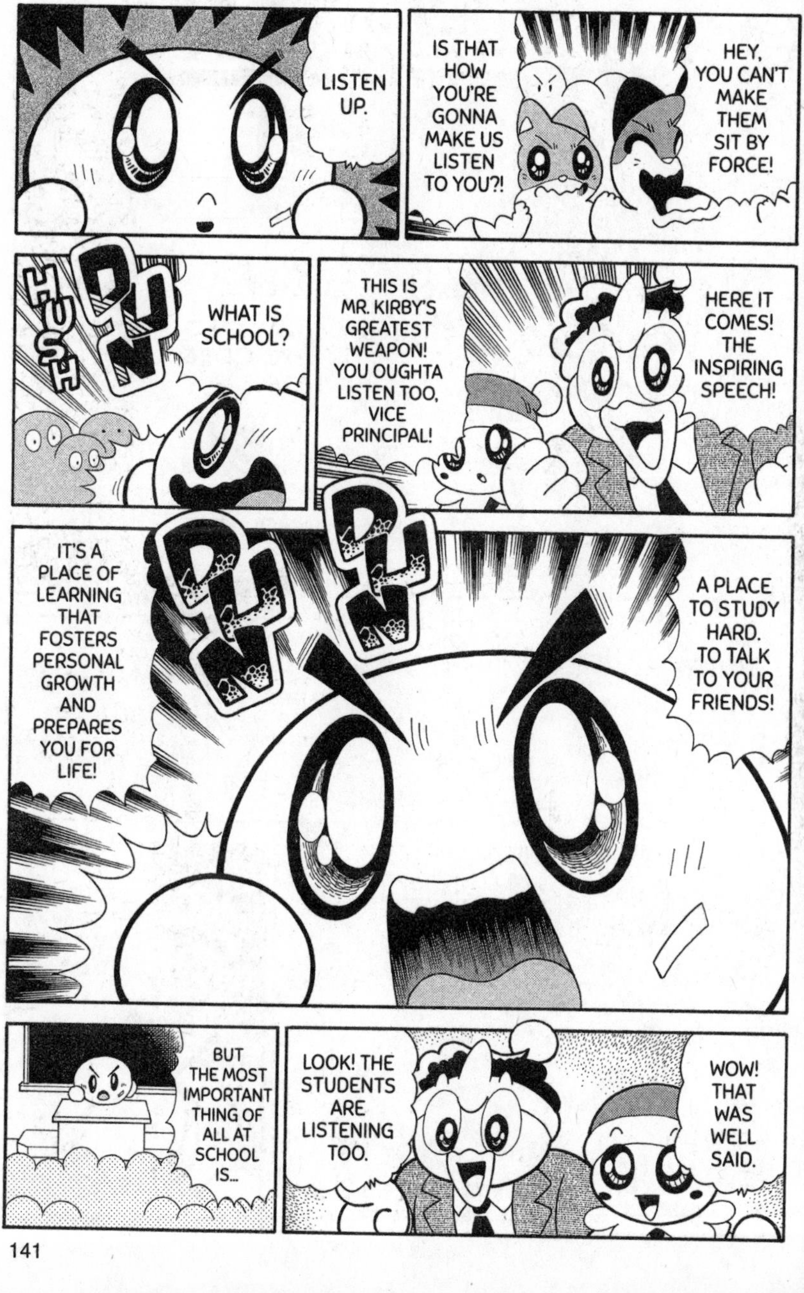
HEY, YOU CAN'T MAKE THEM SIT BY FORCE!
IS THAT HOW YOU'RE GONNA MAKE US LISTEN TO YOU?!
LISTEN UP.
HERE IT COMES! THE INSPIRING SPEECH!
THIS IS MR. KIRBY'S GREATEST WEAPON! YOU OUGHTA LISTEN TOO, VICE PRINCIPAL!
DUN
HUSH
WHAT IS SCHOOL?
DUN
DUN
A PLACE TO STUDY HARD. TO TALK TO YOUR FRIENDS!
IT'S A PLACE OF LEARNING THAT FOSTERS PERSONAL GROWTH AND PREPARES YOU FOR LIFE!
WOW! THAT WAS WELL SAID.
LOOK! THE STUDENTS ARE LISTENING TOO.
BUT THE MOST IMPORTANT THING OF ALL AT SCHOOL IS...

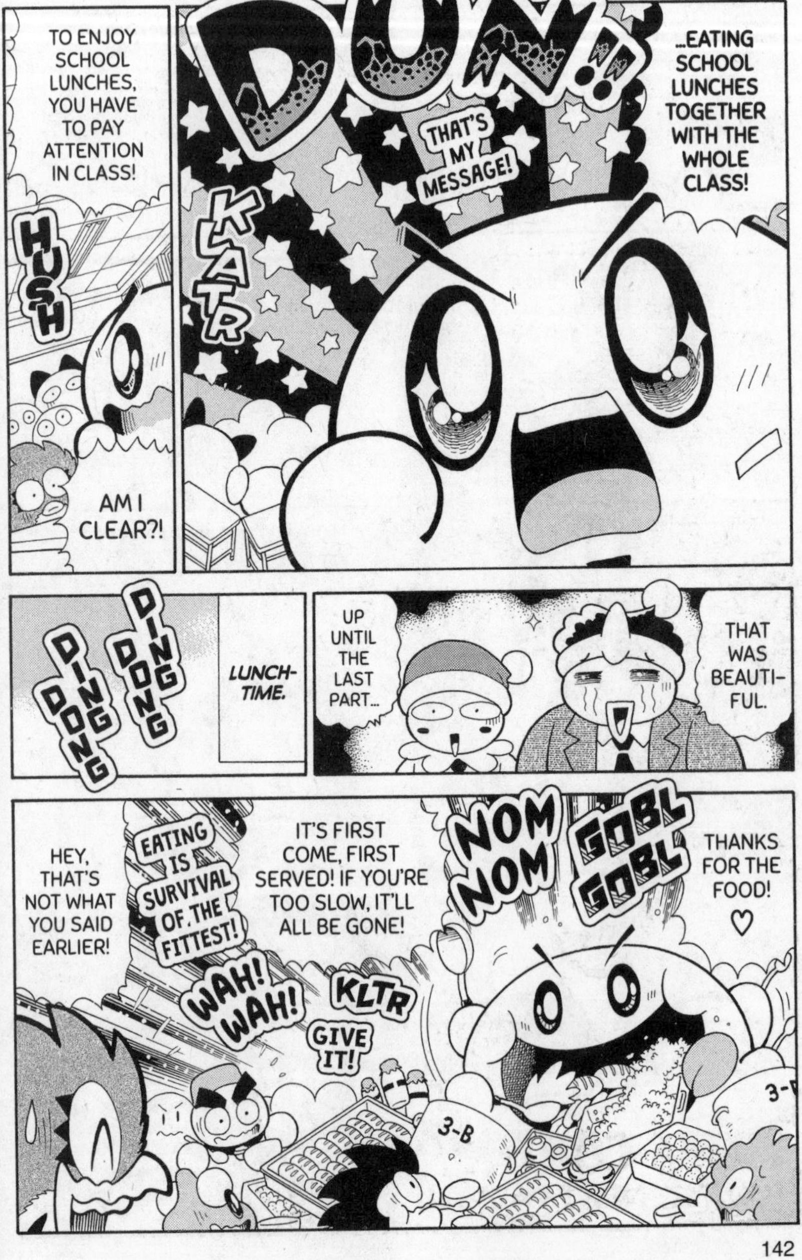
...EATING SCHOOL LUNCHES TOGETHER WITH THE WHOLE CLASS!
DUN!!
THAT'S MY MESSAGE!
KLATR
TO ENJOY SCHOOL LUNCHES, YOU HAVE TO PAY ATTENTION IN CLASS!
HUSH
AM I CLEAR?!
THAT WAS BEAUTI-FUL.
UP UNTIL THE LAST PART...
LUNCH-TIME.
DING DONG
DING DONG
THANKS FOR THE FOOD! ♡
GOBL GOBL
NOM NOM
IT'S FIRST COME, FIRST SERVED! IF YOU'RE TOO SLOW, IT'LL ALL BE GONE!
EATING IS SURVIVAL OF THE FITTEST!
HEY, THAT'S NOT WHAT YOU SAID EARLIER!
KLTR
GIVE IT!
WAH! WAH!
3-B

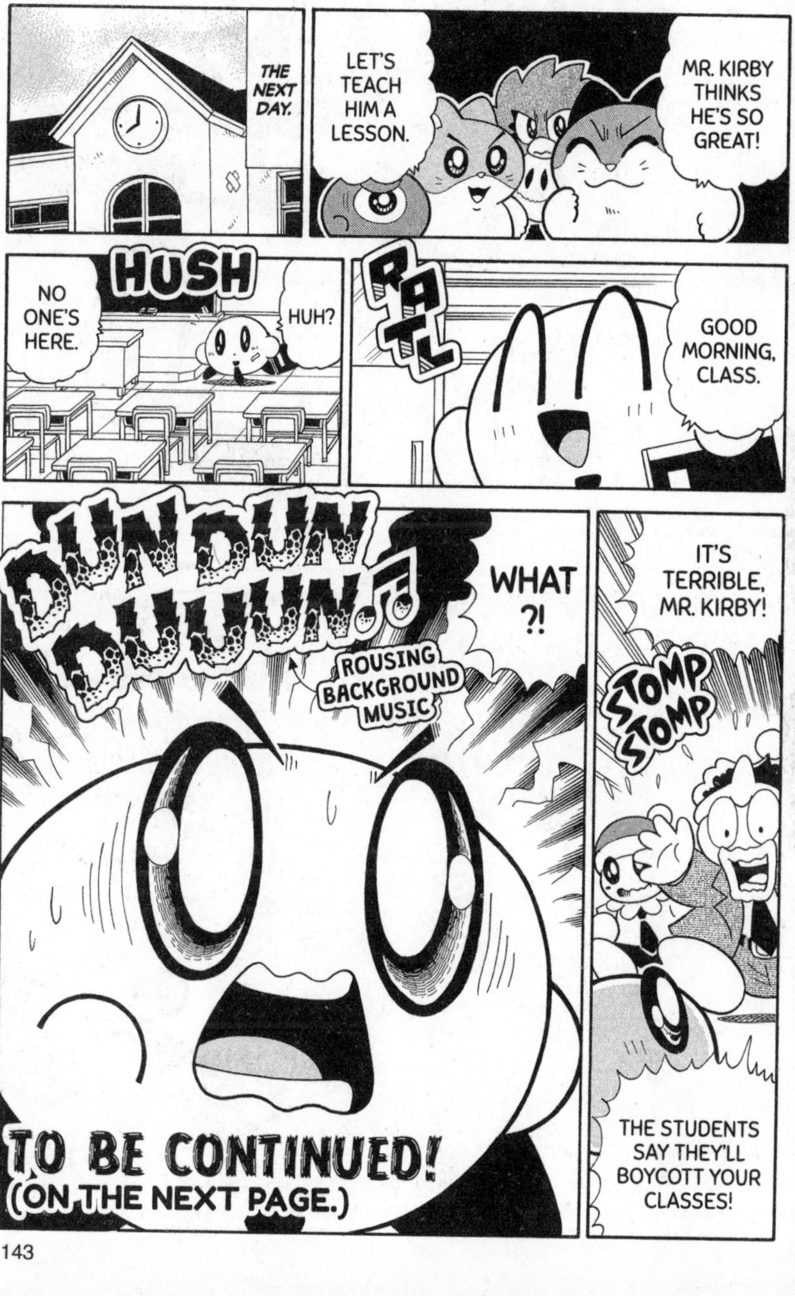
MR. KIRBY THINKS HE'S SO GREAT!
LET'S TEACH HIM A LESSON.
THE NEXT DAY.
RATTL
GOOD MORNING, CLASS.
HUH?
HUSH
NO ONE'S HERE.
IT'S TERRIBLE, MR. KIRBY!
STOMP STOMP
THE STUDENTS SAY THEY'LL BOYCOTT YOUR CLASSES!
WHAT?!
DUN DUN DUUUN
ROUSING BACKGROUND MUSIC
TO BE CONTINUED!
(ON THE NEXT PAGE.)

STORY THUS FAR

MR. KIRBY IS THE NEW TEACHER AT SCHOOL. HIS STUDENTS ARE BOYCOTTING HIS CLASSES. WHAT WILL HE DO NOW?!

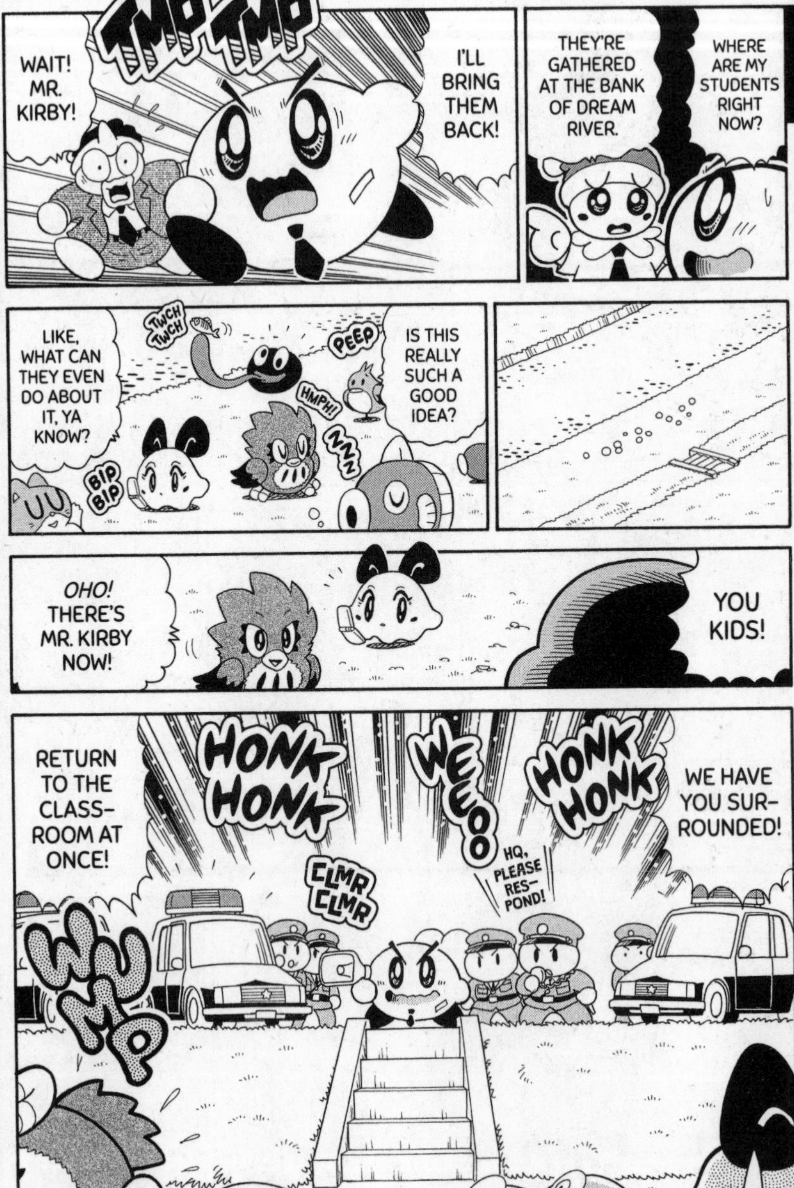
WHERE ARE MY STUDENTS RIGHT NOW?
THEY'RE GATHERED AT THE BANK OF DREAM RIVER.
TMP TMP
I'LL BRING THEM BACK!
WAIT! MR. KIRBY!
PEEP
IS THIS REALLY SUCH A GOOD IDEA?
HMPH!
TWCH TWCH
LIKE, WHAT CAN THEY EVEN DO ABOUT IT, YA KNOW?
BIP BIP
YOU KIDS!
OHO! THERE'S MR. KIRBY NOW!
WE HAVE YOU SUR-ROUNDED!
HONK HONK
WEEOO
HQ, PLEASE RES-POND!
HONK HONK
CLMR CLMR
RETURN TO THE CLASS-ROOM AT ONCE!
WUMP

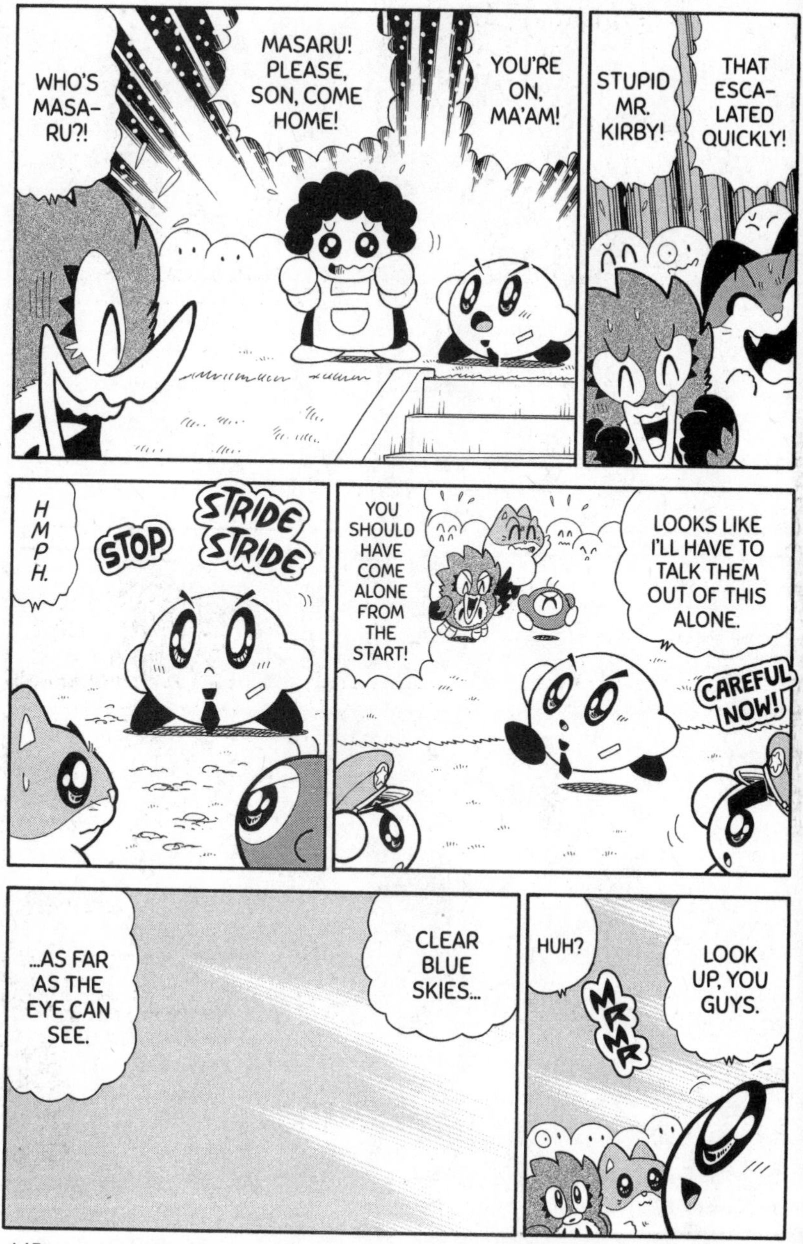
THAT ESCA-LATED QUICKLY!
STUPID MR. KIRBY!
YOU'RE ON, MA'AM!
MASARU! PLEASE, SON, COME HOME!
WHO'S MASA-RU?!
LOOKS LIKE I'LL HAVE TO TALK THEM OUT OF THIS ALONE.
CAREFUL NOW!
YOU SHOULD HAVE COME ALONE FROM THE START!
STRIDE STRIDE
STOP
HMPH.
LOOK UP, YOU GUYS.
HUH?
MRMR
CLEAR BLUE SKIES...
...AS FAR AS THE EYE CAN SEE.

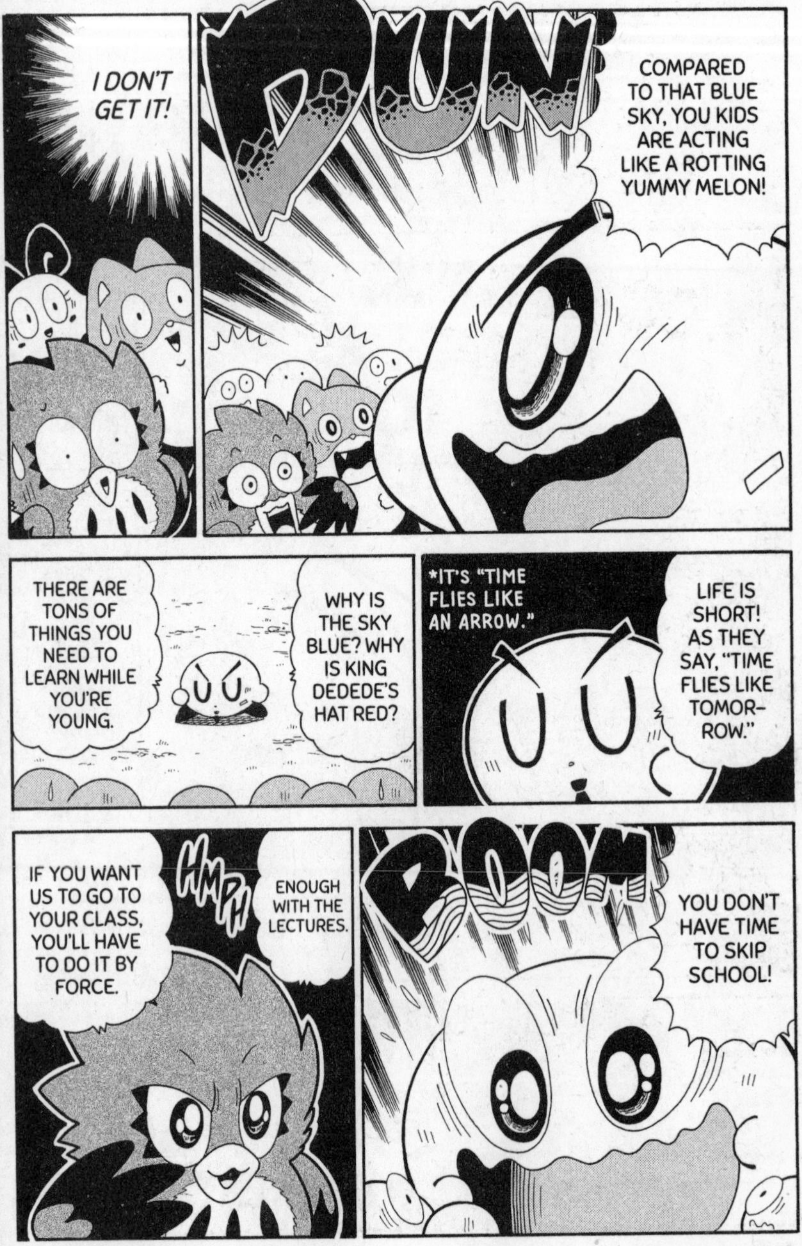
DUN
COMPARED TO THAT BLUE SKY, YOU KIDS ARE ACTING LIKE A ROTTING YUMMY MELON!
I DON'T GET IT!
LIFE IS SHORT! AS THEY SAY, "TIME FLIES LIKE TOMORROW."
*IT'S "TIME FLIES LIKE AN ARROW."
WHY IS THE SKY BLUE? WHY IS KING DEDEDE'S HAT RED?
THERE ARE TONS OF THINGS YOU NEED TO LEARN WHILE YOU'RE YOUNG.
BOOM
YOU DON'T HAVE TIME TO SKIP SCHOOL!
ENOUGH WITH THE LECTURES.
HMPH
IF YOU WANT US TO GO TO YOUR CLASS, YOU'LL HAVE TO DO IT BY FORCE.

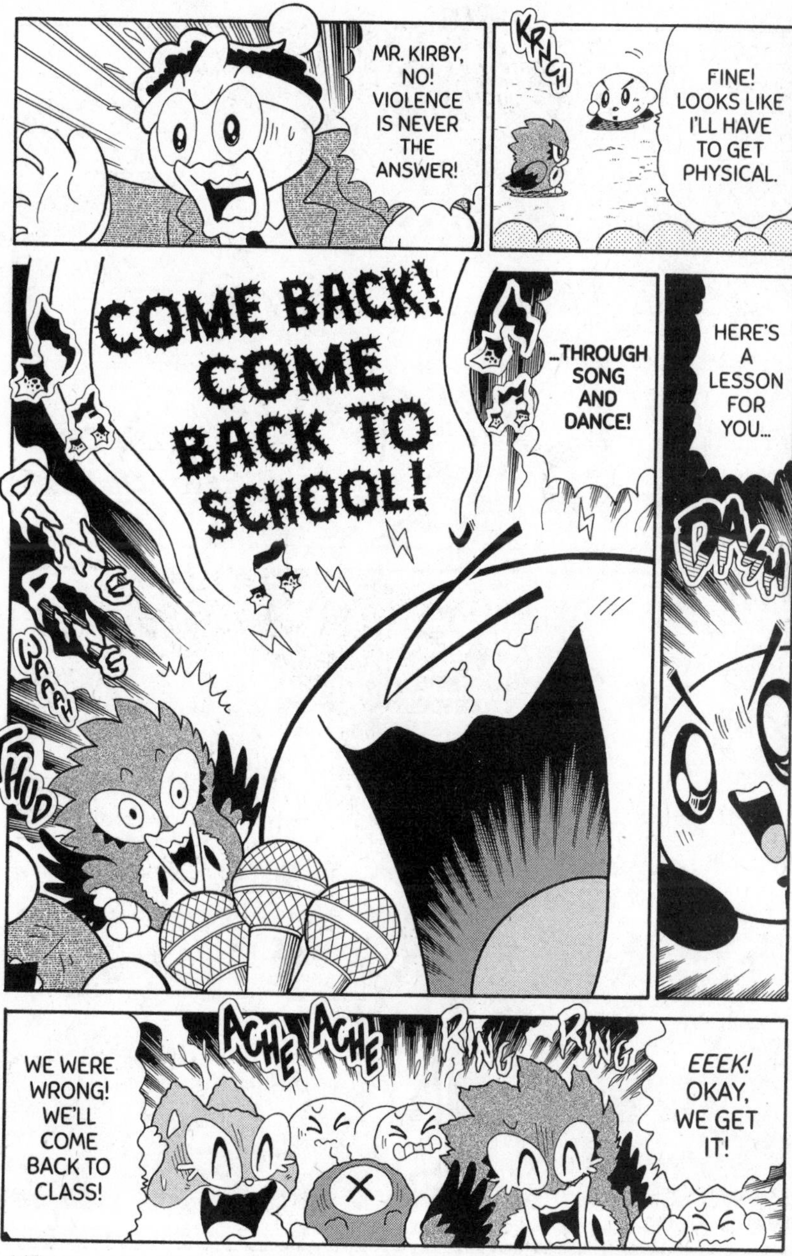
KRNCH
FINE! LOOKS LIKE I'LL HAVE TO GET PHYSICAL.
MR. KIRBY, NO! VIOLENCE IS NEVER THE ANSWER!
HERE'S A LESSON FOR YOU...
BASH
...THROUGH SONG AND DANCE!
COME BACK! COME BACK TO SCHOOL!
RING RING
WAAAH
THUD
EEEK! OKAY, WE GET IT!
RING RING
ACHE ACHE
WE WERE WRONG! WE'LL COME BACK TO CLASS!

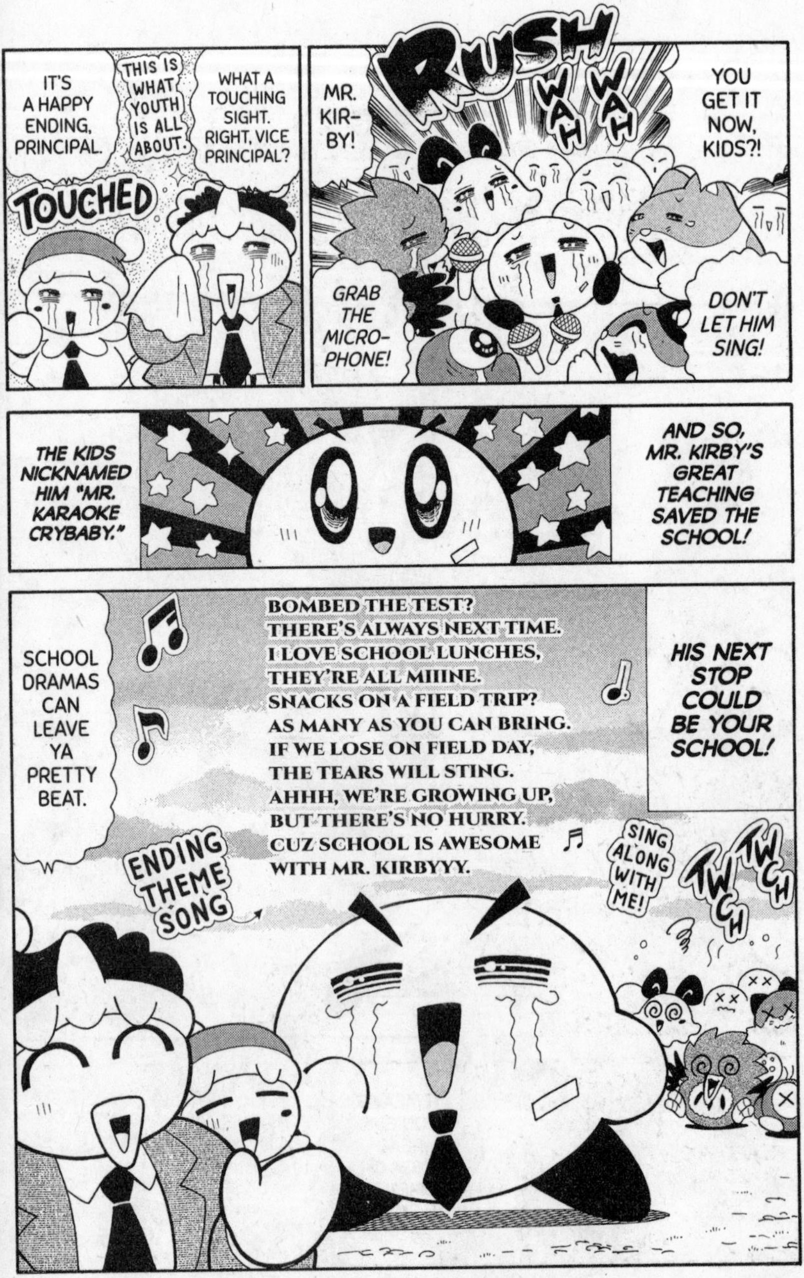
YOU GET IT NOW, KIDS?!
RUSH
WAH WAH
MR. KIRBY!
DON'T LET HIM SING!
GRAB THE MICROPHONE!
WHAT A TOUCHING SIGHT. RIGHT, VICE PRINCIPAL?
THIS IS WHAT YOUTH IS ALL ABOUT.
IT'S A HAPPY ENDING, PRINCIPAL.
TOUCHED
AND SO, MR. KIRBY'S GREAT TEACHING SAVED THE SCHOOL!
THE KIDS NICKNAMED HIM "MR. KARAOKE CRYBABY."
HIS NEXT STOP COULD BE YOUR SCHOOL!
BOMBED THE TEST? THERE'S ALWAYS NEXT TIME. I LOVE SCHOOL LUNCHES, THEY'RE ALL MIIINE. SNACKS ON A FIELD TRIP? AS MANY AS YOU CAN BRING. IF WE LOSE ON FIELD DAY, THE TEARS WILL STING. AHHH, WE'RE GROWING UP, BUT THERE'S NO HURRY. CUZ SCHOOL IS AWESOME WITH MR. KIRBYYY.
SCHOOL DRAMAS CAN LEAVE YA PRETTY BEAT.
SING ALONG WITH ME!
TWCH TWCH
ENDING THEME SONG

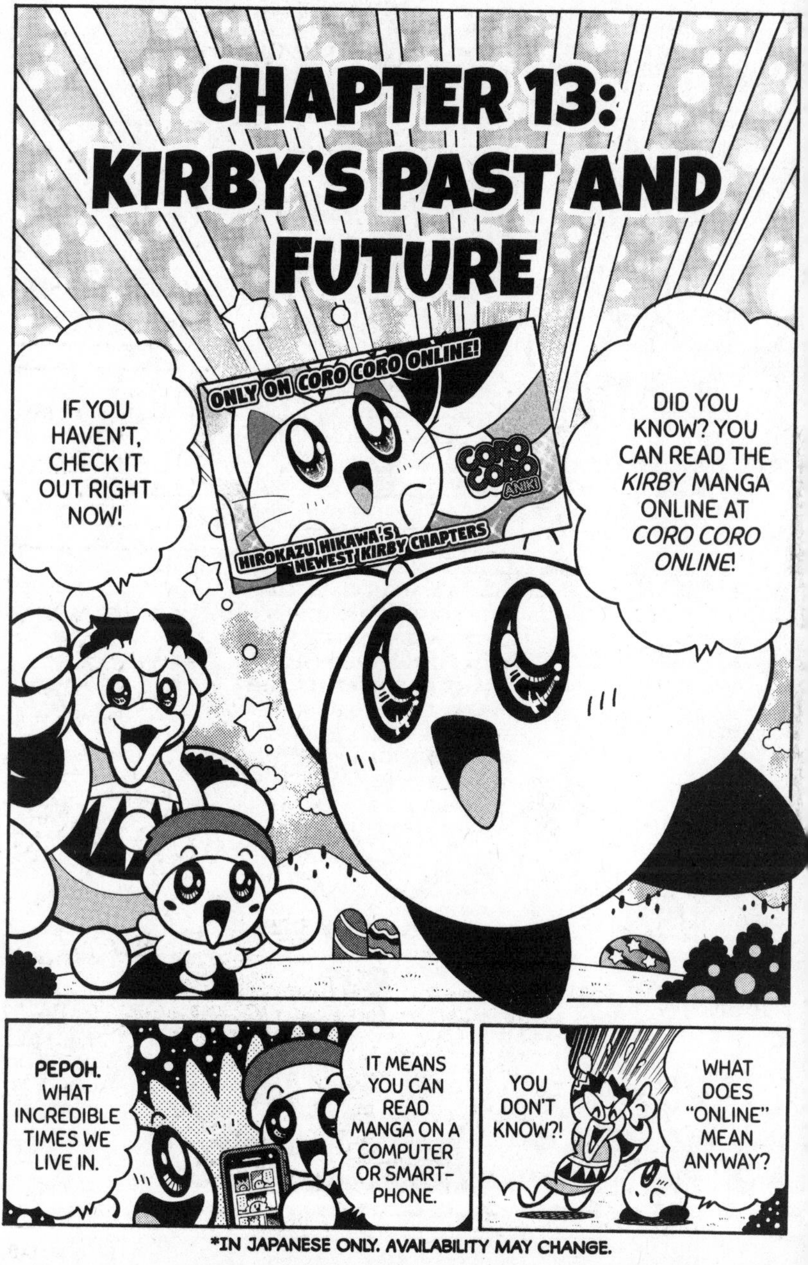
CHAPTER 13: KIRBY'S PAST AND FUTURE
DID YOU KNOW? YOU CAN READ THE *KIRBY* MANGA ONLINE AT *CORO CORO ONLINE*!
ONLY ON CORO CORO ONLINE!
CORO CORO ANIKI
HIROKAZU HIKAWA'S NEWEST KIRBY CHAPTERS
IF YOU HAVEN'T, CHECK IT OUT RIGHT NOW!
WHAT DOES "ONLINE" MEAN ANYWAY?
YOU DON'T KNOW?!
IT MEANS YOU CAN READ MANGA ON A COMPUTER OR SMART-PHONE.
PEPOH. WHAT INCREDIBLE TIMES WE LIVE IN.

*IN JAPANESE ONLY. AVAILABILITY MAY CHANGE.

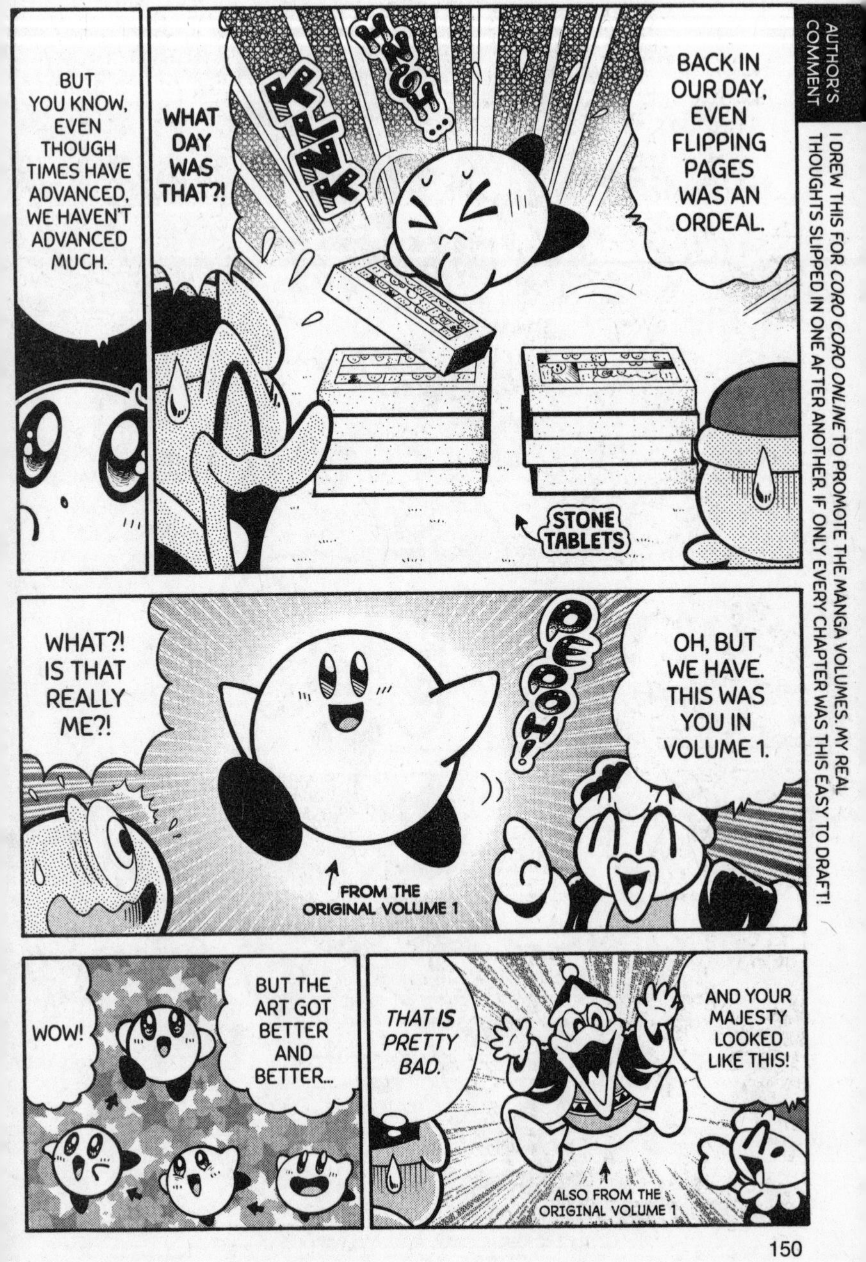
BACK IN OUR DAY, EVEN FLIPPING PAGES WAS AN ORDEAL.
HNGH...
KLUNK
WHAT DAY WAS THAT?!
STONE TABLETS
BUT YOU KNOW, EVEN THOUGH TIMES HAVE ADVANCED, WE HAVEN'T ADVANCED MUCH.
OH, BUT WE HAVE. THIS WAS YOU IN VOLUME 1.
OOF!
WHAT?! IS THAT REALLY ME?!
FROM THE ORIGINAL VOLUME 1
AND YOUR MAJESTY LOOKED LIKE THIS!
*THAT **IS** PRETTY BAD.*
ALSO FROM THE ORIGINAL VOLUME 1
BUT THE ART GOT BETTER AND BETTER...
WOW!

AUTHOR'S COMMENT

I DREW THIS FOR *CORO CORO ONLINE* TO PROMOTE THE MANGA VOLUMES. MY REAL THOUGHTS SLIPPED IN ONE AFTER ANOTHER. IF ONLY EVERY CHAPTER WAS THIS EASY TO DRAFT!

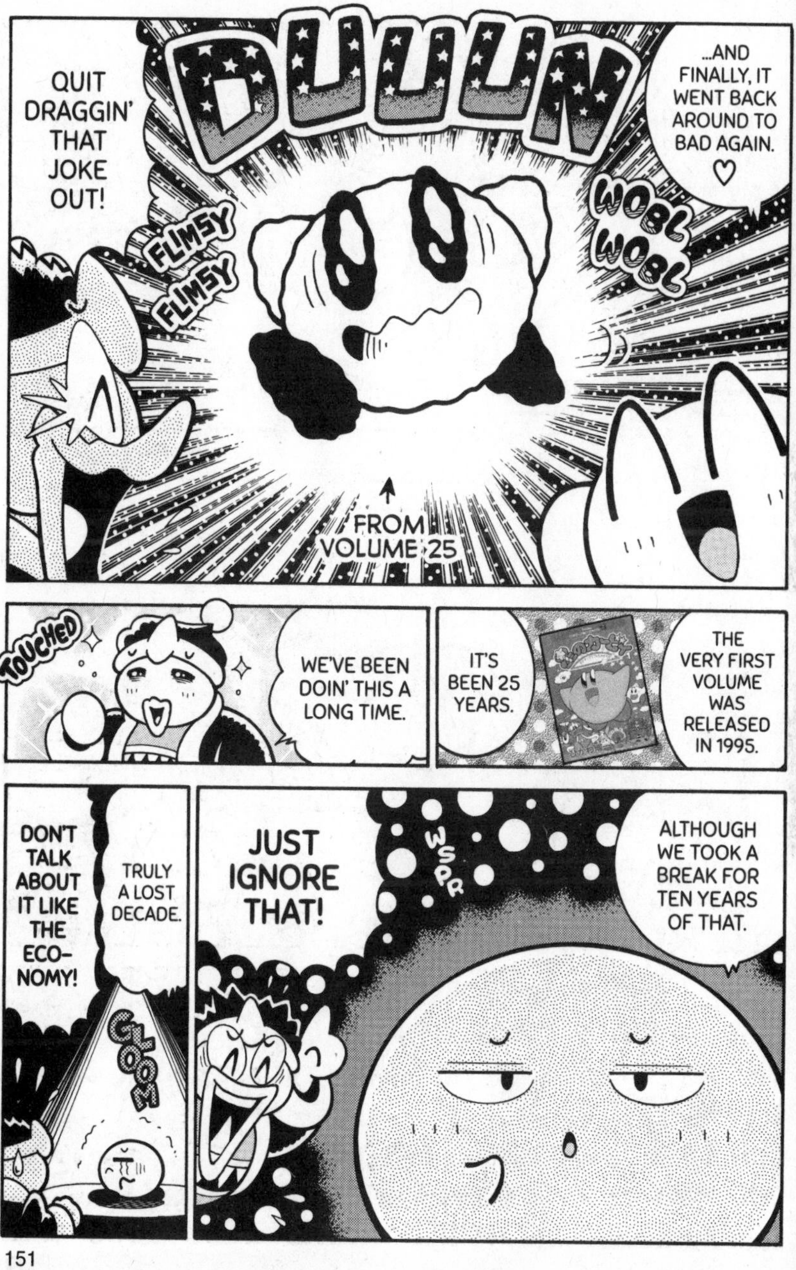
...AND FINALLY, IT WENT BACK AROUND TO BAD AGAIN. ♡
DUUUN
WOBL WOBL
QUIT DRAGGIN' THAT JOKE OUT!
FLIMSY FLIMSY
FROM VOLUME 25
THE VERY FIRST VOLUME WAS RELEASED IN 1995.
IT'S BEEN 25 YEARS.
WE'VE BEEN DOIN' THIS A LONG TIME.
TOUCHED
ALTHOUGH WE TOOK A BREAK FOR TEN YEARS OF THAT.
WSPR
JUST IGNORE THAT!
TRULY A LOST DECADE.
DON'T TALK ABOUT IT LIKE THE ECO-NOMY!
GLOOM

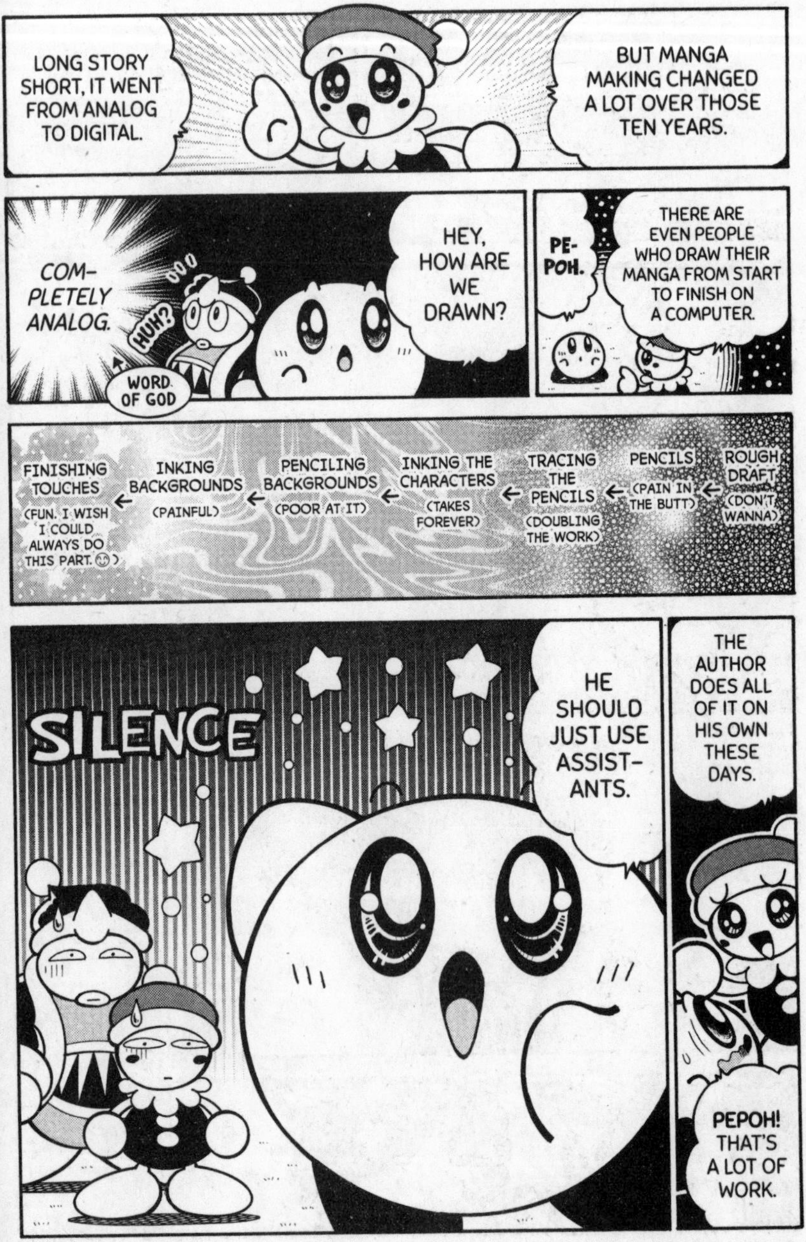

BUT MANGA MAKING CHANGED A LOT OVER THOSE TEN YEARS.
LONG STORY SHORT, IT WENT FROM ANALOG TO DIGITAL.
THERE ARE EVEN PEOPLE WHO DRAW THEIR MANGA FROM START TO FINISH ON A COMPUTER.
PE-POH.
HEY, HOW ARE WE DRAWN?
HUH?
COMPLETELY ANALOG.
WORD OF GOD
ROUGH DRAFT (DON'T WANNA)
PENCILS (PAIN IN THE BUTT)
TRACING THE PENCILS (DOUBLING THE WORK)
INKING THE CHARACTERS (TAKES FOREVER)
PENCILING BACKGROUNDS (POOR AT IT)
INKING BACKGROUNDS (PAINFUL)
FINISHING TOUCHES (FUN. I WISH I COULD ALWAYS DO THIS PART. ☺)
THE AUTHOR DOES ALL OF IT ON HIS OWN THESE DAYS.
PEPOH! THAT'S A LOT OF WORK.
HE SHOULD JUST USE ASSISTANTS.
SILENCE

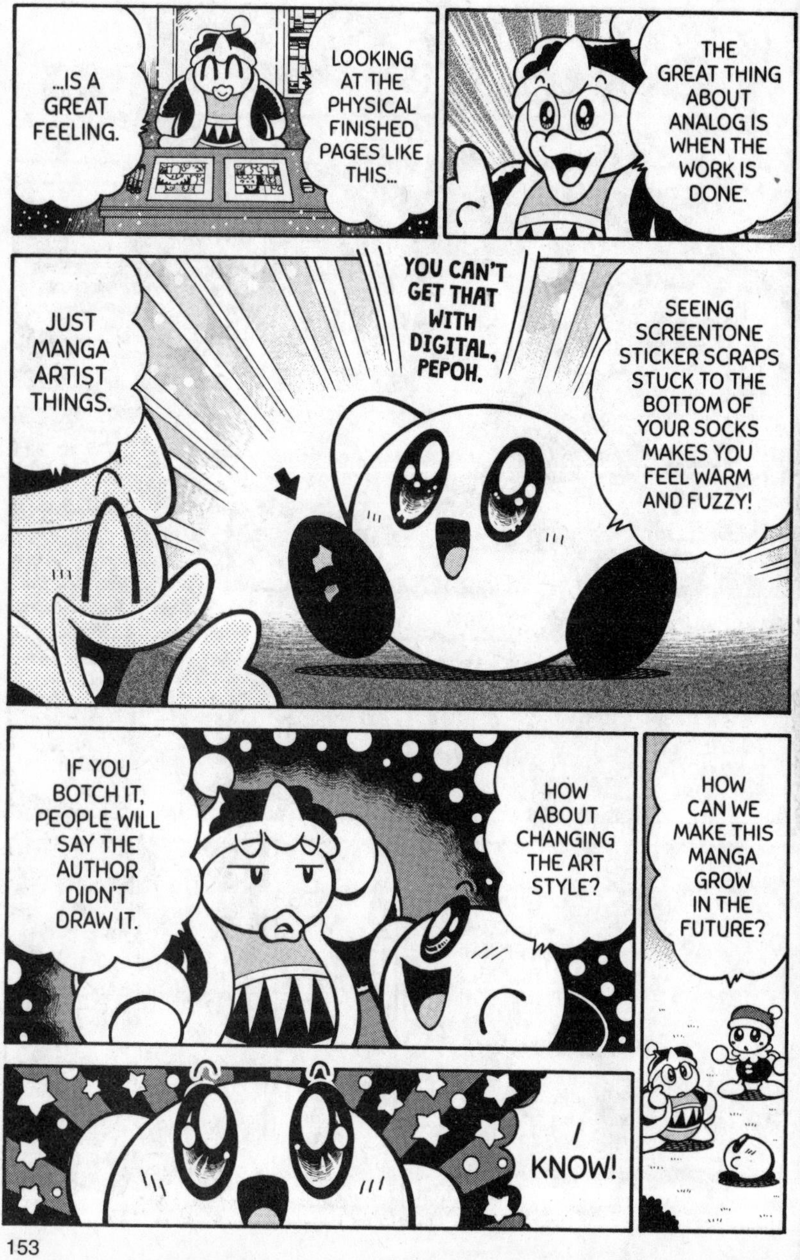
THE GREAT THING ABOUT ANALOG IS WHEN THE WORK IS DONE.
LOOKING AT THE PHYSICAL FINISHED PAGES LIKE THIS...
...IS A GREAT FEELING.
SEEING SCREENTONE STICKER SCRAPS STUCK TO THE BOTTOM OF YOUR SOCKS MAKES YOU FEEL WARM AND FUZZY!
YOU CAN'T GET THAT WITH DIGITAL, PEPOH.
JUST MANGA ARTIST THINGS.
HOW CAN WE MAKE THIS MANGA GROW IN THE FUTURE?
HOW ABOUT CHANGING THE ART STYLE?
IF YOU BOTCH IT, PEOPLE WILL SAY THE AUTHOR DIDN'T DRAW IT.
I KNOW!

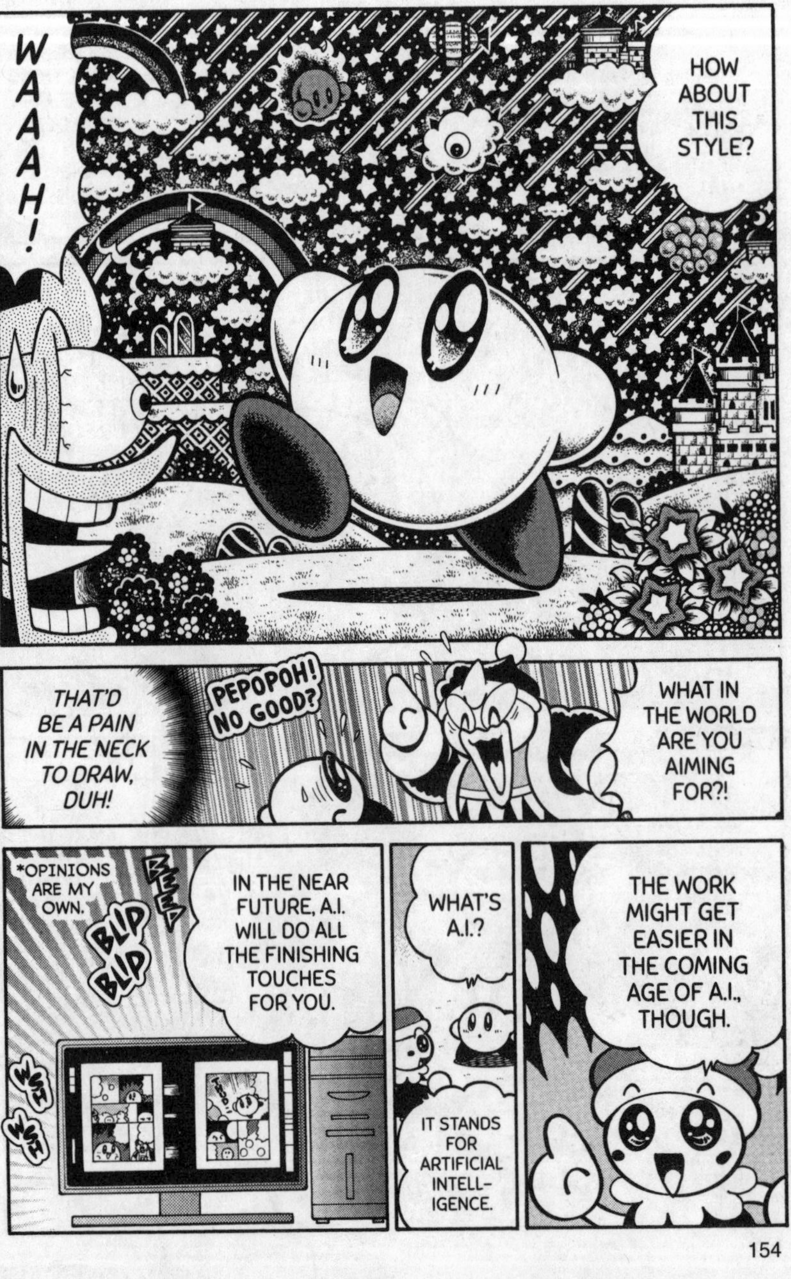
HOW ABOUT THIS STYLE?
WAAAAH!
WHAT IN THE WORLD ARE YOU AIMING FOR?!
PEPOPOH! NO GOOD?
THAT'D BE A PAIN IN THE NECK TO DRAW, DUH!
THE WORK MIGHT GET EASIER IN THE COMING AGE OF A.I., THOUGH.
WHAT'S A.I.?
IT STANDS FOR ARTIFICIAL INTELL-IGENCE.
BEEP
IN THE NEAR FUTURE, A.I. WILL DO ALL THE FINISHING TOUCHES FOR YOU.
*OPINIONS ARE MY OWN.
BLIP BLIP
WSH WSH

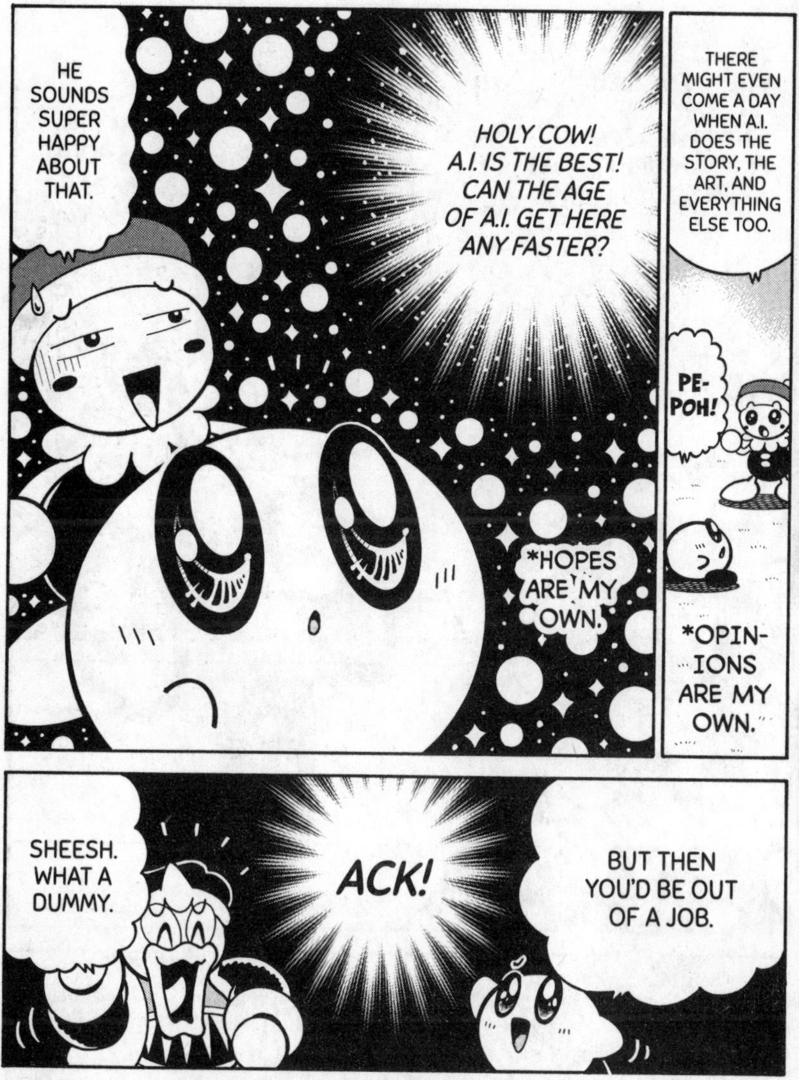
THERE MIGHT EVEN COME A DAY WHEN A.I. DOES THE STORY, THE ART, AND EVERYTHING ELSE TOO.
PE-POH!
*OPIN-IONS ARE MY OWN.
HOLY COW! A.I. IS THE BEST! CAN THE AGE OF A.I. GET HERE ANY FASTER?
*HOPES ARE MY OWN.
HE SOUNDS SUPER HAPPY ABOUT THAT.
BUT THEN YOU'D BE OUT OF A JOB.
ACK!
SHEESH. WHAT A DUMMY.
WELL, FOR NOW YOU'LL JUST HAVE TO DRAW US SLOW AND STEADY!
YUP!
WE'RE COUNTIN' ON YA!

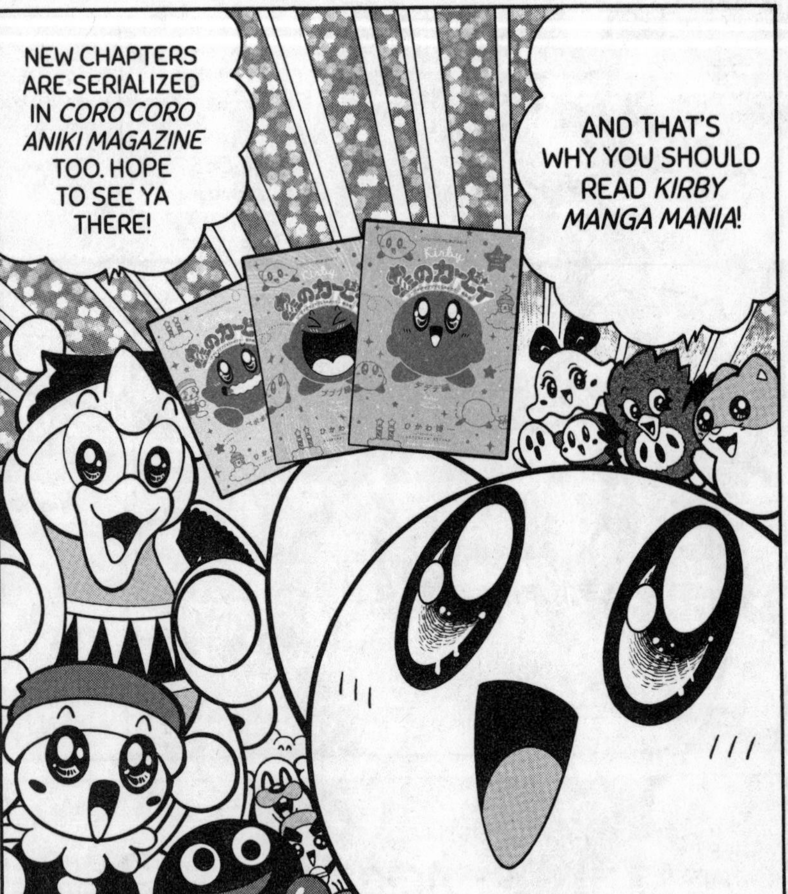
AND THAT'S WHY YOU SHOULD READ *KIRBY MANGA MANIA*!
NEW CHAPTERS ARE SERIALIZED IN *CORO CORO ANIKI MAGAZINE* TOO. HOPE TO SEE YA THERE!

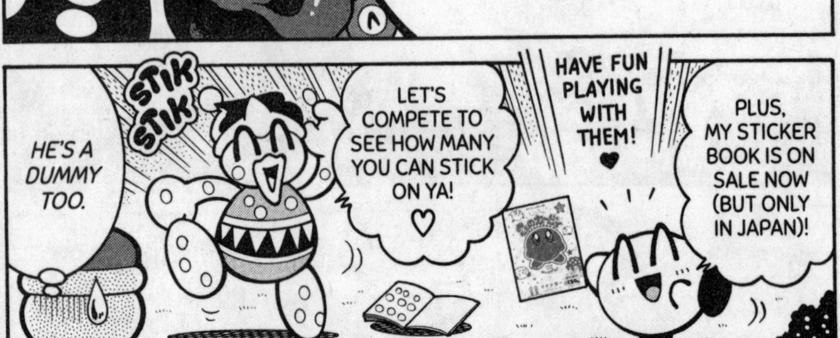
PLUS, MY STICKER BOOK IS ON SALE NOW (BUT ONLY IN JAPAN)!
HAVE FUN PLAYING WITH THEM! ♥
LET'S COMPETE TO SEE HOW MANY YOU CAN STICK ON YA! ♡
STIK STIK
HE'S A DUMMY TOO.

KIRBY MANGA MANIA 4: THE END!

Thank you for reading
Kirby Manga Mania vol. 4.

I've been told for quite some time that books don't sell in this day and age. But I hear *Kirby* books have been selling pretty well.

Fortunately, they even stock these best-of collections on the table displays at my local bookstore. Much appreciated! The covers are just great. They're so cute and eye-catching.

I want to put as many new chapters into the fifth volume as I can, so I'm not sure when it will come out. Please look forward to it.

If there are any classic chapters you want to see in future volumes, please let me know.

HIROKAZU HIKAWA

Kirby Manga Mania Vol. 5 Coming Soon!

FLOAT FLOAT

In my dreams, I live in Dream Land.

This is the fourth volume in the best-of collection.
Not to worry, six brand-new stories are included too.
The Japanese editions are respectively subtitled *Dedede*,
Pupupu, *Pepopo*, and for this volume, *Mupepe*. I'm
thinking next time I'll go for broke and use the subtitle
Farewell, Destined Rival: A New Journey, the Conclusion...

HIROKAZU HIKAWA

Hirokazu Hikawa was born July 4, 1967,
in Aichi Prefecture. He is best known
for his manga adaptations of *Bonk* and
Kirby. In 1987, he won an honorable
mention for *Kaisei!! Aozora Kyoushitsu*
(Beautiful Day! Outdoor Classroom)
at the 14th Fujiko Fujio Awards.

Volume 4
VIZ Media Edition

Story and Art
HIROKAZU HIKAWA

TRANSLATION **Amanda Haley**
ENGLISH ADAPTATION **Jennifer LeBlanc**
TOUCH-UP ART + LETTERING **E.K. Weaver, Jeannie Lee**
DESIGN **Shawn Carrico**
EDITOR **Jennifer LeBlanc**

©Nintendo / HAL Laboratory, Inc.

HOSHINO KIRBY - DEDEDE DE PUPUPU NA MONOGATARI - KESSAKUSEN MUPEPE HEN
by Hirokazu HIKAWA
© 2020 Hirokazu HIKAWA
All rights reserved.
Original Japanese edition published by SHOGAKUKAN.
English translation rights in the United States of America,
Canada, the United Kingdom, Ireland, Australia
and New Zealand arranged with SHOGAKUKAN.

ORIGINAL COVER DESIGN SEIKO TSUCHIHASHI [HIVE & CO., LTD.]

Printed in the U.S.A.

Published by VIZ Media, LLC
P.O. Box 77010
San Francisco, CA 94107

10 9 8 7 6 5 4 3 2 1
First printing, March 2022

PARENTAL ADVISORY
KIRBY MANGA MANIA is rated
A and is suitable for all ages.

viz.com

THIS IS THE LAST PAGE!

Kirby Manga Mania reads from right to left, starting in the upper-right corner. Japanese is read from right to left, meaning that action, sound effects, and word-balloon order are completely reversed from English order.